My Trans Parent

of related interest

Everything You Ever Wanted to Know about Trans (But Were Afraid to Ask)
Brynn Tannehill
ISBN 978 1 78450 956 9
eISBN 978 1 78592 826 0

The A–Z of Gender and Sexuality
From Ace to Ze
Morgan Lev Edward Holleb
ISBN 978 1 78592 342 5
eISBN 978 1 78450 663 6

Yes, You Are Trans Enough
My Transition from Self-Loathing to Self-Love
Mia Violet
ISBN 978 1 78450 628 5
eISBN 978 1 78592 315 9

How to Understand Your Gender
A Practical Guide for Exploring Who You Are
Alex Iantaffi and Meg-John Barker
Foreword by S. Bear Bergman
ISBN 978 1 78592 746 1
eISBN 978 1 78450 517 2

A User Guide for When Your Parent Transitions

Heather Bryant

Jessica Kingsley Publishers
London and Philadelphia

Introductory quotes in chapter sections come from COLAGE and Monica Canfield-Lenfest (2008) *Kids of Trans Resource Guide*. Seattle, WA: COLAGE. Reprinted with permission from COLAGE. The ages reflect the ages of the speakers at the time of the 2008 printing.

First published in 2020
by Jessica Kingsley Publishers
73 Collier Street
London N1 9BE, UK
and
400 Market Street, Suite 400
Philadelphia, PA 19106, USA

www.jkp.com

Library of Congress Cataloging in Publication Data
A CIP catalog record for this book is available from the Library of Congress

British Library Cataloguing in Publication Data
A CIP catalogue record for this book is available from the British Library

ISBN 978 1 78775 122 4
eISBN 978 1 78775 123 1

Printed and bound in Great Britain

For my family, given and found

For anyone who has ever felt different
because of who they are
or because of the shape of their family

Contents

Acknowledgments

Kaley Fry from COLAGE saw the need for an update to the *2008 Kids of Trans Resource Guide*, and Andrew James at Jessica Kingsley Publishers saw the need for this kind of handbook to be out in the world. Without them, this book wouldn't exist.

Thank you to Kaley for being a cheerleader and guide through the whole process, for connecting me with the incredible community of People with Trans Parents through COLAGE, and for being a bright light for all of us.

Thank you to Andrew for encouraging me and giving sensitive feedback throughout the writing.

Thank you to Vicky Phillips for being my first honorary child of a trans parent, for her keen editing and writing advice, and for generally lighting a fire under my behind to get it done.

Thank you to Jess deCourcy Hinds for late-night mid-writing talks, magic writing beans, and sending the "You can do it!" text at just the right time.

Thank you to Andrea Kelley and Olivia Chen for sharing wisdom and experience with research, for your wonderful guides within the guide, and for offering support from proposal to finish line.

Thank you to Monica Canfield-Lenfest for passing the torch from the first guide and sharing your beautiful story.

Thank you to Morgan Green for jumping on board with this guide, too, and for offering your insight and perspective from proposal to final draft.

Thank you to Willy Wilkinson for also seeing the need for an update to the *Kids of Trans Resource Guide* and continuing that update with COLAGE.

Thank you to everyone who shared your story for the time, insight, and gifts of your words.

To my writing group for collectively encouraging me to tell my story in all its forms: Kaylie Jones, Deirdre Sinnott, Stacey Lender, Mary Horgan, Jean Ende, Martha Chang, Ruth Bonapace, Rachel Wong, and all who have joined us along the way.

To my colleagues at Pace for supporting and encouraging my time off to start on this journey: Bette Kirschstein, Jane Collins, Deborah Poe, Karen Berger, and Noreen McGuire.

To the Virginia Center for the Creative Art's Moulin à Nef program and to Disquiet International for providing me with space and community.

To the New York Society Library and the New York Public Library for help with research and additional space to work.

Thank you to Andrea Nouryeh for helping me map the way. To Sigrid for all.

To my true-blues for being there as friends and guides.

To Helene Busby for being a reader, listener, and cheerleader.

Thank you to Donnie for the title, for believing in the power of this story, and for being part of it.

And most of all, thank you to my family: to Dana for

supporting me in this project, for giving me key writing advice and marching orders, and for breaking the silence with me; to Steph for late-night, mid-tornado advice and for helping me stay on track; to the memory of my mom, who told me again and again that I could, even when I thought that I couldn't, and who believed in the power of stories to transform lives; to Lisa for reminding me, "Butt on chair, hands on keys!" more than once.

To my nephews for being yourselves—may you always know that you are perfect, just as you are.

Introduction

YOUR STORY, TOO

"Be proud of your family structure. There are people out there that are like you with similar experiences, you just may not know it."

—CAMERON V., AGE 22

Books like this one didn't exist when my dad was transitioning. I thought I was the only person on the whole planet with a family like mine. We met a few people through my dad's therapist, but none of my friends at school, as far as I knew, had parents transitioning like mine. At the time, there were no trans people on television or in mainstream movies. We had no reference points. We didn't even have a language to talk about it. No one's family looked like mine.

This book aims to fill a gap in conversations about the many shapes of families. I hope that reading this book will provide you with a built-in community of people like you. Like me. Like all the people around the world with trans parents. This book answers questions and gives a space for more questions.

This is the book I needed as a kid, but it's not one I would have sought out. I would have been reading it with the cover wrapped in brown paper under my bed with a flashlight. *Nothing is different about my family. Don't look at me.* I would have had Amazon deliver it to someone else's house and then gone in the night to pick it up. At the same time, I needed to know that we weren't the only ones. I'm still surprised to hear of other trans families, though now I know we are everywhere, across the planet and around the world.

I talked to people in Canada, Australia, Europe, and the United Kingdom, as well as every corner of the United States. Whether we were in Tennessee, or California, or Wisconsin, our feelings were often the same. There was a little boy in Oslo, Norway, back in the '80s whose family also watched the movie *Tootsie*. Our families were looking for our stories even though the story told in *Tootsie* wasn't the exact same as those of our families.

Had I known that at the same time as my parent transitioned, there was a little girl in Michigan named Sharon and a boy in Tennessee named Justin who had parents like mine, I would still have had to go to school every day with kids who didn't have trans parents, but maybe I would have felt less alone. It's important to know that *you're not the only one.* Yet so many of us looked outside and around us while our families were changing, and felt like we *were* the only ones.

I had expected to find a sea change since the days when my parent transitioned, but I was amazed by how similar the experiences of kids with trans parents are today when compared to my story three decades ago. The truth remains that it is still the world that needs to change, not our families. As Becca L. said about the neighbors who drifted away when her dad started to transition, "They just need to get over themselves."

Often what I found in talking with kids in our community

was a sense of isolation, of having to go through this alone. It felt like unknown territory for many families. There were no manuals or guides, no suggestions given for the right path.

In the course of creating this handbook, I reached out to trans families all over the world in search of stories. I interviewed, surveyed, and talked to over 30 kids of trans (people with trans parents), trans parents, and therapists and experts working with trans families. COLAGE, a national organization that supports people with one or more LGBTQ+[1] parent, linked me to the wider community of trans families. The more I shared about the project, though, the more I found people all around me with trans parents. Friends of friends and people I met in writing workshops popped up saying, "Hey! I have a trans parent, too."

I talked to one parent and child who'd just reconnected after 38 years of not talking, and to a girl who knew her parent only as trans. I talked to someone with two trans parents and someone with both gay and trans parents. Some had known for many years and some had just found out. Some had never met anyone else with a trans parent and some are now leaders in advocating for kids with trans families. One of the parents came out before my parent did and one is still coming out today. Her daughter still doesn't know. Some of the kids grew up in the '80s with trans parents, and some are still growing up today. How is it that someone whose parent came out in 1987 and someone whose parent came out this year could have so much in common? I thought by now everyone was broadcasting about their families and parading around their neighborhoods in celebration. Yet backlashes have delayed progress.

1 Acronym for "lesbian, gay, bisexual, transgender, and queer." The "Q" can also stand for "questioning." The "+" indicates the wide range of additional identities, including intersex, asexual, ally, pansexual, and many more.

Pride in trans families is a part of daily life in some small pockets of the United States and other countries. Places where people are more aware. In some places, kids grow up in communities where schools celebrate rainbow days and educate students about gender expansiveness from a young age. As more kids grow up in a world that understands that gender identity is not a matter of checking a box and that this is part of human experience, more families will start with trans at the center instead of in the margins. Jordan L. found that everyone he told in recent years had one degree of separation from someone trans: trans kids, trans parents, trans people in their communities. All across the world, people are transitioning. The more we tell our stories, the more we'll know we're not alone.

We are at the very beginning of a bigger conversation about families. There's no one shape for families, just like there's no one way to be trans. As Jennifer said, "There's not one universal experience that all of us have had. People transition in so many different ways—so many different degrees of being out. That's another thing that people should know—our stories are so different but equally important."

There's still a need for open conversations about our families. My parent still does not feel safe to be open in her community. There are backlashes as we make progress. There are parts of the world that get it, and parts that don't. Communities are forming, but not everyone has caught up yet. We need more stories about our families. Let's keep trading stories until no one thinks there's one way to have a trans parent, to be transgender or just to be.

We need more stories where the fact of our parent being trans is in the background. The everyday moments: eating breakfast, watching TV. It's powerful to look out into the world and see your story. The more people hear about our ordinary lives, the more they'll get to see that this is part of their lives, too.

I didn't expect so much of my own story to find its way into these pages. As I talked to kids and parents around the world, my memories came back. I didn't want to think about times when I'd rejected my parent, when I wanted nothing to do with her, or the times when I laughed along with my friends about something that made fun of crossing the gender lines. It hadn't been too long since I'd played the pronoun game—when you avoid pronouns to try to fit in. I still play it when I don't want to launch into a big long explanation of my family. I had to look at myself, too, at the ways I'd learned that my family was somehow wrong.

There are still more stories to tell. This book doesn't represent all trans families everywhere. More stories are needed from kids all over the world with parents stepping out as non-binary and gender queer. From kids with more than one trans parent. From kids with trans parents from birth. From kids who just found out when their parent was a senior citizen. From kids who identify as trans alongside their parent. Many more stories are coming. As Becca said, "Everyone's stories are unique and different, even though they're all fundamentally the same." Each story I found along the way told my story in different ways.

This book invites you to tell your story, too. Follow along with the prompts at the end of each chapter. Find out something you didn't know about yourself or your family by writing answers to the questions designed to help you explore your own story.

Back when my parent transitioned, there were other families out there like mine. I just didn't know it. I also thought my parent's transition was her journey, that it had nothing to do with me. When I talked to Amy S., another person with a trans parent, she said, "I'm happy that there's something out there that's helping the children understand that they're a part of it, because I really didn't feel like a part of it—I didn't feel like I had any voice at all." You're a part of this. When one family member transitions, the whole family transitions.

When Becca L.'s dad came out, it was her mother who found that her friends in the church community faded away. They didn't understand why she stayed in the marriage. When Jonathan W., a pastor in Brooklyn, decided that his church would stand by his dad and become an LGBTQ+ affirming church, they lost their funding from the network of churches they were linked to. The family is impacted in ways people don't always see. At the same time, as Morgan G. said, "The transition can be something that brings you together with your parent, something that increases your sense of intimacy and connection." The transition can be a chance to get closer to your parent. It's not a linear process, though. There are no instant results.

Wherever you are now in your perspective on your family, start there. It's okay not to be okay. That doesn't mean you don't love your parent or that you don't support the trans community. "No one told me it was okay to be angry," Becca said. "So I felt like crap because I was mad." Trying to fast-forward to acceptance doesn't work. It's not so simple. "I couldn't get rid of me being angry, because that was my first emotion—anger—it was mostly anger, then sadness, then anger again, and then acceptance."

Even B. talked about his own way to acceptance. "I stopped trying to understand it, because I can't, because you have to be transgender to understand it, but I just learned that some people are different, so it doesn't really matter what they are. Don't analyze it, just accept it. We have so much trouble understanding ourselves, you know, trying to understand everyone, we would have a really hard time, so acceptance is a much better way to go."

For me, I still don't have answers to all of the questions, but I'm learning how to name what I don't know or don't understand.

This is a book for us, for our stories, for our lives. So when you have a question and are wondering what to think or do, you can see that there are others like you.

"You are going on a big adventure in talking to all of us," Morgan G. said. And she was so right. It was an adventure, one that helped me see even more the gifts of having a trans parent. Morgan reflected on this, too: "Having a trans parent has better allowed me to relate to my own gender in a way that seems genuine and unique, and I've felt—I think I have felt that it has been easier for me to be a woman and that's also among the gifts that I've experienced." When she said this, I saw how this was true in so many ways for me, too. I never felt I had to fit into a box or a role. As she said, gender "goes beyond the binary, it goes beyond girls and boys and men and women, because everyone ultimately is unique and takes from gender and uses gender in their own way." Her perspective is one that took me a long time to see.

We aren't different from other families. The stuff we struggle with is the same as in every family, and the stuff that brings us joy is the same, too. In our families, pockets of silence still impact our lives. "Nana doesn't need to know." Or, "Let's not tell cousin Brian." Yet being trans is part of all of our lives, not just people with trans parents. It's part of our world. We need to find a way to talk about having trans parents, within our families and within the larger world.

It took me a long time to find my own community. In my family, my parent didn't find a trans community once she claimed her identity. It didn't feel like a community in the way the gay community did. We didn't have neighborhoods or spaces to gather in like those in the gay community. Most of the time, it felt like a part of my identity was invisible. "I'm cisgender," Kara M. said. "So there's also that aspect of being like how do I fit in the trans community?" When I marched in the New York City pride parade, I wore a "Kids of Trans" sign, but people don't see that every day. Still, having a trans parent is a part of me. When trans topics are mis-portrayed in the news, it feels personal. "Hey," I want to yell, "that's my family, too." As I talked to both kids and parents, I saw how we're a part of this community, too; how we have our own unique place.

Olivia C. talked about what it was like for her finding a larger community of people with trans parents: "Hearing all the other voices that were saying exactly how I had been feeling—it was so validating, because I feel like when you're not talking to other people who have been through it, it's hard to be completely honest about how you feel, and even if you are, no one wants to be like—oh yeah—it's just hard to feel validated, so that was really helpful."

I hope you'll find validation within the pages of this book, that you'll hear echoes of your own story, of your family. I hope you'll find what you need to share your story, too.

A NOTE ABOUT PRONOUNS AND NAMES

Our language needs an update. I thought by the time I wrote this book, it would be old news. Maybe everyone would have a link to someone trans or be trans themselves. But people are still getting a grasp on the workings of gender.

I believe we are still learning about pronouns, that we are still behind when it comes to language. One day, there will be a language that won't split us in two. This language will reflect us more fully and tell the story of who we really are. For now, I'm working within the limits of language as it is.

You'll sometimes find pronouns you might not expect like "mom" with "he," and "dad" with "she." Each family chose the pronouns and names that fit. For my trans parent, this means using "she" or "he" with "dad" for the early years and "she" with "Dana" for the later years. I believe the truth lands between or around the pronouns and names, not in one or the other. Still, to see how mis-gendering or mis-pronouning feels, try swapping pronouns for yourself; then you might understand why people choose pronouns that fit.

Some names and details have been changed to protect privacy and anonymity within my own family and others, while staying true to the stories.

Who's Who in this Book

Here are the people who you'll meet in this book (in order of appearance). Some of the names and details have been changed to protect the privacy of the families.

Kids of Trans (a.k.a. People with Trans Parents)

Sharon S., New York, 36
Justin B., Tennessee, 37
Becca L., Massachusetts, 17
Jordan L., New York, 40
Jennifer R., New Hampshire, 20
Amy S., Ontario, Canada, 34
Jonathan W., New York, 42
Morgan G., California, 34
Even B., Norway, 45
Kara M., Wisconsin, 36
Olivia C., California, 31
Monica C., California, 38
Sarah W., Massachusetts, 36
Noelle H., New York, 47
Sandra P., Pennsylvania, 36
Leila R., Oregon, 8
Danielle C., Michigan, 33
Fiona B., Florida, 28
Christy P., Washington, 39
Riley P., New York, 26
Maya S., Minnesota, 8
Jeremy E., Pennsylvania, 7
Tom E., New Jersey, 14
Elsa M., Massachusetts, 54
Jay J., California, 9
Rachel M., Kansas, 23

Brian L., North Carolina, 32
Chelsea W., Nebraska, 31
Sadie P., Australia, 31
Kim A., California, 41
Amber K., Nebraska, 38
Hannah W., Washington, 34
Christina M., Arkansas, 43
Stacey W., Michigan, 57
Ann P., Utah, 32

Kids of Trans Quotes from COLAGE's *Kids of Trans Resource Guide*[2]

Cameron V., 22
Jonathan F., 24
Colleen M., 44
Leslie Q., 24
Elizabeth M., 23
Kevin B., 7
Steve Vinay G., 48
Doug S., 29
Skyela H., 29

Trans Parents

Carson R., Oregon
Sam R., Oregon
Trish S., Michigan
KC, California
Paula W., Colorado
Lily E., Pennsylvania
Anna M., California
Jessica E., New Jersey
Kate S., California
Tricia W., Massachusetts
Stephanie W., Washington

2 These quotes were used with permission from COLAGE. Ages reflect the ages at the time of the publication of the *Kids of Trans Resource Guide* in 2008.

Chapter 1
First Steps

"Okay! Let's go!"

That's what Amy S. said to herself the first week she learned her parent was trans. She latched herself in for the ride. She didn't know where they were going, but in that moment, she was all in.

Maybe you just found out that your parent is trans. Now what? Are you wondering how this will impact your life? What it will mean?

The change isn't only happening for your parent. It's happening for you, too. You might be filled with questions or a sense of relief—it all makes sense now! You might feel like this came out of nowhere.

Or maybe you've known for years. Maybe this is a part of your everyday life, but you're making sense of where you fit into the story. Maybe you're starting a new school, and you're wondering how to tell your friends. Or maybe you're wondering if there's anyone out there with a family like yours.

What does it mean for you?

That's what this book is about. You get to see what other

people did and how it was for them. You get to see how having a trans parent, like any parent, is a zig-zag journey that's all yours.

FINDING OUT YOUR PARENT IS TRANSGENDER

When I first learned that my dad is transgender, I was in fifth grade getting ready to switch to a new school. For the first time in nine years, my family was living together under the same roof. My dad lived on one side of the house and my mom, sister, and I on the other. I had just turned ten, and to me, all that mattered was that we were back together again as a family. My father's hair had grown long, past her shoulders, but she still wore a button-down shirt and jeans. The skin on her face was smooth. She'd started electrolysis and hormones, but my sister and I didn't know this.

The last time my dad dressed as a man was when she had to go to my old school to talk to the principal. My parents weren't happy with the school, and wanted to pull me out and get a tuition refund. It worked. She put on this charcoal gray suit, pulled on a hat over her growing hair, and laced up her black dress shoes. She went to the school and the principal gave us a refund. My mom had tried to go alone, and they wouldn't give it to her. The charcoal suit worked. Soon after that, my dad stopped dressing as a man entirely.

It happened overnight. One day, my dad had long loose curls almost down to her shoulders. The next day, a headband swept the curls back and smoothed them, and the skinny jeans were swapped for a long skirt. Just like that our family changed.

We didn't sit down as a family to talk about the transition, but I remember the day I learned her new name. We were sitting in the kitchen when she told us. Her hair was swept back in a headband, and she wore a button-down shirt and a long skirt that covered her legs.

"Dana Victoria Brown" was the new name she gave herself. It sounded strange to me. The first name, I didn't know what to do with. I'd never met anyone with that name. The middle name I recognized. There were girls in my class named Victoria, and also my aunt and a Queen of England. That part I liked. The third name was another one I didn't know, a family name, but not mine. She would have a different last name now. "Okay," I thought. It didn't occur to me to protest or raise questions. The only thought I had was that I might forget her new name.

"What if we're out together and I shout 'Dad' on accident? What if we're at a bookstore and I shout it across the way?" I asked.

"We'll see," Dana said. She didn't seem worried or afraid.

The name still felt strange to me. I said it, but it didn't feel real. Also, it didn't belong to me like Dad did. The whole rest of the world shared it. Mom said it, too, and all of our neighbors. It didn't occur to me to come up with anything else.

I didn't know that I would miss saying "Dad." At the time, I was mainly concerned with keeping up the façade.

In actuality, the transition had started months before with hormones and electrolysis and years before with my father's internal struggles. My dad struggled with depression when first married to my mother, and then lived for nine years as a gay man, but a piece was missing. To me, though, it didn't start until that fall; until, to the outside world, my dad was no longer Daniel.

The fact that someone might be born and look to the outside world like a boy but feel closer to being a girl on the inside was something I didn't know about yet, but when I did, it felt like an expansion of what was possible.

No one said, "Your dad is transgender." If they had, the word would have sounded strange to me. We didn't use a label. All I knew was that Dad wouldn't dress up as my dad again. Instead, Dad was now Dana. Dana wore skirts and headbands, and flat shoes, and sometimes lipstick when we went out to dinner. Dana, we told people, was my dad's sister, because the rest of the world wasn't ready to know who she really was.

When I learned my dad's new name, Dana, I was supposed to say the new name, but it didn't come naturally, so I didn't say anything. I just let her walk ahead in her skirt and headband, and hoped no one noticed. Even our neighbors who met our dad as Daniel didn't ask questions. They just said, "Nice to meet you" to Dana, and I wondered how they couldn't tell she was the same person on the inside. Even I wondered if she was the same person on the inside since Dana was a little different and wasn't silly goofy wild fun and didn't sing so loud, though sometimes she whistled in the other room. Still, she seemed a little different from Dad, but I went along since this was all I knew.

It was 1987. Reagan was president and the AIDS crisis was spreading across the country. In television, movies, and books, I didn't see a single transgender person. In my daily life, no one I knew crossed the gender lines. At the same time, I was at an age when I didn't question my parents. They knew how the world worked. I looked to them for definitions and explanations about the world. So I went along with this new twist in our family life without asking too many questions.

For my family, the first steps were getting used to calling her Dana and introducing her as my "aunt." It felt like a big trick we were playing on the outside world. The movie *Tootsie* was one we related to as a family. In that movie the main character, Michael Dorsey, played by Dustin Hoffman, dresses as a woman to get a starring role in a TV show. At the end of the movie,

Dorsey does a big reveal to everyone's surprise—Tootsie is really a man! In our story, we couldn't go back. Aunt Dana couldn't just switch back to being Dad Daniel. Instead, we experienced a gradual shifting until Dad and Daniel disappeared. It wasn't a disguise like in the movie. Our dad's body and face were changing.

At first, it didn't feel like a change on the inside. We were the same bookstore-going, pancake-making, movie-watching family. We thought our family only changed for the outside world. *This is my aunt*, we were supposed to say, but it felt awkward to say it. My aunts lived on the opposite side of the country with their own families. Dana was my dad under all the layers, but we couldn't say "Dad" because people would look at us funny like we were confused.

Mostly, we just said nothing, because it felt safer. We swallowed our words, and hoped no one would ask. It helped that we lived thousands of miles away from anyone who knew us before. We could tell this new story, and no one could say it was otherwise.

The transition had already started before my sister and knew about it, but we lived apart from our dad at the time.

Some people I interviewed found out before their parent told them. Sharon S.'s sister discovered some photos in the trash. At the time, Sharon was eight and her sister was five. Her family was living in Chicago. Sharon described what happened: "My sister was going through the trash in my dad's office and found a couple of old photos that had been stuck together and she peeled them apart. They were photos of my dad wearing a dress and so she brought those photos to my mom and said, 'Why is Dad dressed like Grandma?'" This led to a conversation with their parents, who told them then. "My parents decided to just tell us that Trish was transgender, which was kind of amazing in retrospect—I think it was the '80s." Sharon's family moved to Northern Michigan after Trisha started to transition.

Even B. from Oslo confronted his parents about mysterious monthly gatherings at their house. Each month, as a child, he was sent to his grandparents' house and he wasn't allowed to return until the gathering was over. Sometimes, before he left his house, he saw people arriving and noticed that everyone was nicely dressed and polite. At first, he thought his parents were in a cult. As he got older, around ten years old, he asked for an explanation.

"I know there is something going on here," he said. "You have to tell me what this is."

His mother looked at his father, and they nodded. Even's father took him to his office, and said something like, "Your father likes to dress up as a woman."

"Like Carnival?" Even asked.

"Well, maybe yeah—we could say that," his father said.

Both Sharon's and Even's stories happened in the '80s, like mine, before the age of social media and before many people knew about being transgender. As Sharon said, "We didn't know the word 'transgender' or anything back then—we didn't understand." Not having the words to describe what this meant was an obstacle. My sister and I witnessed our father stepping into the role of woman, but we wouldn't have known what to say or how to describe the change.

Monica C. was 17 and visiting her dad, stepmom, and half-sister in Western Massachusetts when her dad told her. Her parents were divorced. She and her sister, age four, were playing together, coloring in a coloring book. Her sister pointed to the people in the coloring book, and said, "Some people are girls on the inside and girls on the outside like you, and some people are girls on the inside and boys on the outside like Dad."

Her dad overheard the conversation and told her the rest. Sometimes a very young child can describe something better than adults. Her sister's description bridged the gap.

Morgan G. was living in California with her family when her parent transitioned from female to male. She doesn't remember the first conversation well, since she was four years old, but she later heard that she said, "I don't want you to be very tall." Her parent tried to explain to her in the moment that she would probably change more physically over the next few years than he would, but she didn't fully understand at the time. She knew her parent was going to change, and her first reaction came from what she pictured that change might look like.

Justin B. was eight years old when his parent told him. They were living in East Tennessee. His first reaction was that he wanted his parent to be okay. "I remember just wanting my parent to be happy. I was like—okay—this doesn't seem like the biggest deal in the world to me. I remember initially being really accepting."

Sarah W. noticed something going on with her dad, but she couldn't quite put a finger on what it was. There were some physical things going on that she couldn't quite sort out. At the time, her dad identified as a cross-dresser, so first he told her that he was a cross-dresser. Sarah said, "It threw me—I didn't quite understand what that was." Her mom struggled too, and her younger sister didn't know at first. "We kept it a secret from her, which was awful." Five years later, her parents separated, and at that time her dad came out as transgender and started transitioning physically.

Noelle H. was in a mall parking lot with her mother, parked in their car, thinking about the jeans she'd just bought, when her mother said, "Your father likes to wear women's clothes and is moving out of the house—we're gonna be away from each other." Noelle was processing this new information about her dad immediately after an ordinary trip to the mall: "It's still burned in my brain—that memory is very vivid of everything and the way the rain was rolling up on the window."

Sandra P.'s mother told her on a shopping trip to Target. It was summertime, and she had just moved out from living with her parents. Her dad told her mom, and then planned to tell each of the kids individually. Sandra recalled, "My mother was heartbroken and shocked and floored, and she told me the next day, while we were shopping at Target."

For Jennifer R., it was part of her daily life growing up in New Hampshire. "When we were younger, she always had long hair and she always wore skirts around the house, but it wasn't something she talked about or really addressed to us." Only later did it come up in conversation. "At one point, she just sat us all down and she was like, 'Listen, this is how I feel, this is the plan, what I'm going to be doing—I'm going to be living full time as a woman.'"

For Jennifer's parent and many others, including mine, doctors required living for a full year in the chosen identity to qualify for surgery. Sometimes it's on the brink of that year when the news comes out in some form. Not everyone opts for surgery, though, so the timing is unique for each family.

After seeing the movie, *Milk*, Amy S., then 23 years old, said to her father, "I don't understand how someone could live with a secret so big for their whole life, it must be the worst and most oppressive thing. I just have no idea how someone would even be able to live like that."

To that, her father said, "Well, I have something to tell you."

At the time, Amy didn't know the difference between transgender, transvestite, and transsexual. Her father explained this to her.

Becca L. was taking a selfie with her dad's phone when they were out together in Boston's South Shore. She went into the camera roll thinking, "I have to send this to myself—I want to post it," and she saw a picture of her dad as a woman, but at the time she didn't know it was her dad. "I thought it was another woman my dad was with." A few weeks later she went back on the phone to try to see what was going on. She found the Facebook app on her dad's phone.

"Dad—let's be friends on Facebook," she said. "This is so cool—you have a Facebook? You're on social media?"

"No—it came with the phone," her dad said.

"Yeah, uh huh," she thought. She went on the app, and saw her dad's account as Dee, which was her new name. All the pieces came together.

Becca said, "I put everything together in a matter of five minutes. That girl that was on the camera roll...was actually not another girl—that was actually my dad, and it was this whole spiraling thing." She didn't say anything at first. Months later, her parents brought it up. "They noticed I was acting very standoffish and just rude and I was just mad all the time—and I was becoming a teenager too."

When they sat her down that fall to tell her that her dad is transgender, her response was "Yeah, I already know."

"We kind of knew you already knew," they said, "but we didn't want to say anything."

Becca's parents were waiting for the right moment. "It was this whole elephant in the room that no one wanted to talk about until we actually talked about it," she said.

Leila, age eight, lives in Portland, Oregon with her two dads, Carson and Sam. Her dads adopted her and her brother, and then decided to expand the family. Like many other trans men, Carson decided to have the baby. "If my dad wasn't transgender,"

Leila said, "I wouldn't have a baby brother, so technically it works out, because my dad can't have a baby if he's not transgender." She found out her dad is trans through a conversation with her family. "He told me," she said. For her, it's a measure of love. "I really love my dad so they're probably going to tell me that he's transgender." In her view, families talk about who they are and how they want to be in the world.

A few weeks before her parent told her, Danielle C. opened the door on the topic. She was in school for a master's in social work in Pennsylvania. Her parents called one day and asked what she was working on, and she replied, "I'm putting together this group presentation on transgender people and their families for my class. This is really interesting to me and I'm trying to find information on family members of transgender people and I can't find anything—there's nothing out there."

Shortly after, she was out to dinner with her parent at a sushi restaurant. In the middle of dinner, her parent shared a dream about choosing between wearing a skirt suit and a dress. Danielle's first thought was, "What's going on? Wait a minute. Is this... Is my stepdad coming out to me?"

Her parent went on to tell her, "When I retire, I want to retire as K." This wasn't a big change, but she still wasn't sure what it meant. Her parent's name was Patrick K. Her whole family used the nickname, "K," but this sounded different.

"Like 'Kay'—'K-A-Y?'" she asked.

"Yes," her parent replied.

The next thing Danielle wanted to know was: "Are you staying together with Mom?"

"Yes," Kay said. "It took her a little while, but we're staying together. We're going to go through the whole thing."

At times, it takes someone outside of the family to connect the dots. Olivia C.'s fiancé saw her dad posting on Facebook with an account using a female name. Olivia had seen the same name on her dad's Twitter a few years before but she didn't think much of it. She just thought, "My dad is checking out the newest frontier of social media—and doesn't want to use his real name. I didn't think much about why he might be using a female name." She decided to look it up, too. She went online and found some pictures from the sports leagues her father played in. "She plays a lot of rec sports—that's her big thing, so I looked up a lot of that stuff online and I saw how she was competing at pretty big things as a female, and she had been living as a woman for quite a long time. At that point, I confronted her about it. It was a really intense experience. I didn't know what was going on." At the time, her whole family was at a wedding in Malaysia. "There were 25 of us staying at my grandma's house. I wanted to talk to my mom about it, but there were people everywhere." She finally found a way to talk to her mom in the middle of the maze of relatives and wedding events. "It turned out my mom had already known for seven years, so she wasn't shocked obviously, but they had never talked about it again. My mom found out and they didn't talk about it for seven years." Ultimately, it took Olivia's fiancé to bring it into the open. Olivia said, "I almost feel like it took someone from outside of our family to bring it to our attention because in retrospect a lot of things in my childhood instantly were clear to me and in retrospect it's sort of like—we really only see what we're looking for."

For some, the news was mixed in with other issues that came up, clouding the news at first: drug use, estrangement, or diagnoses of mental illness. Fiona B. from Florida spoke of hesitating to share her story, because she thought it could ignite transphobia. Her parent came out three years after being diagnosed as bipolar. "He was 52. This was not the culmination of a lifelong struggle or process of discovery. He made the announcement to our family that he was going to become a woman because he had been receiving guidance from a goddess who told him to become a woman. To this day, she maintains that story." The stigma around mental illness has kept her from sharing the story.

Christy P.'s father had been avoiding her for five years when she learned the news. She didn't understand why her father would be avoiding her until one day her cousin asked her a question.

"Do you think since you're Mormon that people don't tell you things?"

"Why would that matter?" Christy asked.

"I don't know. Do you think maybe they don't tell you things because of how they think you'll react?"

"When have I ever reacted badly?"

"You know if I were you and I thought someone wasn't telling me something," her cousin said, "I would call them and I would say, 'I just want you to know that I love you very much no matter what, and our relationship is important to me no matter what happens in your life.'"

Christy took a pause. She thought, "Clearly someone's hiding something from me and I need to make a bunch of phone calls."

She called around and when she reached her father, he told her, "For the last five years, I've been living as a woman."

After absorbing this information, she felt a wave of relief. "Okay, whatever. Are you happy—does that feel better?" she said.

"Yes," her father said. "I thought you'd never want to talk to me again."

For Christy, the biggest challenge came not from the change in gender, but from the rift that had formed after five years of being out of touch.

A parent's knowledge of their own identity can impact their decision to tell and when to tell. As in my family, a parent's awareness can sometimes come over time. My father lived as a gay man for nine years before coming out as trans.

Riley P. had a similar experience. His mom came out as a lesbian when he was five. "I'd always had an experience of my mom as someone who was not like every other parent at school, and in those days, he did cut his hair short and was a bit more masculine." Ten years later, an LGBTQ+ advocacy group called the Yes Institute came to Riley's school. Riley recalled: "My mom went to a parent workshop and saw an interview of a little kid and the punch line of the story was 'I'm not a girl, I'm a boy,' and when that little kid said that, my mom had this experience of—oh that's been me my whole life—that child was me and I've been searching for who I am all of this time, all these years, and never really thought to think about gender as the piece that was missing, the thing that I should investigate the most."

Soon after this realization, Riley's mom sat him and his sister down for a conversation and said, "Look guys, this is going to be a big change in your life, but I am coming out as trans—I'm going to start dressing more like a man."

Riley said that this was "the start of our journey." "*Our* journey"—that's what this book is all about. When one person in the family transitions, everyone does.

INITIAL REACTIONS FROM DIFFERENT PEOPLE

"When [my father] finally did come out, my initial reaction was to ask if we could still make the 2:20 showing of 'X-Men 2'."

—JONATHAN F., AGE 24

I was ten years old when my dad came out, and I just thought, "Okay, this is what's happening." I didn't think of it as a big deal. Sometimes, when I tell that to friends who didn't have transgender parents, they react as if I'm somehow in denial or not being honest, but when I speak to other kids of trans who found out at a young age, many felt similarly. As Even B. said, "It didn't really shake me up or anything—it's just like, okay, my father likes to dress up as a woman. 'Well okay,' I thought, like when I go to carnival, I wanted to be a cowboy or a clown or something. It didn't really change anything—I don't think I spent much time thinking about it." For me, I felt like it was one of the things that people did in the world. I was still learning about the world, so I thought it was simply one of the things to add to my awareness of the whole spectrum of experience. Maybe it was because my dad and I had always been close, but to me, this change felt like the opening of a door that had been there all along. Later, I pushed her away. But at the time when the change first happened, before I even knew the word "transgender," I took it in like it could happen anywhere, like it was a kind of magic my dad was part of, shape-shifting on an ordinary Tuesday. Only this kind of shape-shifting, it seemed to me, couldn't be reversed.

Sharon S. described how she and her sister were just okay. "I think for little kids, especially before you know about what society expects, you're kind of just like whatever—okay. I think a lot of the pressure and the embarrassment happens because of how society reacts and about your fear about people's reactions."

Since my family maintained the story of Dana as my aunt, we avoided some of the difficulties in the short run, but in the long run, I wonder if maintaining our family structure as is and telling the truth would have been better for us as a family. At the time, most people on the outside didn't have a chance to react since they didn't know the full story. We avoided a reaction by shifting our family story.

To me, it was a bigger deal that we'd uprooted across the country, leaving my friends behind in New York. The only thing about this was that we couldn't tell anyone, which made it feel strange. The more we kept it a secret, the more it felt like something I didn't want to tell. That made it harder to tell later on, even when I wanted to.

My sister and I went along like it happened every day. Inside our house, we witnessed a gradual transformation and we didn't wonder why or how. We simply went along for the ride at first. At home, it felt like we slipped across a threshold. I didn't question the change. I just thought, "This is what can happen in the world." Dana showed me a book she was reading, *Second Serve* by Renée Richards. I looked at the striking blonde on the cover and book jacket, and at the man in the photographs inside. "This is what's possible in the world," I thought. It was like learning a new idea in school. I didn't question or challenge it at first.

Dana's therapist encouraged my parents to come up with a story that would help us blend into our social world, which was part of why Dana was now our aunt. One of our neighbors walked by the house one day in our new neighborhood in Berkeley and my mom introduced Dana to her as "Daniel's sister."

"Oh—you look so much alike!" our neighbor said.

"You should see the rest of the family," my mother said.

That marked the start of my dad adopting a new identity. Dana had her own history and family, her own separate life. She was still my dad to me, but to the outside world, she was someone else.

We kept it as a family very much in our house, and then outside of the house, she was my aunt. I'd say, "This is my aunt," and it felt really weird to say the word "aunt" connected to my dad, but no one asked questions.

People out in the community met Dana as my aunt. In that way, I didn't know how the larger world would respond to this change for a while. I only knew little snippets, like how Dana's mother, my grandmother, felt that my dad was messing with God's creation, and how some people still said "he" and sent cards addressed to Daniel Bryant.

When I first found out, I didn't think I would have any feelings about this shift in my parent. Others spoke of the feelings shifting and changing with time. Olivia C. said, "My initial reaction was to be so supportive and minimize my own feelings. I went overboard, saying, 'I need to see pictures and you can borrow all my clothes, and this is amazing.'" The wish for a never-changing, ongoing closeness can sometimes mask initial feelings and questions. For me, I felt very protective of my parent. When we were out, I was very careful not to say, "Dad," not to out her to the world. How close we are to our parents can impact our responses, too. "Me and my dad are really close," Olivia explained, "so I was saying, 'this is the best—we'll be best friends—nothing will change', stuff like that." I relate to the part about being really supportive initially and discounting my own feelings. I was also very close to my dad, so I just wanted her to be okay.

When Jonathan W. got a phone call from his dad calling a family conference, he wondered what the news might be. Was his dad sick? Was he in financial trouble? He prepared himself for what could be difficult news. So when his dad shared the news, he was initially relieved. "There was 30 seconds of being relieved, and then there was this 'Oh my God, no, wait a second. You're not in trouble, but you're going to change fundamentally who you are.'" Even though Jonathan felt supportive of people in the world who wanted to claim their identities, the fact that it was his parent wanting to change made it more difficult for him. "For me, objectively speaking, I'm pro LBGT+ and if someone wants to transition or if someone comes out that's wonderful, we applaud it, and then when it was my own dad, I was like, 'Oh no, I don't want this.'" He wanted to find the root cause or reason at first. "I immediately went on the offensive, and was like, are you sure it's not because you're this way or because this happened to you or whatever. I started blaming him for everything at that point—I was probably a little harsh." Jonathan went on to write a book about the experience, *She's My Dad*, which tells the story of his experience with his dad's transition and the new understanding of his religion that came about in the process.

Christy, who also reconciled the change with her beliefs, said, "I grew up in a family that was definitely like 'live and let live,' so I felt like, 'Oh my gosh—this is something that makes her happy and doesn't hurt anybody. That's a good plan.'"

Sometimes, feelings can come out in other ways. Olivia spoke of traveling through Japan, right after she found out, with the news on her mind. "Immediately after, I was in action mode, but I was also somatically reactive. I wasn't processing anything, because I think I had no means of processing it, but I also could not digest anything." She was upset late at night, but couldn't voice it. "I think my whole body was in shock or trying to protect itself."

An initial rush of support can be followed by more complicated feelings. As Amy described, "The week she came out I ended up going to her trans support group with her as an advocate—I was just like—okay great! Let's go." As time went on, she went through a period of struggle and adjustment. "One of the hardest things for me was this big shift in personality and in interests, because all of a sudden our interests weren't the same at all." Sometimes, Amy felt like her parent's newfound freedom had a flip side. Who had her parent been for the years when she was little? Amy said, "[My parent told me] 'I've been living a lie for my whole life—now I can be who I really am.' As a child, you're sitting there thinking, 'What does that make me?'"

Becca found herself questioning a lot of her childhood leading up to that point. "I thought that everything was a lie, because at that point my dad was like, 'This is not how I've felt for my entire life.' I totally get that, but then you start thinking about everything that you've ever done with him." She started to rethink and reconsider their history together. "The sports and the training and the—just any activity—and you're like, 'Well was that all a lie now?'"

If our identity has been shaped by this person, then who are we?

WHAT DOES IT MEAN FOR YOU?

So, what does this mean for you? How will this impact your life?

Monica described navigating this confusion: "I was trying to make sense of what it possibly meant for me. I was partway through my senior year of high school. I had gone through my parents' divorce when I was really young, and so I was kinda mad that this other thing was happening that was gonna change things."

One part that I never considered at the time was how my father and I were on parallel journeys. I was on the cusp of becoming a woman and she was doing the same. Each of us was on a rollercoaster of hormones and physical changes.

Monica experienced something similar at age 17: "I was

becoming a young adult woman, and then my dad was becoming a woman." She spoke of an initial sense of overwhelm, but at the same time, said, "Despite how emotional I felt about the whole thing, I also felt protective of my dad, and recognized what it took to do something—to follow through with this need to fully realize your identity." At the end of the initial visit when she found out, driving back in the car, she turned to her dad and said, "No matter what, I love you—I want you to know that." She said, "I really meant that, even though I didn't know what it meant that I felt that way. I just knew it was really important. I knew that she needed to hear that at the time."

I, too, felt this need to protect my dad and I didn't fully understand it, but I just felt like I would do whatever I could to be protective when we were out. I would think, "Okay, so I'm not going to say 'Dad' anymore when we're out together—okay—I hope I can remember that." At the time, I hoped that I could do whatever was needed to help her with this stage of change. And then a little while later, I entered junior high and I wanted both of my parents miles and miles away. So even with the initial acceptance, other stages came after that. My reaction didn't stay the same over time.

Riley described an initial plan to navigate the changes together. Looking back, he could see that they were setting out into uncharted territory. "I think I couldn't have a clear picture of what trans would look like on my mom, what trans would look like in a relationship, so on that first day, both my sister and I were just like—okay great, we know you love us, we love you, so this is happening, without really getting into the details of physically what would change—anything like that. Just baseline—we're going to work this out together."

Trying to understand and navigate a parent's wishes and our own understanding is ongoing. "I definitely had my difficulties in the beginning," Danielle said. "Mainly because I was holding it in. I didn't want to out her to anyone." She asked her parent key questions to get some clarity. Name, pronouns, and coming out. "I'm calling you 'Kay' now—great. Am I using feminine pronouns for you? Yes—okay, good. But you're not out to anyone else yet, so how do I navigate this?"

Self-knowledge is a part of the experience. "At the time, I hadn't even fully come to terms with who I was," Jennifer said. "I didn't do a whole lot of research on my own about what being trans was and being involved in the community until a little bit later, so it's not something that was a shock necessarily, but it was kind of a transition, I mean." Our own transition comes with a growing understanding of what this means for us, for our parent, and out in the world.

It's important to give voice to any difficulties you're having. Amy said, "One of the biggest things for me was the fact that I felt really uncomfortable having any issue with it, which I feel like is such a disservice." There's a sense that if you have an issue, you're not supporting the trans community, but denying an issue can come out sideways. It's important to talk to someone you trust about any issues that come up.

Acting like you have no issue at all might help in the short run, but not in the long run. As Sarah W. said, "I just told my dad what I thought she wanted to hear, which was, 'Oh no, of course it's cool Dad—yeah it's really awesome,' even though inside, it was really, really heart wrenchingly hard for me." Expecting acceptance right away can backfire in the long run, so it's important to be open to a whole range of responses over time.

A SHIFT IN YOUR WORLD

More than one person I talked to spoke of having their sense of the world shift. They thought they knew their family and what it would look like for years to come. It's almost like a rupture of solid ground—an earthquake that shakes up the pieces and puts them back in another order.

Questions can come up at any point: "Who am I?" "Who is our family?" "Can I really know for sure?"

A year or so after the transition, one of my friends who knew my dad before the change came to visit. The way she stared made me glad that no one else knew the whole story. She stared and stared like she was at the zoo. Dana had to step into another room to get away from the staring. I don't think my friend realized what she was doing, but it made me want to protect my family and our story even more, to make sure no one ever found out. If they did, I might still have friends, I thought, but they would probably talk about how weird it was. I wasn't going to risk that, and we had a family story in place, so I hid behind that story, kept it like a shield for as long as I could.

As a child, I liked to parade my dad around and introduce him to my friends. "This is my dad." He was funny, silly, and handsome. From the start of the change, though, it felt irreversible. It never occurred to me to ask her to go back to who she was before. She didn't tell us until she knew absolutely that this was who she was becoming. Until she'd looked into all the options and found none. At that point, it didn't feel like she could go back.

CHANGING FAMILIES

Our whole family was changing. Who we were to the outside world. Now, my parents acted like sisters instead of partners. They shared clothes and books and make-up. People didn't question that my dad was my aunt. We looked closely related, but no one looking at us would have said, "Oh, that's her dad."

Noelle H.'s parents split up around the same time her dad came out, which changed her world, too. "I still found it a little shocking when it happened, because, you know, your life is normal to you and you have rituals and so all those rituals get upended, so it was still a little bit shocking." The family routines changed, too. Her relationship with her dad was different now. "Over the course of high school, I would get the divorced dad visits. Every Saturday we'd go out for burgers and we never did stuff like that when my dad lived with us. We literally never spent time—the two of us—ever, so that was the first alienating factor. And then my dad started physically morphing, a little bit all the time." The shift in her parent was accompanied by a change in the family, too.

In my family, we didn't have any models in the media and very few in books, so there was a lot of guessing and trying things out, improvising as we went along, as the shape of our family changed. We met some other people in transition, and once we even met another family with a parent in transition and little kids younger than me and my sister, but we didn't connect with them, so we went back to being mostly alone and isolated in our experience. We had to find our own way.

MAKING SENSE

Sometimes, it can feel like the pieces coming together. Now, all those parts of our parents make sense, like for Jennifer, whose father dressed in skirts and dresses for years in the house before coming out, or for Olivia, who found her dad's female name on social media.

It can feel like things settle down and make sense.

Olivia looked back in her journal and found entries where she was so close to knowing, but she didn't make the leap from what she saw to what was happening. Once, at a restaurant, a waiter mistook her dad for a woman and her mom got upset. She just thought her mom was overreacting.

Becca looked back at family vacation photos, from when she was four or five, where her dad was shaving his legs. At her sports games, her dad gravitated to the other moms. This part of her parent's identity was there in some ways all along. It might be there in other dads, too, even cisgender dads. Not every change in gender expression has a meaning. For Becca, clarity came later. Once her dad came out, she made sense of all the pieces.

YOUR TRANSITION, TOO

As much as it feels like it's your parent's transition and your life is separate, it's not. It's your transition, too. That's not to say that this defines who you are, but you will have your own zig-zag path through this. It will be yours. And you'll need your own community, too. I didn't think that I needed a community. My family felt like a community of four. I could talk to my sister and my mom. If someone had offered me a community or a place to go, I would have probably said, "No, thanks." What I found out later was that community can take many forms. It can be one person who says, "Yeah, I've been there." It can be a group or an online chat. It can be a book or article. It can be someone in your family who really listens.

As Leila said, if your parent really loves you, they're going to tell you they're transgender. It's about trust. People who care will share about who they are, inside and out. If you've only known your parent as transgender, like Leila, you might come to a place where they share what this means to them from their experience.

There might not be a conversation if you've only known your parent as transgender. It will come out like the rest of their life and yours—in pieces. You will learn over time what it means for them and for you. At one point, they might not share openly in the wider community, and then they might change their minds, too. You can do the same.

Your parent might be crossing the lines of gender or they might have already crossed, but all along you can find out where you fit in. And wherever you are in terms of understanding, that's where you can start.

Toolbox for First Steps

1. Awareness: Learn what it means to be trans for your parent first. Ask questions if you need to.
2. Acceptance: You may land on acceptance quickly, but don't rush there if you aren't feeling it just yet.
3. Action: Take an action on behalf of yourself and your trans parent that feels good and right to you.
4. Know that this will be a transition for you, too. You'll need help and support through this shift in your family. Whether you need help navigating the shape of your family or your parent, don't be afraid to ask.

LEARNING THE BASIC TERMS AND IDEAS—WHAT DOES IT MEAN TO BE TRANSGENDER?

"Do your research. Knowledge is strength."

—VICTORIA T., AGE 32

The word "*transgender*" wasn't in my vocabulary when my dad first transitioned. At the time, if I had to define what was happening, I would have said that my dad was slipping on a new skin and a new identity. To me, "transgender" implies occupying more than one gender, being "across" genders, but what I saw was a transfer from one body to another, a metamorphosis. It was more like shape-shifting than overlapping. If you had stopped me in the street to ask what "transgender" meant, I wouldn't have known what to say.

I was given the word "transgender" later, and it was one I hid with shame. I didn't have any friends with a transgender parent, so I had no idea what it meant. People at the time associated "transgender" with things that were hidden and taboo, with prostitutes and gigolos, with people who didn't fit in. I didn't like the word at all. I also didn't know what it meant. I just didn't want anyone to know that the word was connected in any way to my family.

"Before I could even deal with my own feelings, I had to educate myself about what 'transgender' is."

—COLLEEN M., AGE 44

So, let's talk about some definitions. Language and concepts of gender are changing all the time. As new ideas evolve, we learn more about ourselves and our families. Keep in mind, too, that everyone has their own unique preferences for language and how it relates to their identity, so when in doubt, respect those chosen terms. Your parent might teach you something new about gender that you didn't know. With that in mind, let's get started.

Sex

According to the GLAAD Media Reference Guide, our sex is our classification at birth as either male or female. Check your birth certificate—it's probably written there. It's based on the appearance of our anatomy. In actuality, it's a mix of factors including "chromosomes, hormones, internal and external reproductive organs, and secondary sex characteristics."

Subconscious sex

Our subconscious sex, according to Julia Serano is "a deep-rooted understanding of what sex...[our] bodies should be." She shows how you can determine this by asking an audience: "If I offered you ten million dollars under the condition that you live as the other sex for the rest of your life, would you take me up on the offer?" This points to our underlying sense of our identities.

Gender identity

GLAAD defines gender identity as that "internal, deeply held sense of...[your] gender." For some this might be man or woman or boy or girl. For others, it exists on a spectrum and might be described as non-binary or gender queer. Gender identity is invisible, unlike gender expression.

Gender expression

What's that?! Gender expression is the way you show your gender on the outside—this includes things like your name, pronouns, clothes, hair, how you act, voice, and/or body presentation. Other people see this as gender, and the way they see it is very much influenced by culture and society. Transgender people want their gender expression to match up with their gender identity—not with the sex assigned at birth.

Sexual orientation

This is who you're attracted to—who you want to date. It's not defined by gender. Someone transgender can identify across the spectrum of sexuality: straight, lesbian, gay, bisexual, queer. A transgender man who dates men might identify as gay, for example.

Transgender

The GLAAD definition is "an umbrella term for people whose gender identity and/or gender expression differs from what is typically associated with the sex or gender assigned at birth." People under the umbrella might describe themselves using one or more of a variety of words. Don't assume! Ask what they prefer. A transgender identity doesn't depend on how someone looks or on any medical interventions.

Transsexual

This word was developed in medical and psychological communities to describe someone who permanently sought to change their sex assigned at birth through medical interventions. The word has also been adopted by some living full time in a sex other than the one assigned at birth. If someone prefers this term, they'll tell you. This word is not interchangeable with transgender, though, so don't assume.

Trans

This is a prefix often used as a shorthand in reference to the transgender community. It derives from the Latin word meaning "across from" or "on the other side of." Many consider "trans" to be an inclusive umbrella term for gender expansive identities. At the same time, it's important when using it to consider the context. Not everyone understands the meaning.

Gender expansive

An umbrella term for anyone who expands notions of gender expression and identity beyond gender norms expected by society. This is the term I would have adopted if given a choice when talking about my family. Trans contains a hidden binary, while this term feels more open and all-encompassing.

Transphobia

Transphobia is a term often used to describe the "fear of" or "aversion to" trans people or trans concepts. The word can also be used to describe the assumption that cisgender identities are "more natural and legitimate than those of trans people." Additional helpful terms include "trans-antagonistic," "trans-suspicious," and "trans-unaware."

Microaggression

The act of invalidating another's identity or experience through a subtle verbal or behavioral slight, whether intentional or unintentional. One example would be when someone asks Kim, who has two female-identified parents, one trans and one cis, who her "real" mom is. "I have two moms. Period," Kim says.

Cross-dresser

Anyone and everyone can wear clothes of a different sex, but this term refers to those for whom it is an integral part of their identity.

Transition

This is the process of leaving behind one's sex assigned at birth. This may include, but is not limited to: telling family, friends, and co-workers; using a different name or pronouns; legally changing one's name/sex on official documents; hormone therapy; various types of surgery. The timeframe and choice of this process is unique to each person.

Sexual reconstruction surgery/gender confirmation surgery

This refers to any "doctor-supervised surgical interventions," which make up only one small part of any transition. These terms are preferred to "sexual reassignment surgery" or "sex change."

Gender dysphoria

This is a clinical term referring to any symptoms that arise when one's assigned gender/sex doesn't match with felt experience. This is the term used in the *Diagnostic and Statistical Manual of Mental Disorders*. Some advocates believe the inclusion is essential to advocate for medical coverage for treatment. Others believe it creates a false sense of pathology. The term might be helpful for some, but not all.

Cis

A prefix or adjective meaning not trans originating from the Latin word for "on the same side as." Can be used as an umbrella term to describe those whose gender identity and/or expression is the same as what is typically associated with the sex or gender assigned at birth.

Cisgender

This is also an umbrella term and is used to describe people who identify and express their sex or gender with what is typically associated with the sex or gender assigned at birth. It can be shortened to "cis."

Gender non-conforming

This is a descriptive term for people whose gender expression differs from the societal and cultural expectations of masculinity and femininity. Being transgender doesn't make someone gender non-conforming. In fact, many transgender men and women adopt conventional gender expression according to societal expectations.

Non-binary

This is the preferred umbrella term for all genders other than female/male or woman/man. Non-binary individuals might define their gender as falling somewhere on the spectrum between man and woman or as wholly different from those ideas. Some also use the term "gender queer." Another non-binary identity is "genderfluid" when gender identity or expression shifts and changes over time.

Kids of Trans

People with one or more transgender or gender nonconforming parent. Can be abbreviated as "KOT." Another term used is "People with Trans Parents" or "PTPs."

These definitions were compiled using the *GLAAD Media Reference Guide*, Julia Serano's *Whipping Girl* and "Julia's trans, gender, sexuality, and activism glossary!" on her website *PFLAG's National Glossary of Terms*, and the *National Center for Transgender Equality*'s reference guides. All of these texts include additional helpful tips on understanding and etiquette within the larger community. See the References and Resource Guide at the end of this book for details on these and additional texts.

??

Prompts for First Steps

1. How did you find out your parent is transgender?
2. What was your initial response? How did your family respond?
3. How do you feel about it now?
4. Which words in the definitions section were new to you? Which words would you add?

Chapter 2

Coming Out or Not

What if everyone in your school had a trans parent? Or in your neighborhood? On your block?

Flip the world upside down so that every family is like yours. How would that change your idea of your family?

What if we didn't have to decide how and when to tell about our families? What if we didn't have to "come out" at all?

"Guess what? I have a trans parent!"

You might want to shout this from the rooftops or you might want to hide under a rock. Both are acceptable responses based on where you are today. It can change tomorrow. What I didn't know when my parent came out was that I would have to come out, too—to friends, to bosses, to people I met. That coming out would be a process that would continue through my life. Sometimes it would be easier than at other times. And it's not entirely about my parent, though they're a part of it. It's about me saying this is a part of my story.

The more we say it, the more people see this is part of our lives. Someone at Christy's church was telling her about how she was taking her kids out of softball because the coach was transgender.

"Okay," Christy said. "I guess I'm confused about what that has to do with teaching softball."

"I just don't know if I want my kids around that—I mean—what would you do? Would you let your kids be around that?"

"Well," Christy said, brightly. "My dad's a woman now, so I don't really have a lot of other options—we just—yeah—they're around it."

There was a big group of ladies standing around, and they all looked back at Christy, dumbfounded. Christy shrugged.

"Yeah so, I don't know, you get used to it." She walked off.

Christy said, "I was like, 'Mic drop!'"

Her response snapped the woman's story into focus. This was no longer something happening *over there*—to *them*. It was happening right here with her friends and community. It was happening right next door. It's important, too, to know how your parent feels and not to inadvertently out them to someone who might respond with hostility or excitement or advice for your parent that they don't want. Coming out is also about your own understanding and where you're coming from, so let's get started.

WHETHER YOUR FAMILY DECIDES TO BE "OUT" IN THE COMMUNITY

Some families tell their extended family and community all at once, maybe even throwing a coming out party, like Noelle H.'s family. Some families tell a handful of people, or the community finds out over time. Some keep it within the family. Some opt not to share widely for various reasons. There's no one right way to do it. Whether the family decides to be "out" in the community or not, this choice impacts each family member. Whatever the family decides to do, it can also shift and change over time.

My family was not "out" in the community. My trans parent was known as my "aunt" to all but very few. Later, when she wanted to reclaim being a parent, people assumed she was my mother. I didn't want to "out" her, but I also felt conflicted by this perception.

I wasn't told directly to hide the truth about my father; just that the new name we should say was "Dana" instead of "Dad," and that if someone asked, this was our "aunt," our dad's sister.

I got really good at reading social situations. I would assess: What kind of situation is this? What kind of person do I need to be here? I did this a lot in school—I learned to show certain versions or ideas of my family.

For Justin B., in Tennessee in the early '90s, coming out didn't feel like an option. "I was told then, and for the next four to five years, that it was a secret." Keeping it a secret was a protective measure at the time. "We had to keep it from everyone—family members because of my mom being scared of me being taken away or some kind of retribution, and the people around us, for safety." The culture around them wasn't welcoming of differences. "We had no idea how people would react." Once the transition started and they came out to people over time, some people disappeared from their lives. "A lot of the friends that she lost and the friends that I lost stepped away in maybe not a graceful way but in a way that wasn't violent. Nothing bad happened." It was the fear of potential violence or hateful responses that kept them quiet.

When Noelle H.'s family threw a coming out party for their

extended family and community, it was designed to celebrate, in part, and to face any misunderstandings head on. "If you kind of threw it in people's faces and were really up front about it, people would feel forced to be accepting, even if they didn't want to be accepting," Noelle said. When I first heard about the party, it seemed like the ideal solution. To tell everyone at once instead of keeping a secret and having to tell people one by one. While it worked for a time and for many people, some parts of the community—in particular her father's work world of advertising—distanced themselves later on. "It became really hard to tell during the years that followed whether she had lost work because she was trans or because she was a woman and they didn't know she was trans." Over time, the door that had initially been flung open closed with some in the wider community.

People might ask when they see your parent around town. As Sarah W. described, "One of my mom's friends was driving by our house one night while my dad got out of the car dressed, and she asked my mom, 'Who was this person in your driveway?'" After a while, her dad decided to come out by simply dressing and showing up on people's doorsteps. This strained her parents' relationship, especially when her dad told some of her mom's friends and family before she was ready to tell.

For some, parts of the community might already know, but that doesn't automatically make it easy to talk about. Sharon S. described moving to a small town in Michigan when her parent transitioned. "Everybody knows everybody. As soon as we moved up there, everybody in town knew Trish has two daughters and they're Laura and Sharon and she's married to Marsha." She went to a friend's house for a playdate, and Trish was going to pick her up. "I knew Trish was going to show up in a dress and I didn't want Trish to come to the door and I was very agitated." As the time approached for Trish to pick her up, she didn't know what to do.

Her friend's mom sensed this and said, "Sharon it's okay—we know."

Sharon didn't know how to respond. She recalls, "I just couldn't talk."

She looked at her friend's mom and said, "What do you mean? Know..."

Even if others know, it's not an immediate open door to acceptance and ease.

COMING OUT AT SCHOOL

In sixth grade, my school had a Father and Daughter Dance. As soon as I heard about it, I knew my dad couldn't go. Already, her hair had grown long, past her shoulders, and her skin was smooth. Each week, she came back from electrolysis with puffy red skin. Even if she wanted to, she no longer looked like my dad to other people. That's all I thought about—what other people would think.

In my sixth grade class, no one else had a dad who was transgender. I went home to a parent who, more and more each day, was changing, but none of my friends knew this. To me, it was private and belonged only to us. When I found out about the dance, I went home to my parents. "What are we going to do?" I wanted to know. My parents had a solution. Donnie, my dad's ex-partner, would take me. This felt like the best possible solution. I was excited to have Donnie take me to the dance. Still, it didn't change the fact that I knew I had to hide this one part of my family, and that I had to bring someone to stand in for this role.

At the time, all that mattered to me was that I would be

there with someone who looked the part and fit in. I didn't think of the fact that it wasn't fair. The other girls got to celebrate with their dads, but I didn't, because my dad didn't fit that role in society's view. At the dance, I still worried that Donnie didn't quite fit the part—that he stood out in the crowd of dads in gray and navy blue suits with his gelled hair and white cardigan sweater. If Dana had brought me, though, no one would have known how to respond.

Sharon S. remembered bringing Trish to her Father and Daughter Dance. "It was Trish with a ponytail and then a billowy shirt with a Western tie, and that's my dad showing up to the Father and Daughter Dance and nobody else is dressed like that! I was just thinking, at least Trish isn't wearing a dress right now... That used to give me a lot of anxiety." In school, the desire to fit in can trump any other wish. The desire to look the part. Sharon kept quiet about it for the most part. "I never told anybody when I was younger, I never spelled anything out, but everybody kind of had an idea, but still it was just terrifying to talk about it."

Over time, hiding the truth was ingrained in me. "They wouldn't understand," I thought. "No one needs to know." We came up with a simple story made up of a mix of lies and truth: My parents were divorced [true]. My dad went to London [true at one time, in 1982, but a lie now]. My dad's sister came to stay with us [lie].

We lived far enough away from family and friends who had known Daniel well that the story stuck.

At the start of high school, my parents brought me to boarding school. They came together as my mother and aunt. I watched Dana like a hawk to make sure she was playing the part of aunt—that she was fitting in. They met my new roommate's parents. Everyone was smiling and no one seemed to think anything was wrong. As soon as my parents left, though, I felt a huge wave of relief. It was so much better without them there—that's what I thought.

Most teenagers have this sense of rebellion, but most teenagers don't get a chance to move 3,000 miles away from home. That's what I did. For four years, I kept the truth about my family a secret. Even my closest friends, who I confided in about boys and my period and everything else, didn't know.

It didn't occur to me to tell my friends the truth. It wasn't something that I struggled with—wanting to tell and not having the words. It was simply a closed door. No way was I going to tell. All through high school, I simply told people my dad was in London. The summer before my senior year, I spent a month in London.

"Will you see your dad?" a friend asked before I left.

A beat passed.

"Yes!" I said. I'd almost forgotten the story I'd told.

That summer, I visited a couple who had known my dad before and after the change. I felt pinned under a microscope as the man asked me questions about my experience. I didn't know what to say. I talked about it so rarely, I didn't have the words. Also, when it happened, there was an ordinary aspect to it, an everydayness that people didn't understand. It wasn't strange inside our house; only when we went outside.

I thought the aunt story was unique to us, but Sharon shared a similar story from her high school years. "I introduced Trish as my aunt to my boss at this little clothing store when I was in high school." Her boss knew the truth, but didn't say anything. "I was old enough to know better, and to know that adults would probably know already, but I still was sticking with this charade."

The aunt story was the one I felt most comfortable with for

a long time. In high school, I would announce to friends that my aunt had sent a care package. What if I had told them that it was my dad sending baked cakes and cookies? My friends might have asked. "Why does your dad sign the letter 'Dana'?" I didn't want to answer any questions.

When Morgan's dad came out as trans, they sent a letter to the preschool community asking for their support of the family, but especially of Morgan. The preschool distributed the letter, so the school community knew, as well as her friends at that time. In later grades, she was more selective about who knew. "I started hiding details about my family life in a protective sort of way because I was being ostracized based on my own appearance and I felt so vulnerable around that that I just didn't want people to have any other information about me that they could use to hurt." At the time, her parents were living apart, and she kept both of their identities secret. "Not only was I hiding that my dad was trans but I was also hiding that my mom was a lesbian."

When Morgan reached high school, she had a different perspective. "I wanted to be myself, I wanted to better express myself, I wanted to be more comfortable in my own skin, and I didn't want to be ashamed of myself any longer." This wasn't just about her family. It was an overall feeling that she had. "I no longer wanted to keep this information secret, so I began to talk about it more openly." The first person she told was a new friend of hers in her math class. "Her response was so welcoming, verging on excited for me, that I think it helped me in going forward and sharing with other people."

We often think of bullying as happening between students, but teachers can be bullies too. Sharon's sister had a math teacher in high school who held her after class and said, "I know what your dad is doing and I don't approve." At the time, her parent was sharing her experience in a gender studies class at a local college, and the teacher didn't agree with this.

"How devastating for my poor sister, you know," Sharon said. "And it's like how do you go through and finish your semester after he says something like that?"

As schools start to educate about gender expansiveness, more responses are changing. Leila L. described the range of responses from her friends at her school in Portland, Oregon, such as "Cool!" or "That's awesome!" or "Oh..." It's not a big deal, which reflects the changing times. As new people join her school, she has a chance to tell her story, which doesn't set her apart but makes her special or unique. "There were two new girls and they still didn't know what my story was, so I told them about it and they were kind of really surprised." That's a shift from the times of trying to fit in at the Father and Daughter Dance or avoiding pronouns to hide the story.

WHAT IF NO ONE KNOWS?

"Since virtually no one knows that I do, in fact, have a transgender parent, the only challenges I have faced thus far are internal."

—LESLIE Q., AGE 24

At the time when my dad transitioned, "passing" was encouraged by the therapist and doctors. To qualify for surgery, she had to live full time as a woman for a whole year. She had to be a part of society in this new role. She wasn't given the option of living in between. "Passing" raises questions about our expectations about gender.

It used to be that the goal was to "pass," to slip by unnoticed, but more people are recognizing that all of us are more gray areas than black and white. We're still cracking open our gender codes. There's still more to learn for all of us, more parts of the spectrum we have yet to see.

"Passing" felt like a superpower at the time—that practically overnight, she could slide on a headband and a skirt, and disappear into this new role. It felt like magic. No one asked and no one stared. As my "aunt," she could say things that would sound like bragging if people knew she was my dad.

"Passing," for me, meant telling only part of the story, hiding in a way from the whole truth. To my parent, it was a comfort to slip by unnoticed, to not stand out or be put in the spotlight. To me, it was complicated by my own desire to fit in, while also wanting to tell the truth.

I became watchful of the world around me. Once, Dana and I went to a soup and sandwich place for lunch. Half of my attention went to checking the faces of the people around us to see if anyone was staring, and the other half was simply going out to lunch. I became a guard, whether I wanted to or not.

If my parent slips by unnoticed, I don't face the direct discrimination that can come up if my parent stands out. As Noelle described it, "I didn't have to deal with the challenge that might have been facing us had people been able to tell." She also emphasizes that it was a choice of her parent. "Now there are people who don't even seek to pass." Like my parent, hers disappeared in the crowd. "That was my dad's goal—she was really good at it—nobody could really tell." That was the same in my family. It felt like we were succeeding, but at what?

For me, I didn't experience bullying or ostracization from my peers, but the desire to pass and that goal to fit in built up an internal resistance to being different. It put the focus on how we looked to the outside world instead of who we were on the inside.

If people don't know our parents are transgender, then where do we belong? I wanted to fit into the straight, cisgender world, but that didn't always feel like the place for my family. At the same time, my family's place in the LGBTQ+ community shifted with transition, too.

SHIFTING IDENTITIES IN THE LGBTQ+ COMMUNITY

I once went to a gathering for COLAGE, a national organization for people with one or more LGBTQ+ parent, where I saw a family that I perceived as straight. I wondered what they were doing there. Later, I learned that one of the parents was trans. They looked straight on the outside, which changed how the world and the queer community saw them.

For me, the opposite happened. My parents, who the world once saw as straight, now looked like lesbians when they went out together. As a teen, this was mortifying to me. Still, my mom didn't identify as a lesbian, and they weren't a couple in the way that they used to be, so it was confusing.

When my dad was gay, there was no question about that identity. We were folded into a bigger community through partners. When my dad was trans, it was like being alone and navigating through rough terrain. There wasn't the same strong community of support. We found ourselves on the outside, even in the LGBTQ+ community. For a long time, it felt like the "T" was silent.

The trans community was more dispersed, with some in hiding, trying to "pass," and some in families. Dana's therapist connected her with other people in transition, but it didn't feel like a community. It was one person here or there, coming out in secret. It wasn't a group that embraced us and said, "Here, you belong with us." In a way, it felt like we didn't belong anywhere; not to a bigger group who shared the same identity.

I used to see our isolation as simply part of the fact that there were fewer trans families at the time; but, in fact, the medical model was designed for isolation. Julia Serano talks about this in her study of the problematic science at the time. The gatekeepers required a "real-life test" of living full time in the chosen gender. Each step of the way, gender ambiguity was discouraged and silence encouraged. The hoops and steps led to isolation and invisibility, serving society more than families.

Most people with trans parents who I spoke to shared a sense of isolation, of not feeling connected to a wider community. That is one of the biggest obstacles they faced. It impacted coming out for them and their families. The wider the community, the more support for "coming out" and all things. Now, there's a wider community, but there's still a way to go in terms of supporting families in transition. The "T" is no longer silent in LGBTQ+, but the community for trans families could still be strengthened further.

YOU "COMING OUT"

What about your own "coming out" about your family? When do you tell your friends? Many children with trans parents consider themselves and their families when it comes to sharing with their community.

Monica C. lived in a separate town from her parent, which gave her a sense of choice. "It was kind of nice that we didn't live in the same town, so I got to choose who knew and who I shared the information with and to make my own choices." The question of who to tell came next. "It was this interesting experience deciding which of my friends to tell and who could I trust with this information and who did I want to talk about it with." Sometimes it can clarify friendships and give perspective on who we trust.

Jennifer R. was initially selective about who knew. "There were some of my friends that I told right away—I was like, 'Listen—this is what's going on' and they were fine with it, but there were also friends that I hid it from." The friends who matter will stick around, but it's hard to see this sometimes. "There were just some people that I hung out with and I was like, 'You're just not going to get it or not going to accept this.' Now I'm like, 'Well, shouldn't have been friends with them.' I have a bit more perspective now." This can be the gift of having a family that's unique. It's a built-in way to find out who your real friends are. The real friends won't judge or criticize. They'll just want to know more and support you with whatever's going on.

I didn't tell any friends outside of our immediate family circle and the few close family friends who knew until I left college. Even my closest friends from school didn't know. Some of them described their surprise when I finally told them. I'd told them everything else under the sun, and here was this big part of my life that I didn't share.

The first person I told outside my immediate family was my college boyfriend. A friend was there to help me tell him, but it was still hard to say out loud. My friend told most of the story. He didn't reject me as I thought he might. Still, after telling him, I kept it mostly to myself. I told myself that I didn't want to tell anyone, but the truth was I was afraid to tell. Afraid of ridicule, rejection, judgment, other people's assumptions, and that they would look at me differently.

Justin talked about how hard it was to tell anyone at first. "When I really started to tell people in an open way, it was—it felt like near panic attack every time—heart pounding, and real, real, real fear every time, but it felt like something I really had to force myself to do."

I related to the fear, the uncertainty of how each person would react.

Positive experiences telling can open the door. Sharon S. started telling friends more in college. She had a group of gay and lesbian friends. She decided to tell, figuring that "this is probably about as safe a space you can ever have." When she told them, their reaction was positive. "They were just like, 'Oh my God, that's so cool... Like, tell me more!'" This gave her the courage to share with more people. "It's nice to not have to pretend."

Coming out can really be about letting people in, a friend told me once. People talk a lot about "coming out of the closet," like you're jumping out from this dark place into the light, but another way of looking at it is letting people in. We can invite people in as we trust them and want them to see more of who we are.

Before coming out, I talked about "my dad" and avoided pronouns. I found a lot of ways to tell half-truths. Only around close family friends could I fully relax. Once I started to tell my own friends, though, my circle widened. I started to let more and more people in.

My initial fear was that this difference would set me apart. What I've found, paradoxically, is that the more I share those differences, the more connected I feel. At times, it has felt lonely to tell someone who reacts in shock or awe. Yet no one has rejected me because of my family. And in all cases, it only made our relationship more open, and in some cases more close.

Jonathan W. shared the sense of loneliness that came with holding a secret or telling those who might not understand. On the one hand, he was connected to a church community where he couldn't tell right away; and on the other hand, when he told friends, he felt they didn't always understand the complexity of the experience. He and his dad were both pastors, and coming out could impact his dad's career and also his own if he chose to be openly supportive.

He said, "It felt a little lonely. To not say anything in that world—this is brutal—I need to say something, but I can't. In the other world, these people are people I love, but they can't understand the complexity of keeping a secret in this world or the fact that this is going to upend everything professionally for my dad, so they said, 'It's going to be fine—it's her truth.' I'm like, 'It is, but you don't understand.' That was hard—that was really hard, it was a hard time."

It did feel safer sometimes when no one knew. As soon as they did, they brought their own assumptions and ideas into the mix. Many of my friends I knew for years before telling them. Right before I told them, I faced my own fear that came from believing that not telling was what kept me safe. I had to break through the fear, to say it anyway, however messy or sloppy it came out.

Here is a snapshot of one of those times: I sat across from my friend Tara at a café in Berkeley. I'd known her for 12 years but I hadn't told her about my dad. The words came out slowly. I think I looked down at the table a lot while I told her. She encouraged me, asking me questions and letting me tell the story at my own pace. That conversation was a turning point in our friendship. We became closer. She shared more about her family. I felt less guarded around her. Bit by bit, I opened up. But she did, too. That's what I didn't expect about sharing my story; that it would bring others to open up with me, too.

"Everyone's family has something," Tara reminded me over the years whenever I went back to the place of feeling like the only one whose family didn't fit into some cookie cutter picture on the mantle. It took a while for me to see that, and I still sometimes fall back into feeling like my family is forever different, but under the surface, the emotions, the struggles are often very close.

With "coming out" come questions and responses. Years later, when I did start to share the story, little by little, different responses came up.

"But you seem so normal," one of my friends said. I laughed, and kept on with the conversation, but her words sank in. I thought people would look at me differently if I told them, and in some cases, this was true. I wanted to know what she thought, why she thought this would make me different.

"For a while, there was no right reaction for me," Justin said. "The first few people I told had this big reaction like, 'That's crazy—wow—I'm so sorry. And what did you do?' And that was so hard. And I was just like, 'No—please stop.'" But then he told some more people, "and they were like, 'That's not really a big deal.' And I was like, 'Wait, are you kidding?' It was revelatory to my idea of sex and gender. It was a really big deal." He happened upon the right response unexpectedly: "Someone said, 'Whoa, you've had some wild times.'" Sometimes we don't know the right reaction until we hear it. "It was this confluence of humor and understanding and respectful seeing that I was like, 'Oh, okay, that's the right reaction.'"

"People don't know how to react," Olivia said. "A lot of responses were like, 'Oh my gosh—how liberal.' Or something like that. Their own discomfort with trans people comes to the forefront and then they say something like, 'I like trans people.' This isn't about that really."

For Olivia, the best responses came from "friends who have

had kind of...something happen in their life that they truly didn't expect that changed the way they looked at the world. Those people had a more empathic reaction."

Coming out is something that's not done just once. It's a continual process. Noelle said, "You have to kind of keep coming out and it's a way of life for all of us. You always have to, because if you use the right pronoun, that's a conversation or you have to at least acknowledge it."

If you decide not to be "out," know that there are people just like you who have been there, too.

Remember, you don't have to answer every question, especially intimate questions about body parts and private parts of your parent's life. You can choose what you want to say to whom and when.

TIPS FOR TELLING

If you don't know what to say to your friends, keep it simple. Don't try to explain everything all at once. You don't have to sum up your parent, your family, the state of the world, and all the shows on television all at once.

"What do you think of *Transparent?*" one person asked me. What I think of *Transparent* is the same, more or less, of what I think of *Six Feet Under* or *Jane the Virgin* or any show I've binge-watched. I get swept up in the characters and story. *Transparent* was another door opening on the conversation, but it was also just a story about a family.

You don't have to be an expert.

Keep it brief.

You don't have to explain everything.

When you tell your friends, tell it like a story that makes the world bigger. Tell it like this is the family you chose, even if you don't always feel that way. Tell it like you're inviting them in to know more about your life; like a gift you're giving; like it's a part of you, but not all; like you're expanding your own world by letting them in.

With telling friends, Becca L. said, "It's all about how you bring it up." In middle school, she told her friends like it was a big deal, but in high school, she just let them know as a matter of course. "I noticed that the more casual you were about it, the more casual they were about it." If you present it as no big deal, they'll take it like that. "If you make it dramatic," Becca said, "it's this whole dramatic thing. If you don't make it dramatic, they don't care."

The way you say it can make a difference.

If they say something ignorant or confused, just let them be confused. Not everyone knows about this and people are still learning. Think of them like they're sitting in a classroom packed with people and they blurted out the wrong answer. Oops! It happens. Be nice to them. Don't close them out. Give them a chance to learn, too.

Some people will want to ask questions but hold back because they don't want to make you uncomfortable. You can open the door, too. All of us have questions. As with any subject that has been silenced or ignored, we all have blind spots. The non-binary is still a blind spot for me, an area where I have questions, but it's part of my experience, too. Just because my parent was asked to check one gender box back in the '80s doesn't mean it fit. She told me recently that neither binary gender identity fits for her, but it was the path she was given, the one that fit most at the time. The questions I have about being non-binary can help me learn that it's part of my family's experience, too. The questions your friends have about your parent and family can help them see that something they previously saw as foreign is part of their experience, too.

WHAT IF YOUR PARENT ISN'T OUT?

Dana is still not out in her community. Years of rejection and meanness keep her very guarded about what she shares. After I left college, she wanted to be known as my parent, not my aunt, but she also didn't want to be outed in the community. This left me and my sister in a difficult position. On the one hand, we didn't want to out her to strangers. On the other hand, when Dana introduced us as her daughters, people automatically assumed she was our mom. It felt like we were lying to people all the time.

Dana went by the Mary Poppins principle: "First of all, I never explain anything." This was nice in theory but didn't always work in real-life situations. Sometimes it left questions hanging in the air unanswered.

I can be open, but when my parent's more protective of who knows, it makes things complicated. Sometimes the excitement I have from the freedom I found through telling makes me want to drag her along with me. I want her to feel the same freedom. But I haven't walked through the years of prejudice and assumptions. I haven't experienced the rejection and fear she found when people learned her whole story. I choose to share my family story with friends, but she doesn't share with everyone. Both of us have a right to our choices.

Each of us has our own separate way to navigate coming out or letting people in. What's important is getting to know when or how you feel comfortable sharing your own story. Start there. Your family might influence some of that, but at some point you can make it your own. If your parent decides not to tell, you can still share it with close, trusted friends. Maybe you won't rent a billboard with your story, but try to share it when you can. This is your story, too.

Danielle C. described how her family navigated this. "She very slowly told people and I let her take the lead on that. She told a couple sets of friends she knew her whole life, and my mom and her therapist and me. And that was it." Over time, her parent came out to more people, and Danielle started to tell more people, too. First, she told her supervisor at work. "I cried in her office a little bit, because I just didn't know how to handle it!" She was dating the man who became her husband at the time. It took her a month and a half to tell him. She told him on a car ride. At first he didn't believe her. Turns out, she picked April 1, April Fool's Day, to tell him. It took her a little while to convince him that she was serious. As she told more people, her own community network grew.

Before going to parties, Dana and I usually have a conversation to agree upon the story for the night. We match our stories up and go out into the world.

At a Christmas party with Dana's friends, someone I'd just met said, "I like your mom—she's got spunk," and I wondered briefly how he knew my mom. Then I realized he was talking about Dana. I smiled and nodded.

This is something we're still navigating. For now, I respect wherever she's at and let those overlapping communities be hers to shape. I have plenty of people I can share the whole story with. I don't need to tell everyone all at once.

Sometimes keeping secrets for so long can make us want to share more of our stories. Noelle said that after keeping a secret for a long time, she became eager to share as much as possible. She became resistant to the act of keeping secrets. "I am almost congenitally incapable of doing it or going along with it, even in other areas of my life." After keeping this inside, we might want to shout it from the rooftops, but we can first check to see who might be coming along for the ride.

STORIES WE TELL

"My mom told me he was transgender when I was eight, which was just before he switched. The biggest challenge is other people's reactions, and trying to explain the situation, or avoid explaining it without actually lying."

—ELIZABETH M., AGE 23

The story my own family invented matches almost exactly the recommendation given frequently to families at the time. Regarding family, some in the medical community suggested, "Young children are better told that their parents are divorcing and that Daddy will be living far away and probably unable to see them." This is similar to the story we created.

It took years before I could talk about it out loud. Those who wanted to be there for me left the door open. One of my mother's friends pulled over once while driving when the topic came up. He didn't pressure me to talk about it. He just left the door open, and when I was ready, I walked through it. He made it clear that he was ready to listen, and left the rest up to me.

"It feels a little confusing to tell people what it feels like to me. So I wish they didn't ask about it."

—KEVIN B., AGE SEVEN

FAMILY SECRETS

Of all the things that impact a family, the strongest for most are the secrets. Five years without telling. Estrangement. Not sharing with some family members. Not telling the truth. The longer and more buried the secrets, the more difficult to unravel.

In my family, we didn't tell my extended family for years. By the time we did, almost 20 years later, no one knew what to say. The silence continued because none of us had any way to talk about it. We avoided the subject because we didn't know what to say.

I remember a cousin asking me once if I would see my dad on a trip overseas. This was before she knew the truth. I don't remember exactly what I said, but I remember seizing up inside, feeling a momentary panic. "What should I say?" I thought. After a pause, I replied in the affirmative, keeping my response vague. The fact of the matter was I *would* be seeing my dad that year— just not overseas, and not in the form that she once knew.

We spent years with secrets that kept our family in hiding. It took a long time to untangle them and bring them out.

The ability to talk about it, to say what we're feeling is something that doesn't come automatically. It's something that must be learned and practiced. This learning curve happens alongside the changes in your family and your parent. If you're wondering where to start, look for the secrets. Find out where those are and pull them out if you can. Uncover the secrets. Don't let them sit in the dark. Try to bring them out into the light of day. Start there. Start anywhere. Let this be a chance to know more about your family, not less. Let the conversations start.

"COMING OUT" ON SOCIAL MEDIA

Social media also impacts the ways we, and our family members, come "out" (or not). How can we avoid outing a parent who is not yet out? What do we do when we have friends or followers who have differing beliefs about trans people or issues? How do we handle trolls, misinformation, and people who are just plain mean?

My trans parent avoids social media, but there are times when I want to share about my experience. Some people, even friends, still don't know my whole story, so what do I do? Safe spaces like COLAGE's Facebook page and the COLAGE People with Trans Parents (PTP) community on Facebook give me a chance to share more openly.

Still, social media remains a key territory for people with trans parents to navigate safely.

"I think social media's a big part of this now," Becca said, "because that's where everyone gets their news, their information, how they learn about new things." At first, she jumped into arguments and debates. "I always used to fight with people and comment back but then I realized there's no need, there's no point. I'd rather put my energy into educating people than fighting with people." She posts articles that educate, and ignores the responses for the most part.

Charlie Craggs, an author and activist for trans rights and education, has this recommendation for navigating social media: "Social media is rife with transphobia, but so is real life. So I just navigate social media the same way I do real life and I just ignore the haters." It may sound easier said than done, but try focusing on the communities that support you and your family. In the long run, those are the ones that matter the most.

SOCIAL MEDIA CHEAT SHEET

Andrea D. Kelley, Ph.D.

Andrea Kelley is a lecturer of sociology of health and medicine at the University of Michigan, Ann Arbor. Her research focus is on gender, sexualities, and health, with a specific focus on people with transgender parents.

Social media can be an important gathering place for learning and sharing information! This cheat sheet will offer some suggestions for navigating social media.

When reading others' posts and gathering information:

- You can learn more about transgender people and families by following trans activists and organizations that support trans people and rights. For starters, try searching online for "transgender activist." Some organizations to consider following are:
  - COLAGE
  - National Center for Transgender Equality
  - Transgender Legal Defense & Education Fund
  - GLAAD
- There are a lot of people out there posting negative or harmful things about transgender people. Sometimes they call themselves gender-critical feminists, and they may be referred to as TERFs (trans-exclusionary radical feminists) by trans activists.
- Some people just post harmful things about trans people for various other reasons (ignorance, transphobia, etc.), and it can be upsetting to read. It is always your choice whether to engage.

When creating your own posts:

- Follow your parent's lead if you post about them, whether or not they are also on social media! Talk to them about their name and pronouns, talk to them before posting old photos or tagging them in posts.

- If you are going to post broadly about trans rights and issues, read work written by trans activists and organizations. They are doing fantastic work, and so much of it is available online. Link to them!
- If you are not trans yourself, be open to trans people's suggestions or criticisms about what you post

Things to keep in mind:

- There are safe spaces where you can ask questions and be supported. Check out COLAGE's website to join the Facebook group for people with trans parents. It's secret, meaning nobody else can see what you post or even that you're a member!
- Take care of yourself, even if that means unfollowing, muting, or unfriending people whose posts or opinions are upsetting to you.
- The trans community is incredibly diverse in terms of background, identity, and gender expression—and so are their families!

Some general safety tips to remember, adapted from the Social Media Cybersecurity tip sheet available at cisa.gov:

- Think! Before you post, consider that you may not be able to erase it completely. Once it's up, someone probably saw it.
- Connect! Consider who you connect with and try to link up with those you trust.
- Protect! Stay safe and protect your information and yourself. Don't share your own location or your parent's.
- Speak up! If someone posts something you find offensive or harasses you online, tell someone about it and take action to protect yourself.

??

Prompts for Coming Out or Not

1. Is your family out in the community?
2. Have you shared about your family with friends? If so, with whom and why?
3. How did your friends respond? Which responses were most helpful? Which responses were least helpful?
4. Is it important to you that your parent looks a certain way or "passes"? If so, why?
5. Are you out on social media?
6. Have you encountered transphobic comments on social media? How did you respond or process these?

Chapter 3

The Transition

Electrolysis. Hormone treatments. Surgery. Clothes. You might notice that, for the first time ever, your parent looks comfortable in their skin. You might have some initial feelings of discomfort. It can feel like getting to know a new person, a new identity. For me, the changes in my parent's dress and hair, the hormones, and electrolysis didn't impact me as much as the surgery. Dana still felt like my same parent pre-surgery. For you, it might be a change in clothes or voice that marks the shift. It's different for everyone.

The transition is not a process with a definite start and finish. No one says, "This is what you must do." Each person defines it for themselves. It can begin and end with a name change or shift in gender expression. It can involve some surgeries or none. For you, it will mean some change to your parent, one that makes them more comfortable in their skin. For you, it's a process of understanding your parent, your family, and yourself.

Back in 1988 when my dad transitioned, there was a clear path based on binary principles: *You must live for a full year in your chosen gender identity before you can have the surgery.*

This was to ensure that the person could integrate into the world in this new identity. It also reduced the number of people who might want it reversed. As a child, I saw the end result as our goal. Everything in between was a dress rehearsal. The surgery felt like the grand finale.

Some parents don't have surgery and others wait for years, amassing the resources and support to do so. For my dad, surgery happened just a couple of years after she started the hormones. When she first started electrolysis, she told my mother once that her face looked like a billiard ball. The swelling and irritation lasted for days. For anyone who questions whether being transgender is a choice, they can look at the hoops that must be crossed, at the sometimes arduous and painful physical changes that must take place.

At the same time, the transition doesn't always start with these physical changes. It can start before that or later. If your parent identifies as non-binary or gender fluid, or even if they don't, each transition will follow its own unique pattern. It will be different for you, too, because you're also part of this transition.

WHEN DOES THE TRANSITION START?

The transition can start with the telling. It can start with the name change, with asking for different pronouns. It can start with a change in dress. There's no one starting point. And in the same way, there's no finish line. When Dana transitioned, I thought the surgery was the big finish line. That was when she would be who she wanted to be inside and out, but it didn't happen like that. The truth was more complicated. There's no one way to be trans, and likewise, no one way to transition.

For you, the transition starts wherever you are and follows you through the changes in your family.

CHANGES IN GENDER EXPRESSION

"Whether she's wearing wingtips or high heels, she's my dad. I love the person in that body."

—COLLEEN M., AGE 44

On days when Dana went for electrolysis, she lay on the couch with a beard of aloe on her face. Her skin turned red and puffy. It took so long to zap the hair from growing at its roots. She told me about a guy who looked like Tony Danza who went every week to get his uni-brow zapped. I pictured the actor in the waiting room at the electrolysist's office. Anything was possible, I figured then. Anything could happen.

Hormones made her softer, her whole body growing a new layer. She wore her hair swept back and pinned to the sides. On her chest, two tiny buds appeared—the start of breasts. Still, as my parent, she was in the background, off to the side. There, but not all the time. I ran in to see her if I needed to know a word or ask a question. I didn't call out her new name the way I used to call out "Dad," but I still went to her with all of my questions and looked to her to explain the world.

You might be used to seeing your parent in a certain way, and this new way of expressing their gender can feel like an unexpected shift.

As a child, I paired people off: boy–girl, boy–girl, boy–girl. I grew up watching Disney princess tales where the prince came along to rescue the princess just in time. I thought of the world in boy–girl pairs. In the same way that I thought of couples only as boys and girls, I thought of dads only as men. As soon as my dad started wearing skirts, he couldn't be my "dad" to the outside world. All the button-down shirts and skinny jeans got boxed up, along with the topsiders and blue-striped sneakers.

These were all things my mother might have worn, but for now, they were off-limits in Dana's wardrobe. To me, as soon as the dress changed, the shift felt absolute. This wasn't a temporary change. This was who my dad would be from then on.

Noelle H.'s dad had been gruff and boring to her, so this new aspect of her parent didn't quite fit. "I didn't know how to process the women's clothes part of it," she said. "I had pop culture references for it, and they were all kind of cartoony. In the *Tootsie* vein or, at the time, the *Phil Donohue Show*—daytime talk shows and movies that felt over the top." In '80s talk shows and movies, people who crossed the gender lines were often shown in exaggerated contrast with a fake moustache or lipstick and heels. As she tried to reconcile the person she had known as her dad for 15 years with the new person emerging, she also started to see that this was about more than clothes. "The way it was presented initially, was like, 'Your dad likes to wear women's clothes sometimes. Not in front of you, but just sometimes.' It became clear to me after the first year or two that this wasn't just 'I like to dress as a woman.'"

Your parents will probably try to talk to you and explain what's going on, but you'll see through the stories. Your own observations and experiences will fill in the missing gaps.

For years, Danielle C. watched her stepdad go to work dressed in an almost uniform of sorts. "She worked for the federal government, and every single day wore a short-sleeved, starched white button-down and slacks." Seeing her stepdad dressed like that all the time made her gender seem fixed. Danielle didn't expect at all that her stepdad was planning to change, in part because she'd watched her go to work each day in that almost uniform. In their first conversation about the change, her stepdad had talked about the dream of choosing what to wear, of deciding between a peach skirt suit and a black and white dress. As she told Danielle about the dream, it dawned on her what her stepdad was saying. All those years going to work in those slacks and short-sleeved shirts, she wanted something else.

Jennifer's parent wore skirts and dresses around the house for years before she decided to transition. For her, the clothes weren't a big part of the change or shift. They were already a part of who her parent was.

For Morgan, it was similar. Her parent already dressed according to his chosen identity well before the change. "There were physical changes that I observed in my dad gradually over time. His dress didn't change significantly. His way of speaking and relating to other people didn't seem to change a whole lot."

Even described growing up with a parent who was outwardly very manly. His father was "a really macho man with big muscles, and he even had a beard—he was dressing up as a woman with a beard, but that was at a point in time when he was trying to sort of suppress it in a way." Over time, his dad changed more, and that gender expression shifted until his dad was "a very subtle woman—more like a house mother in a way."

When Amy's parent wanted to go for a makeover together, Amy didn't know what to say. This wasn't something they'd done together in the past, and Amy had no interest or knowledge about make-up at all. "She asked for me to go with her to get a makeover and I said that I wasn't comfortable with it because I don't wear makeup—I don't care about clothes, shoes, makeup—I'm not that person." When Amy expressed her discomfort, her parent got emotional. "She cried, and I was just like, 'I don't know what to do.'" Amy didn't want to share in the makeover, which came across to her parent as a kind of rejection or sense of discomfort with the change. A conversation later helped them both understand the other's perspective.

If you can, be open and talk about these changes. Of course, that might be easier said than done. It's not always easy to open up about these things, and we might not even know exactly what we feel.

As a teenager, I had no sense of what my feelings were about my family. My mother had zero interest in make-up. It was my dad who taught me how to put on eyeshadow years before the change. At the time, I was so excited, I went and told my friend Katie.

"My dad taught me all about make-up—how to put on eyeshadow and everything."

"Your dad? What are you talking about?" Katie said, like she didn't believe me.

Later, I asked my mom about it.

"Katie said men don't wear make-up," I said.

"Men wear make-up all the time," Mom said. "Matthew Broderick wears make-up—he has to wear make-up for work. Actors wear make-up."

We'd just seen the sneak preview of *Ferris Bueller's Day Off*. That made it kind of okay, but I also knew not to tell my friends. I tucked the knowledge into my pocket, but kept it to myself.

In a moment of frustration, while still learning about make-up and clothing styles, Sarah W.'s dad said, "My friend's wife goes shopping with her and teaches her how to do make-up. Why don't you guys want to do that with me?"

This came up in different ways, her dad wanting to know, "Why are you having a hard time?"

"Look we're trying," Sarah W. said. "We're really trying—this is just hard for us."

Sometimes it's okay for it just to be hard. There doesn't always have to be a reason. I loved clothes and make-up but didn't always want to share this with Dana. I didn't know why.

It wasn't about the change, either. It was just a time of adjusting and getting used to this part of our lives.

I used to think if I didn't accept everything about her, I was being a bad daughter. But when I forced acceptance, it came out sideways or unexpectedly. It came out in the middle of a trip to a bank or a party with friends. I thought the solution was for her to just leave, go away, and become someone else. Had I let myself have a hard time with it right then, I wonder if it would have been different.

My mother went shopping at Loehman's and brought back extra clothes for Dana. I found Loehman's so awkward with the group dressing room where everyone was getting undressed and showing their lumpy girdles and granny panties. Still, the racks and racks of clothes had enough options for all of us.

My mother also went with Dana to find new suits and clothes and have them tailored for her. Once, I went along to a branch of the fancy tailored clothing store Aquascutum, and I wanted to be anywhere else on the planet. I would have picked the moon with no oxygen or visible life in exchange for that store with Dana. This was my teenage self that wanted nothing to do with any part of my family, except maybe my sister. Both of my parents were an ongoing source of embarrassment to me. All those reactions and rolled eyes were not about Dana. It was my own discomfort and the changes in me that made me want to reject everything about my family. Still, Dana was a prime target. I didn't want to be at that clothing store with her. I wanted to trade in my family for one that fit in with everyone else.

If you struggle with your parent's changes in gender expression, try connecting with the trans community overall. Sometimes, if you see you can accept someone else's gender, you can get perspective on your parent. What if your parent was someone you just met going through this? What if they were a friend? What would you say? It's not always easy to get that distance, but some perspective helps. You might also find that these changes are no big deal or part of the background for you. Your feelings might change over time.

HORMONES AND BODY CHANGES

Now, Dana wore skirts and headbands all the time when we went out. Her body got softer and softer, but she was still mostly sharp angles. The surgery would change that. That would give her the body she wanted. We just had to wait and get through this trial period and then the surgery would make everything be the way it was supposed to be.

The body changes on hormones. My own body was starting to change the year Dana transitioned. Living with my parent during the transition, the changes were subtle—a little bit every day. If you live apart from your parent, the changes might seem more pronounced each time you see them. It feels like an evolution, someone changing bit by bit.

Noelle described how it happened gradually, almost imperceptibly. "My dad started physically morphing, a little bit all the time. It was so slow, because my dad was trying to keep other people from noticing." They were seeing each other for visits on weekends, which was part of the new routine after her parents separated. In between visits, the changes continued, and she would notice new things when they met up. "She started losing weight and her nails got longer, and the hair. Certain things kept shifting. Every couple of weeks, there'd be something different." As it was happening, Noelle didn't know what to say. "I found that disconcerting, but we didn't really talk about it—I didn't really want to talk about it."

As Justin's mom started transitioning in rural Tennessee, they didn't talk about it much, either. His mom hid behind humor and made jokes that Justin half understood. His imagination filled in the gaps. "At one point, I thought that I was just going to wake up one day and everything was going to be different and I would have to instantly acclimate to it, and that really scared me, because I felt like I didn't know what was going on." Would he recognize his parent? Who would his parent become?

You might have questions about these changes. What will it be like to have your parent change like this? How will it be different between you? You don't need to answer the questions right away, but if you can find a way to say them out loud, you can start to come to your own understanding of what this means for you.

My parents thought if they didn't make a big deal about it, then it wouldn't be a big deal. We didn't talk about any of the changes going on, in part because they didn't want it to seem like a big issue. If someone had given me a handbook or guide back then, I would have dropped it and picked up the nearest *Sweet Valley High*. You don't have to force a discussion. Opening a conversation can be as simple as sitting down as a family or as a parent and child and listening to each other's point of view. Becca L. described weekly meetings with her family, with donuts to entice the kids. Whatever shape it takes, you can find a way to talk about it, or just say you don't want to talk just yet.

A blurring of roles can happen in different ways. Amy described how in the midst of transition, her parent became a teenager again. "She ended up wanting to be a younger sister to me instead of my father." Sometimes, when a parent is more vulnerable, they become like a child. Or an aunt or uncle can stand in as a parent. As a parent changes, the roles might shift. *Who are we to each other?* This question comes up in any relationship at different times.

You might have to forfeit your idea of a father or mother, give up having that figure stand in at school events and community parties. At the same time, you might gain an ally later in life. When I encountered sexism out in the world, Dana understood. "It's real," she said, having lived on both sides of the fence. As she moved into a new role in the world, the world acted differently toward her. Our relationship changed, too. All of this was part of the transition

THIS IS ME

As you get to know your parent under all the layers, you are seeing a side of them you might not recognize. You get to know who your parent is, after all. Questions might come up. If this is your parent's authentic self, then who was that other person before, the one you knew and loved for years? Who is your real parent?

When Noelle H. met her dad fully dressed as herself, she didn't know what to expect. Her dad stepped into the room in a striped blue and white top, wearing sensible shoes. "When I saw her, I started laughing—probably more from nerves than anything, but also because she looked like a substitute teacher." She didn't stand out or look flamboyant as Noelle had expected. Noelle said, "She looked nice." From that point on, they spent more time together with her dad dressed as herself. The moment was a turning point for them. "That opened this new horizon—we started getting used to each other, with her being her." In a way, they had to get to know each other all over again. It's a reboot of the relationship, starting from scratch.

Becca L. saw her dad dressed for the first time at First Event, a conference for the transgender community in New England. "Seeing my dad with hair and make-up, I got this feeling in my chest—it hurt—I don't know what it was." Her dad looked so happy. She didn't know how to respond. "To see your dad for your entire life one way, and then another way and he looked ten times happier." She felt conflicted. "I couldn't even be mad, I couldn't even be disappointed. So I was mad that I couldn't be mad, mad that I couldn't be disappointed. I didn't know what to feel." She looked back on her life with her dad—the sports training and other activities they did together—and wondered if that was all a lie. Who was her parent?

In my family, the year before surgery felt like this in between time when my dad lived on the cusp between Daniel and Dana. I have memories from that time where I can't quite remember if it was Daniel or Dana talking to me or taking me to a lecture or bookstore. Once she was Dana, there were pieces of Daniel there, but the rest of the world didn't see them. They only saw Dana. She used to come to my plays at a community theater as Dana, and no one ever looked twice. At one play, I saw her come through the side door and felt slightly anxious, like it was another layer of stuff I had to remember and think about. If Daniel was still part of her, then why was it hard having Dana there?

The therapist who Dana was seeing through the transition told us over and over that Dana was the same person on the inside. Only the outside was changing. But what I saw was that outsides do change insides. Who she was out in the world did change our relationship inside the house. We couldn't split our lives apart and continue having the same relationship.

As our parents change, we sometimes grow apart for a while. Amy S. said, "One of the hardest things for me was this big shift in personality and in interests, because all of a sudden our interests weren't the same at all." She envisioned a future of trans families who don't experience this shift. "I'm hoping that transgender individuals will be able to come out earlier and be themselves and be comfortable by the time they have children, so it's not a transition for the kids." Getting to know your parent all over again adds another layer to the transition.

Sometimes I wonder, "What if I had only known my dad as Dana?" It's hard for me to imagine that. The memories of Daniel are fixed into my brain, even before my own memories started. It was an innate connection. Noelle has a beautiful passage about this in a book she wrote, *Dress Codes*:

> As far as I can tell, babies learn who their parents are through sensing them—the tenor of Mom's voice lulling them awake, the feel of Dad's chest, the strength of his hands, the whiff of her pheromones. What if all those sense associations were suddenly to cease? Would we recognize our parents anymore? Would we think someone else had taken their place?

Before I distinguished shapes and gave them names, there was this unnamed shape called "Dad." Coarse blue jeans, shirts covered with buttons to grab and pull, chunky watches with accordion wrists. Before I knew the name for collarbone, I leaned there and rested my chin in the crook. Ear, heart, skin. The flat, broad chest provided a wall, a haven for my fuzzy head and stubby fists. The hum of pheromones, the smell I knew so well. Before DNA printed the story of genes, a secret knowledge joined my dad and me. I could touch his face without looking and recognize who he was: the shapes and grooves had familial roots, patterned first in the thumbprint and swirling out. Would I always be able to do that? What if the skin became smooth like a hand covered in lotion? What if silk blouses and twill skirts took the place of the jeans and button-downs? What if the voice changed and took a higher pitch? Would I still know from that place deep inside that this was my father?

Those early memories of my dad's body are in there—that's the body I reach for. There's a pattern of recognition that may be linked to survival. We recognize the ones who take care of us, who are essential to our survival. When one of them changes, how do we remake the pattern? How do we recognize them on that innate level?

What if there are parts of our new parent that we don't like? Sarah W. shares her frustration with a self-centeredness that came out in her dad. "It's a lot of me, me, me, which wasn't the way my dad was before the transition." Making sense of it, she wonders if it's some underlying need for validation of her parent's new identity: "I need you to tell me that I am this person now." You look to your parents for support and validation. When your parent is looking to you, it's another time when the roles are blurred, which can make it confusing.

You may also find new parts of your parent that you like and admire. Riley described how he watched his mom transform, becoming more outgoing and taking on community projects with a sense of "freedom of self-expression and feeling like who he was really in our community for the first time." He witnessed a coming out "not just in terms of gender expression, but as a political person, as an outgoing member of my family and our community." This "growth of self-expression" strengthened their relationship.

It could be a mix of both. As your parent says "This Is Me" to you and the world, you might find parts of them that weren't there before or rediscover old parts in a new way. You'll also find out who you are. New parts of you will come to the surface, too.

NOT A BOX

On medical forms, there are boxes to check which designate our chosen or given gender identity. Sometimes it looks like it's an either/or choice. One or the other. The truth is that none of us fit into these boxes, labels, or roles.

Dana told me recently that she didn't know what gender she was. For years, she identified as female. Now, she stands in between. Maybe she always did, but the medical world didn't give her a chance to be otherwise. She had to choose, to fully transition, to fit into that other gender.

The understanding at the time was that if she didn't identify as male, she was female. There was no room for anything in between. There were no gray areas, no non-binary options. In the therapeutic community, there was a push toward the binary.

One non-binary parent I spoke with told of struggling to claim their identity fully, and to come out to their daughter.

Your parent might not want to choose one box either. You might feel like you wish they would. But if your parent doesn't ask you to change who you are, then maybe it's possible to let them be, too. It's never so easy as that, but Christy's "live and let live" idea can apply here. You don't have to fit into a box and neither does your parent.

SURGERY AND POST-SURGERY

One year: 365 days. That's what the doctors thought was needed. To live in her body as a woman. To be in the world as a woman. After that, she could have the surgery. It felt like the surgery was what we were waiting for. The big happy ending when her body would be complete.

Not everyone opts for the surgery. Both costly and difficult, the surgery is not accessible to everyone under current health-care standards. Furthermore, it might not be what your parent wants. You might find that the surgery comes and goes without a big impact. On the other hand, you might find that all the other changes felt minor in comparison.

When Riley's parent went for surgery, it brought about a sense of finality and a bigger change. "I think the stronger reaction for me personally came after my mom got top surgery," Riley said. Before the surgery, he'd been more flexible with pronouns and his parent was still firmly fixed in his mind as "Mom." The surgery brought up bigger questions. Who was Riley's parent to him now? They sat down to have a conversation.

"Your role in my life as my mom..." Riley said. "You don't have my mom's body anymore. When I hug you, it's different." The physical change made it feel like the roles could change. "You sound different," he added. His mom had started hormones, which changed his voice. He tried to articulate some of his feelings that had been there, but unexpressed. "That was a much more emotional conversation," Riley said. Riley's parent said that regardless of the physical changes, he would still be Riley's mom. That role was still firmly fixed. Once Riley knew that, he felt better. His parent's body was changing, but not the role.

The surgery can feel like a turning point, a shift for the family, a milestone for the parent. It can feel like the place where there's no going back.

Morgan G., at age four, felt confused about the surgery. She talked to her older cousin, age nine, who stepped in to "clarify." "They take somebody who wants to be a man and somebody who wants to be a woman, and they lay the people on twin surgical tables and then they cut off their parts and sew them onto the other person." Of course, this was far from how the surgery actually worked. "I thought that would be happening to my dad. I just remember feeling terrified," Morgan said.

As for sharing details of the surgery, we may want to know some, but not all. Amy told her parent, "I don't want to hear anything about your new vagina. I love you and I support you, but how much did you know about your mom's vagina? Because if you did, then that would be weird, but you probably didn't, and so I don't want to know about yours." Parents can feel rejected when you don't want to hear about some details, but thinking of their own relationship with their parents can put it into perspective.

Sharon S. described her parent lying inside with the shades drawn, recovering from facial surgery, her face black and blue. Your parent might opt for some surgeries, but not all. Know that the surgery is not an end point or destination. The transition continues after that for the whole family.

My parents crossed the Rocky Mountains to go to Trinidad, Colorado, for the surgery. All week, my sister and I waited for news at Donnie's house. We talked to our parents on his kitchen phone. Our parents told us that one of the nurses at the hospital desk looked from one to the other and asked who was there for the surgery. They laughed about that. At the time, Trinidad was known as the "sex change capital of the West." Dr. Leland set up his clinic there and offered some of the first sexual reconstruction surgeries in the country. I pictured a place in the middle of the desert where people walked around waiting for their bodies to become whole.

All along, I thought of the surgery as an end point. I was looking forward to it—everything would be complete. The day my parents got back from the surgery, my sister and I waited by the door of our house with Donnie. We heard the car pull into the driveway and stepped outside to see them. Our mom got out of the car first and came around to hug us. She'd recently cut her hair short and got mad when people called her "sir." She helped Dana out of the passenger seat. Dana moved slowly, deliberately, her posture hunched over. She carried a donut to sit on that looked like a toilet cover for old people.

My sister and I were excited, but Dana was more subdued. When we got inside the house, we found a place for her to sit down and rest. We wanted to hear all the stories, but when she opened her mouth, her voice came out in a raspy whisper. Did they change her voice, too? I was confused. The change wasn't on purpose. The anesthesiologist had botched the intubation and damaged her voice. We had to get very quiet to listen, and when she spoke, she turned pale and looked pained, like it was a strain to make any sound come out. Singing was a great joy in her life. She had a voice that carried through whole churches and rooms. She sang, "On a Clear Day," once to a packed church. She sang "Edelweiss" at my parents' wedding.

So much for my happy ending. After the surgery, for a long time, Dana retreated into herself. A sadness filled our house. Here was the step that was supposed to make her "complete," I thought, but it left her without her voice. I wanted her to be okay, but she wasn't. It felt like a fairy tale trade. Like *The Little Mermaid*. You can live on the land, but you must give up your voice. I wanted my old parent back, the one who was silly and sang and whistled around the house. The one who lived in the in between and laughed at everything I said. Where did she go?

The dramatic change in her personality split the transition in two in my mind. Before: Dad who was silly, doting, and fun. After: Dana who was bitter, angry, and sad. Maybe if I'd seen more of my dad, I would have seen them as two sides of the same person. As it was, it felt like two completely different people.

HOW IS THE FAMILY IMPACTED BY THE TRANSITION?

"See the transition as not being about the [parent] going through change, but the whole family going through change. Everyone needs support."

—STEVE VINAY G., AGE 48

Families go through the transition too, even if they aren't the ones taking the hormones or changing physically.

Your parent might shift some of their interests and activities. As they connect to their own trans community, they might find a missing piece of themselves. Where do you fit in all of this? At times, your parent can seem self-focused. They could be preoccupied with changes, both inner and outer. You're going through changes, too. The change of your relationship and who your parent is out in the world is a part of this.

Amy described feeling invisible during this time. "I was not seen at all in that transition. That was really painful. It took me ten years to feel comfortable saying, 'I completely support and understand you, and it was really difficult for me.'" On the one hand, you want your parent to be happy and have the life they want and on the other hand, you might be struggling with the change in your world.

My family didn't stay together after the transition. We moved into separate places: my mom, sister, and me in one apartment; Dana in another, smaller place. She came over, but we weren't all together anymore. It was a confusing time for our family. Our mother urged us to spend time with Dana, but my sister and I dragged our feet. Everything was supposed to be the same on the inside. So then why did everything feel so different?

The transition is ongoing. As Anna M., a therapist who focuses on gender identity, said, there's a lot of focus on the years of the initial physical and social changes. In the media and elsewhere, the spotlight is on that first change. But there are years after that to consider. It's not complete and done once. It's a continuous passage. And the family is part of this passage.

There are more changes than just the physical parts of our parents. The whole family changes, too. Without my dad, we didn't have someone who the world stopped to listen to. Dana grew sad and felt isolated. When it feels like your family is in pieces, what do you do?

You can start with what you share with your parent as a jumping off place. Are there things you still like to do with your parent? Think of five things you and your parent share today. Start there. Don't start in the fissure, in the gap. Start in the places that are already whole.

WHO CHANGES?

In many ways, I changed as much as, if not more than, Dana did. I started out with my mind wide open to anything in the world. In time, as I entered junior high, my mind closed shut and my whole goal was to be the same as my peers. I wanted to blend in and disappear.

At my high school, there was this group of blonde girls who had one honorary brunette as a friend. I thought at one point, if I was blonde too, I could be in their group. Or if, like the honorary brunette, I had a parent who flew in a private plane, then I could be friends with them. I also wanted to have an everyday dad, a dull and boring dad, one who mismatched his clothes and did taxes for fun.

I didn't want to have anything to do with Dana. She was

secretly my parent, but no one knew this apart from a handful of people. I didn't invite her to my high school graduation. I sent out formal ivory invitations to everyone in my family but her. In the end, I was the one who changed the most, who wanted to find my family somewhere else—anywhere other than where it really was.

HOW DID I FIND MY WAY BACK?

The Wizard of Oz was my favorite movie as a child, hands down. My dad gave me my own copy in VHS, and it was the first movie I owned. In that movie, Dorothy clicks together her heels and says, "There's no place like home." She finds that she was home all along. All she had to do was believe it for herself. The same was true for me. My family was in me wherever I went.

All through college, while I told so few people, I thought about what I had learned from my family. I studied ways that gender is constructed in society, but I already knew this. My parents never told me: *There is only one way to be*. Both my parents encouraged me to live according to the quote often attributed to Oscar Wilde: "Be yourself, everyone else is already taken." Anytime I dare to be myself, I return to my family. Over time, the more I accepted myself, the more I accepted Dana, too.

YOU BE YOU

Sometimes it takes the perspective of someone who has been there to understand what you're going through. Your parent has also struggled through a lot and has a lot to offer in terms of advice on handling challenges. If it feels awkward to talk to your own parent, here are some tips from KC, a non-binary parent, who wants her child to remember to be true to herself:

"First, you just have to be true to yourself and always trust yourself. Don't be as worried about what other people think. That's where I always limited myself—I was always scared about how people would see me. Second, accept yourself for who you are—don't limit yourself because you're scared how other people are going to judge you. I liked being different, I liked being the black sheep. At the same time, I didn't let myself fully be myself because of the fear. Third, know who your friends are—who you can trust. Know who your team is, who your allies are, who you can go to and just say anything openly and question openly without being judged."

So be yourself, find your team, and be honest. Don't let fear of what other people will think stop you! If your parent can be true to themselves, so can you, during the transition and the changes in your family and for years to come.

Prompts for the Transition

1. How does it feel to see your parent develop this new identity?
2. What role does your parent play now in your life?
3. Which parts of the change have been easy? Which parts have been hard?
4. How has the whole family been a part of the transition?
5. What lessons have you learned so far?

Chapter 4

Names and Naming

Names matter. The names we use, whether terms of endearment or proper names shape our relationships. We're given names based on our roles in our families. My nephews call me "Auntie Heather." I'm also a sister, a daughter, a niece, a granddaughter, and a cousin. Of those, "cousin" is the only one that doesn't also designate my gender.

In the card aisle at the drugstore, there are sections labeled "For Her" and "For Him." I used to walk past all the Father's Day cards feeling like the only person in the world whose dad didn't fish or play golf.

The names we use for each other and in our family are our constellations and reference points for our lives. When these change, we change too. Who we are and who we want to be is bound up in our names.

Claiming a new name is part of claiming a new identity. Your parent might choose a new name that you have to get used to, and they might want you to call them something different out in public. It can feel like learning a new language. It can feel funny at first to say the new name.

What you call your parent can change over time, too. It did for me. For a long time, Dana was my "aunt" out in the world. That changed when I left college. I had to get used to her introducing me as her daughter, which was true, and the fact that people immediately assumed that she was my mother, which wasn't true in the way they saw it.

You can also find a name of your own for your parent, one that belongs only to you, a term of endearment that fits your relationship. Or you might keep the ones you've used all along.

WHAT DO YOU CALL YOUR PARENT?

"Dana!" I call out across a bookstore in Tucson. The person we're with thinks she's my mother, so I catch myself just after I call out, remembering the story we've told. Still, I don't say "Mom," because that's not a name we've ever used. We ditched "Dad," too, back in 1987, though I sometimes use it when talking to friends. It doesn't have the same strong male connotations as "father," which immediately makes me picture a guy with a long white beard.

Some say "Dad" and "she." Some switch to "Mom." Some say "Mom" and "he."

Riley told a story of a co-worker checking out a family photo on his desk.

"Ok, walk me through the photo—say who they are in relationship to you," the co-worker said.

"That's my dad," Riley started. He pointed directly at his dad. Then he skipped across the picture, vaguely pointing, and adding, "Oh—that's my mom, that's my sister, that's my stepmom." The co-worker backtracked in the photo.

"Wait—who's that?" the co-worker asked.

She pointed to the man standing in one of the rows.

"That's my mom," Riley said. There was a pause. "Yeah, my mom's a trans man." The name "Mom" fit their relationship, but not the co-worker's picture of a "mom." As he showed the picture to his co-worker, he had a chance to make the world a little bigger.

Leila, age eight, said that "having a transgender parent is awesome" because they defy roles. People think that moms do this and dads do that, but trans parents shake up these categories. "Some people say, moms should stay home and clean—blah blah blah—but when you're a man and you transform into a woman, they say, 'Dad should take us out.'" In her family of two dads, she said, "Sam is the one who does the cleaning and Carson is the one who does the work and he takes us places—traveling." Defying roles is just one way having a trans parent can be a gift. The names can reflect the new roles, or you may keep the name and switch the pronouns.

Saying "Mom" and "he" or "Dad" and "she" catches some people off guard. Most people immediately assume that moms are female and dads are male.

Noelle H. says "Dad" and "she," which not everyone understands. "We decided to try and untether 'Dad' from male and it's a harder fight to make with people because—even to this day they'll just say, 'Why don't you just say mother?'" Saying mother creates a whole history for her family that isn't true, and impacts her mom, too. "It creates this image of what my upbringing was, which is totally false, and to whatever experiences I ascribe the word 'mother,' I don't envision my dad."

Jonathan W. also says "Dad," which came out of a conversation the two of them had. "When I asked my dad what she wanted me to call her, she said, 'I want you to call me "Dad" because I've always been your dad.'" The one exception was when they were out together in public. "I call my dad, 'Dad,' but then in public, I say 'my parent' because not everybody knows and I don't want to throw that off." He also uses her new name, Paula, when they're out together. He admits, though, that it's still hard navigating that shift.

Other changes might come before the name. "Pictures of my dad from before are no longer up in my house," Sandra P. said. "That person is gone." Her dad asked her to say "she" and "hers." These changes she accepted, no problem. When it came to the name, though, it was her dad who compromised. "My dad has accepted a few things. She will never be my mom. My dad still lets me call her, 'Dad.'" Sandra uses the name in private conversations at home. "In public, people get confused!"

Some choose to switch names in private and public, while others keep the same name in both. Even B. kept "Dad" both in private and public. This evolved naturally. "I didn't change that," Even said. "As a kid I'd say, 'Dad! Dad! Dad!'" People nearby would raise their eyebrows or look twice, wondering, 'Who is dad? Is that his mother?'" That happened a few times," he said. "People just were watching, like they were wondering why I was crying 'Dad.'" It didn't faze him, though, he just kept saying "Dad." Like Noelle H., he untethered "Dad" from male.

If you switch to "Mom" from "Dad," some people might ask who the "real" mom is. This happens to children with lesbian parents, too. The distinction between "real" mom and "trans" mom is not helpful. As Kim A. from Oakland, California, said, "Don't decipher between my two moms as 'real mom' or such—it's disrespectful and simply untrue; I have two moms. Period." The name, "Mom," is a name that can be shared by both. The name, "Mom," can expand and stretch to include Riley's mom, who now identifies as "he" and Kim's mom, who was once "Dad."

In Justin's family, they said "Mom" from the start, and that was the name they continued to use as he grew older. Christy struggled at first to say, "Mom," though that was her parent's preference. Also, it made sense for the community they lived in. "I know lots of people do it different ways, but to be honest, we live in a very conservative community." At the same time, the name "Mom" just didn't fit for her. "I have this really strong emotional bond with my mom. Calling my dad my mom felt like a betrayal." To her, moms were solid, stable, and steady. Her dad hadn't been that in her life. After struggling for a while, she talked to her mom.

"'Oh—who cares?" said her mom. "Just say she's your mom."

Her mom saying, "Oh who cares?" made Christy feel better about it.

"Okay," Christy said.

The next time they were out together at one of her children's plays, Christy decided to try it out. She told a friend in advance that she was bringing Dee Dee to the play and that she was going to practice saying the new name. "I said, 'This is my mom, Dee Dee,' and my friend's like, 'Oh hey!' and the world didn't disintegrate into chaos—everything was fine—it wasn't a big deal. After that day, I was good."

I felt the same way about saying, "aunt," like someone might pop out of the sky and say, "No, she's not." The "aunt" story came up in a lot of stories of dads becoming women. It also comes up in stories of people with lesbian moms. "Aunt" is the story that fits for blending in and disappearing. My parents, together with Dana's therapist, came up with the "aunt" story in part for me and my sister so we wouldn't be ostracized at our schools. While it seems far-fetched that we would be left out because of our families, I remember being grilled by one girl about what kind of car we drove. Her family, she said proudly, drove a Jeep Cherokee. Apparently, a Volvo was okay, but I felt like I'd narrowly passed the test. In junior high, anything slightly off could plunge me into the social abyss.

The "aunt" story was supposed to help us fit in. We introduced "Aunt Dana," our dad's sister who happened to be visiting. Forever. "Aunt Dana" did pretty much everything our dad did except out in the world she was our "aunt." Overnight, we didn't have a dad, not here. Our dad lived far, far away. That's what we said. After a while, it started to feel true, though. That's the flipside of naming, of the stories we tell. The more we tell these stories, the more we lie, the harder it is to know our own truth. Over time, we might lose track of the real family, the one we're trying to hide.

As a child, I learned the name, "Dana," and recited it like a poem or verse. It took a long time to get used to saying it. Later on, I rejected the name, and wanted to get as far away as possible. It was a name linked with shame, one I wanted to hide. I shone bright lights on the part of my family I wanted my friends to see. *Look at my grandparents who live in a big fancy house! Look at these pictures from our family trip to the Bahamas!* I kept Dana hidden along with her name. Even with the aunt story, I didn't want to have to answer questions about which side of the family she belonged to or whose sister she was, though I had the answers prepared. I just avoided talking about her. Her name felt hollow to me, like a stand-in for the real thing.

My sister and I adopted the name our parents gave us, however begrudgingly. We never came up with a shorthand name, a term of endearment, one that belonged to me and my sister and only to us. Sometimes I wish we had. Calling her "my aunt" was the cover story, but we had our own truth, too.

Your parent's new name might click into place right away or it might take a while. You might never quite get used to it.

You can also come up with your own name for your parent, one that belongs to you and your siblings. Maya P. calls her parent "Momdad," combining the two parents in one.

It can take a while to get used to saying the new name. "Dana" felt like a foreign name to me. It came out of nowhere and landed like a planet in our kitchen the day she told us. Even when I practiced saying it, it felt like a shell, like a temporary name. Not a forever name.

If your parent adopts a new name, you might see right away that this is the name that fits your parent, or it might take time. You might never get used to this name. You might want to hold onto your parent's old name, because that's the one you knew.

If you have to learn a new name, think of that name as a protective shield, a superhero alias, a name your parent picked out, just like they picked out your name. Try saying it like that for a while and see what happens.

On the way to learning this new name, you might find out something new about your parent, too. The names my parent chose were important to her, and part of our family history. The first name was one that could be either he or she, and so reflected her stance on gender. The middle name was one that belonged to a cousin who was a writer. The last name was her grandmother's maiden name. Each name had a story for herself and for my family.

Sometimes I see it as just a name. It doesn't represent our whole relationship. It's just what I call her. It's just what I say when we're out at a bookstore together and in that moment, the word "Dad" doesn't fit. It's a placeholder, not a definition. Who we are to each other goes beyond words, so we can find the names that work for today.

If I could go back, I would change the world around us instead of changing us. I would make them see that a dad can be she, that someone can walk the line between he and she and land somewhere in the middle. Then we wouldn't have to change our story. I would flip it upside down and change the world, instead.

HOW DO YOU SAY GOODBYE TO A NAME?

I have a book Dana gave me for Christmas in 1986. It's inscribed: "To my special Heather. Love, Dad." It's still a treasure to me, because it has that word inside it: "Dad." A name I connected to pure joy. My handsome, doting dad. I had no idea that I would miss saying that word, and that years later, when I did say it, it would feel like a lie.

We didn't come up with another word to replace "Dad." Because in the world, she was our aunt, and in the house, she was still our parent, so it didn't feel like we needed one. We could say "Dana" in her birthday cards and letters, but even a few years into writing that, it felt false to me. I wrote it anyway, but I didn't have a name of my own, one that belonged to me and my sister and no one else.

Jennifer's family came up with a new name: "Mem." "Mem" was close to "Mom," but not exactly, so it fit and was easy from the start. "We call her Mem, because it's not the same as Mom, and it was also kind of like, 'How do I think of her now?'" She tells people she has two moms. "That's how I think of it," she said. "It's that she's just like a mom."

Becca always called her dad, "Da." It started from a young age, when she couldn't quite finish the whole word, and then it stuck. That name fit even after her parent changed. It was open enough that it didn't tag a particular gender. Now, even her friends use the name. "What does Da think?" they say. She said it sometimes feels funny for her friends to say "Da" instead of

"Mr. LaValle," like they used to, but the name works for everyone, even outside of her family.

Sometimes families start with the original name, like "Mom" or "Dad," and then find that they need something else. At a movie theater when he was six years old, Jeremy told his dad, now Lily, that he needed to go to the bathroom.

"Okay, just go," Lily said.

He didn't want to go alone. "Come with me," he said. "Dad, come with me."

Lily was wearing a dress. People stopped and looked. Lily sent Jeremy with his older brother. When they got home, they sat down as a family.

"Okay, guys," Lily said. "I think we need to come up with a different name for me." The boys agreed. "I will always be dad in your hearts, but when we're in public, people are going to question if you say 'Dad' to someone who's wearing a dress." It was very simple.

The boys came up with a solution. "We'll just call you 'Mom,'" Jeremy and his brother said.

That worked for a while. Once, though, when Lily dropped the boys off at their mom's house, their mom came to the door. Jeremy said, "Bye, Mom!" and ran inside. Their mom flushed. She stepped outside to talk to Lily. To her, she was the only one who was Mom. It felt to her like Lily was taking her identity, and that the world would now see her as a lesbian, which simply wasn't true. Lily disagreed, but saw her point. She sat the boys down again. What could they say that wasn't "Mom" and wasn't "Dad" and still fit? They landed on the name, Ema, the Hebrew word for mother, which was different, but also fit since Lily is Israeli.

Not too long after, Jeremy was with his Hebrew school class when Lily came to the synagogue. This was one of the first times she was there as herself. Jeremy was walking down the stairs with his class when he spotted Lily. He gave her a look, like, "What are you doing here?" Lily waved him on as if to say, "Keep going with your class."

"Who's that?" his teacher said.

"That's my Ema," he said. "He used to be my dad, but now she's my mom." It was that simple. The class went on to their next activity.

On the show, *Transparent*, they say "MaPa," which I liked since it's a mix of both parents in one. When I heard the name on the show, I started to think about a name that would work in my family. One that took the place of "Dad." It felt important to have a term of endearment, like it was something we were lacking. Maybe it's easier to say goodbye to one name, too, if you have another to take its place. I didn't come up with one, so it's still a work in progress.

If there is a sense of loss in the name change, it can be hard to admit. Your parent might feel freed up by their new name, so they won't always see why it would be hard for you. People don't talk about grieving a name, whether it's "Mom" or "Dad" or the old name your parent went by. There's no one way, no recipe or guidebook. It helps to know that others have been there.

If you really miss that old name, especially a term of endearment, talk to your parent. Maybe you can use the name sometimes, when it's just the two of you, or together you can come up with a strategy for moving on. Maybe when you hear more of your parent's side or perspective, it will make you want to give up the raggedy old name that doesn't fit, after all.

IN THE NEWS

To officially change her name, Dana had to list it in the newspaper as an announcement. We lived in a big city, so the announcement got buried in the back of the paper. No one called us or said anything on the day it was listed. It just got printed in black and white, and then we moved on. I was grateful for that. I didn't know who would find it and read it. It felt like we were being exposed, having to list the name change like that, but it was part of the law. Now, it was official, set in stone. It got printed on all her documents and cards: passport, driver's license, credit cards. This name that I still had trouble saying out loud was now everywhere. Her new name was Dana, forever and ever. She wasn't going back.

POWER OF NAMES

There's a power in names. We become what we say we are. For Dana, naming was a declaration of her new identity. When KC asked her colleagues to start saying "KC" instead of "Keeth," the human resources department didn't blink. For her, though, it was a big step in claiming her truth.

In my family, everything connected to "Daniel" got boxed up and put away. When we got mail addressed to "Daniel Bryant," we knew it was junk mail. Daniel didn't live here anymore. Most of my extended family didn't know, so they just thought we had this deadbeat dad, Daniel, who didn't show up for anything in our lives. He'd been conveniently erased, along with his name, and most of our family thought he was just gone. The ones who did know and still sent mail to Daniel seemed to be saying that they didn't accept Dana. It's called "dead-naming," when you call someone trans by their old name. I didn't know the word then, but it just felt wrong. That name, Daniel, just didn't fit anymore.

When we started calling her my "aunt," it was just a cover story. After years of calling her my "aunt," though, our relationship changed. Her role in my life became more peripheral.

We became more aunt and niece than parent and child. I also pushed her away a lot as a teenager. I kept her at a distance. Still, it felt like there was a power in naming, in calling her my "aunt." As if by saying it over and over again, it became true.

PRONOUNS

For a long time, I avoided pronouns when I talked about my dad. I danced around pronouns when I talked to my friends. "Who ever says, 'She's my dad'?" I thought. The book *She's My Dad* by Jonathan Williams wasn't out in the '90s when I was in high school. Yet for me, this was the truth. I had a dad who I loved and who was now very much a woman, with "she," "her" and "hers" all over her new life. People still get confused when I talk about "Dana."

"Who's Dana again?" they'll say.

"My dad," I say, or "my parent," but that sounds more formal.

I'm learning I don't have to do the pronoun dance. I can say "she" and "Dad," and "she" and "Dana," and clarify as needed as I go along.

Noelle H. talked about this dance. "If I'm not in the mood or it's someone who I'm like, 'This person doesn't need to know,' I just find ways to not use a pronoun. I'll say, 'My dad's coming' or 'Yeah, my dad'll be here tomorrow.'"

In part, not saying any pronouns is a way to avoid being disrespectful of your parent's wishes. "I can't say 'he,'" Noelle said. "I can't do it—it feels like a betrayal to me."

I feel the same way, which sometimes leads to this dance with words. It's called the pronoun game—when you dance around pronouns to avoid saying the one you want to hide. For me, it was the pronoun, "she," the one my dad had claimed for eight years, the one I still couldn't bring myself to use when talking to friends. So either, I said "my dad" a lot or I said, "he," and felt like I was lying. I didn't know how to do it differently.

The pronoun game became the dance that I did when I didn't want to tell the full truth. I talked about my parents together: "My parents are both writers." "My parents live in Colorado." I left out the messy parts and the in between.

My own pronouns are "she," "her," "hers," and sometimes I take that for granted. I wouldn't want someone to use "he" pronouns to talk about me. Each of us should have that choice, to choose the pronouns that fit for us.

Some relatives used to keep using the "he" pronoun, and sometimes I looked down on them for doing that, like they didn't know better. Sometimes it brought up shame for me, that I had a parent who did something that people so violently objected to that they refused to acknowledge it.

Jennifer suggested that using "they" could be a good in between pronoun when moving from "he" to "she" or "she" to "he." If you can't yet make the leap, that's one to try. For a while, it might sound false, and maybe forever it will, but we can try. We can stop playing the pronoun game and simply try the ones that fit.

What if you say the wrong pronouns? Sometimes, when talking to friends, I used the wrong pronouns. Dana was nowhere in sight, and it still felt wrong. Other times, my friends said the wrong pronouns when feeling around for the right ones. With my friends, I just said, "Usually, I say 'she.'" Or "I call her 'Dana.'" When it came to my own use of pronouns, it just took time. Sometimes my sentences got tangled up in explanations.

Your friends will follow your lead when it comes to names, too. You can say "my parent, who I call..." Or you can say, "Now, I call my dad/mom..." This is a chance, like Leila said, to expand the idea of family roles, to claim the name that works for your family, the one that matches your relationship right now.

We are still learning how to use language to describe our

lives. Maybe somewhere down the line, pronouns will be tossed out the window or we'll share one pronoun. There's more to be revealed about pronouns in the future. There's a lot we still don't know.

CHANGES OVER TIME

Names can change over time. A new term of endearment can come up or a parent may shift identity.

After I graduated college, Dana no longer wanted to be known as my aunt. She introduced me as her daughter and people would immediately assume she was my mother. Since she wasn't out, I couldn't say, "No, she's my dad," which felt more true. When she introduces me as her daughter, I don't contradict her, but this is still an area of struggle for me.

Even my college boyfriend, when I saw him years later, asked, "How's your 'aunt'?" He used quote marks when he said, "aunt," because he knew that this was the story we told. It felt comforting somehow that he said, "aunt." It was the story I knew. It was an old, familiar story, but it no longer applied.

Dana saw that this story had cheated her out of the role she played as our parent.

In truth, I didn't like the aunt story, either. It felt awkward and strange to say she was my aunt when she wasn't, when she was my dad and she—both and all at the same time. Still, it was the story I got used to, just like I got used to hiding my family.

When Dana decided to ditch the aunt story, it made sense, but it also led to some confusion. Overnight, I was given two moms, who were both seen by separate social circles as my only mom in the world. The social circles didn't overlap, so on one side, they thought I'd grown up with one mom and on the other side, they thought I'd grown up with the other. In both cases, my dad was missing.

Dana shouldn't have to explain her whole story to every stranger passing on the street, but it felt like we were creating a false history in which she was my only mother. My other mother disappeared. If Dana wasn't my aunt and she wasn't my mom, but she was my parent, how could I present this to the world without outing her? I didn't want to out her, but I felt caught in between.

I never corrected people who saw Dana as my mom, but on some level, like Christy said, it felt like a betrayal. She didn't inhabit that role in my life and the one who did wasn't there in those moments to say, "That's me!" We entered another phase of half-truths that didn't feel entirely comfortable.

Once, my mother and I spotted one of Dana's friends on the street and we bee-lined in the other direction. The friend thought Dana was my one-and-only mom, and we didn't want to improvise a story. When Sandra P. was out with her dad, now Liza, and ran into people who knew her mom, she said that Liza was her stepmom.

Maybe the problem lies in the limits of language. There's no shorthand word for "parent." There's "mom," "dad," "ma," "pa," "pop," but there's no word that takes out the gender unless we invent one. If we make one up, we have to teach it to everyone we meet. And if your trans parent wants to be invisible, to just live their lives without explaining, a new word might call them out.

So what should we do? Live on the moon until the world has evolved enough that they understand? There's no single answer, no one-size-fits-all name that works for everyone and in every situation. If you're faced with an awkward social situation, have a plan you share. Hopefully, we won't need a plan in the future. We can just say, "Meet my parent," and move on from there.

Until then, we might have to improvise sometimes or say a word that feels not quite right. Think of it as a trajectory, a direction you're moving in. Are you closer to the words that fit?

What feels right to you and your parent? Sometimes that might be different. Is there a compromise? I wish I could snap my fingers and see Dana the way she wants to be seen—as another mother. I still think of her as my dad in all the best senses of the word: my guide, my teacher, my carer, the one watching over from a distance, giving me perspective on the world. She doesn't want to be known as a dad, so I can hold her as my dad in my heart, and say the word she chooses; maybe think of it as a translation of "dad," and set aside the rest.

Now, I follow Dana's lead. I say her name and claim her as my parent. The rest of the world comes up with labels. Let them. As Christy's mom said, "Oh, who cares?" You can throw up your arms and wear the labels loosely. Yes, I'm a sister, an aunt, a daughter, and there's no one way to be those things.

If you can, set the world aside and figure out first in your family what works for you. Try not to think about what other people will think. I thought too much about what the world would think and too little about what made sense for my family.

When it comes to choosing names, we're still a work-in-progress. Try to figure out what's true for you and what's true for your parent, and go from there.

MOTHER'S DAY/FATHER'S DAY

Holidays like Mother's Day and Father's Day raise more questions. Which do you celebrate now, if at all? For a while we didn't celebrate Father's Day. The day skated by with no recognition. Then, for a while, I called Dana on Father's Day, saying, "Happy Paternal Birth Parent Day!" After a while, though, that felt wrong, too.

Jennifer talked about how her family sorted out this question. "I don't want to celebrate Father's Day because you're not my male parent, but I still have a biological mom, so that was a little weird at first." The solution for her was a triple Mother's Day for her parents and her stepmom. "I just celebrate Mother's Day three times and that's just easier." She added, "It's just kind of figuring out the little things like that."

It seems minor, but sometimes it's the little things that catch you off guard. Becca described grocery shopping with her parent in their neighborhood in the south shore of Boston. The clerk sometimes fumbled with whether to say "sir" or "ma'am." After a while, it grew so uncomfortable that her parent decided to have the groceries delivered.

Parts of our daily lives and routines change, and we have to decide how to handle this. Schools sometimes have assignments and crafts linked to Mother's Day. As Elizabeth M. said, "Advice to others: Do not ever tell your grade 5 class on Mother's Day that your mom is a man—or you'll have to live with people bugging you for the next seven years." She added, "Tell people you trust individually, and they are usually very reasonable about it." You can decide what you want to tell your class, and how you want to approach the holiday.

One year on Mother's Day, Dana sent a link to an article about a trans woman who wanted her daughters to call on Mother's Day. It was the year after my mom died, and I couldn't imagine anyone taking her place. For better or worse, she took on the role of my emotional, physical, and, at times, financial support even into my adulthood. She was the one I called when anything went wrong, when I needed anything. She could have probably claimed both holidays: Mother's and Father's Day.

I suggested choosing a day of our own to celebrate. Dana liked the idea, but we never picked a date.

Now, there's a "Transgender Parents" Day, but sometimes Dana doesn't identify as trans in the larger world. So, I guess we need our own holiday, or we can throw all these holidays out the window and decide to celebrate each other in little ways as we go through the year.

Now, we take Mother's Day and Father's Day for granted, but each was started by one individual who believed recognition was needed for those roles in society. For Mother's Day, it was Anna Jarvis of West Virginia. For Father's Day, it was Sonora Smart Dodd of Spokane, Washington. We could make a change like that, too. It could be started by one of us to declare a day for parents who don't land in the binary, but somewhere in between, or an overall day for parents and guardians of all stripes—an umbrella day for anyone who takes on that role.

Maybe "mother" and "father" will become obsolete. If it had been a "Parent's Day" all along growing up, there wouldn't have been a question. If my school had hosted a parent-child dance, I could have chosen which of my parents to bring, and I wouldn't have felt like our family's shape was set aside.

We could start a new holiday or boycott all holidays that put people in boxes! We can celebrate our parents in our own ways.

Prompts for Names and Naming

1. What name do you call your parent? Do you have a term of endearment?
2. How do you handle when someone mispronouns or misgenders your parent?
3. What about your own name and pronouns? Do those fit for you? Do you think we should come up with new pronouns that don't create a binary?
4. When a baby's born, we often say, "It's a boy" or "It's a girl." How could we change that to acknowledge that gender exists on a wide spectrum of experience?

Chapter 5

The Shape of Family

CONFLICT AND DIVORCE, HARMONY AND PARTNERSHIP

The phone rang in the room I shared with my sister. She ran to pick it up. I followed her down the back hall, waiting to see who the call was for. When I got to our room, her face was sheet pale. She slowly lowered the receiver from her cheek.

"Mom!" she called. Our mom came down the narrow hallway to our room. My sister passed over the phone.

On the other end of the line, Dana held a bottle of pills. She planned to take them, every last one. A year after the surgery and she couldn't see her way out. Our mother had started dating someone, which was something Dana supported at first, but now she felt left behind. The surgery had damaged her vocal cords, so her voice came out in a raspy whisper. My grandmother said it was a punishment from God. Dana had moved into a tiny house in Sonoma, and now she felt isolated and alone. She went to see a doctor who had given her a cocktail of pills. At the time, being trans was seen as a pathology, so the doctor gave her drugs meant for major disorders. She found herself in a hole, and the people meant to help her out only made it worse.

These are the parts we don't always talk about, the part where things get dark. We want to present a front of comfort and acceptance lest our families be rejected. So we put up a façade, and feel even more alone. The more we try to pretend our families are perfect, the more we get lost in that pretending, the more we lose ourselves.

Standing in that room with my mother and sister, I felt jumpy and afraid. I pictured Dana in a dark room holding a bottle of pills. In just over a year, she had become a stranger to me. That silly, doting dad who seemed to know everything had been replaced by someone who was afraid of everything, who hid herself from the world. Only a few people knew that she wasn't our aunt. Before she became a woman, everything came easy, or so it seemed. People handed her jobs on a silver platter. Doors opened in every corner of her life when she lived as a man. Now, she found closed doors and locked rooms. She lived, for the most part, in fear. I didn't recognize this side of my parent, and as a child, I felt helpless.

My mother took the phone and started speaking in low tones. She talked Dana into setting down the bottle of pills and walking out of the dark bedroom. After they talked, Dana called a doctor. On the wall in Dana's house was a painting by another trans woman, showing burial mounds with crosses planted inside, representing all the tiny deaths and endings that came with a transition. At that point, it was all too much for Dana. She had to climb out from a very low place, and none of us felt we could help her with the climb.

CHANGES IN THE SHAPES OF OUR FAMILIES

What happens when our families come apart? Or when our parents repartner? What happens when our families stay together, but don't look the way we expected them to? Where do we fit in the changing shapes of our families?

The transition initially brought my parents back together. For nine years, my parents had been divorced and living apart while my father explored relationships with men. The last relationship came apart as my dad emerged as a woman. It wasn't the only reason the relationship ended, but the end brought my parents back together. They decided to move back in together as a family through the transition. In some ways, the divorce impacted me more. Right before the transition, when we moved back in together, my response was, "Oh yay! We're moving back in together." I didn't know *why* we were all back together again.

We spent two years living in the same house. During that time, the dad we had known changed fully into Dana, surgery and all. At the end of the two years, I now had this "Aunt Dana" in my life. But I didn't need an "aunt." When my school had a Father and Daughter Dance, an "aunt" didn't help me. That night, Donnie stepped in and came with me. Over the years, the gay men who had been my dad's partners and friends became a bigger part of my life. My family grew bigger. Still, I didn't have a "dad"—not on the social level.

My parents stayed close, even when we moved into separate places again. Sometimes, when they walked down the street, I worried that people would think they were lesbians. Both my parents dated other people, and now that my dad was a woman, their dating pools overlapped. As a man, my dad was attracted to men primarily. Now, as a woman she appeared straight. She dated one woman, Susan, for a while. Dating women, she looked like a lesbian.

I didn't understand how she could switch between the two, but later she told me that she was attracted to souls, not genders. That sounded very advanced, but my own attraction to boys didn't seem to come with the same flexibility. Boys were the ones I wanted to kiss. Most people know that our gender and sexuality develop on their own, independent of our families, but I know this through experience. All the doors were open, and still I became myself, a cisgender girl who likes boys.

Some parents stay together through the transition and others split up. These decisions can impact us more than the transition itself. We don't choose the shape of our families or how they change shape over time. For you, the relationship with your parent is changing, and you might look at your family, thinking, "This wasn't the shape I had in mind." On the other hand, the shape of your family might get better. You might come to appreciate the change and freedom that evolves.

Morgan's parents split up during the transition. Her mother repartnered with a woman. When her parents came to her school, now, they looked like a divorced straight couple. Before her dad's transition, they, too, looked like lesbians out in the world. Her family changed shape, and it looked a certain way on the outside that didn't always match her experience. "People, because of heterosexism, are expecting to see a mom and a dad. When they see my mom and dad, there's nothing to explain there. They would appear straight unless you went over to my mom's house and saw her partner at the time." At the same time, she watched her dad change, getting involved in the trans rights community. "That role impacted how we spent time together or structured our time or what I witnessed him doing as a kid." As our parents take on new roles out in the world, that can shape our relationships with them, too. Morgan now had a trans dad and a lesbian mom, and while they appeared as a divorced straight couple in some contexts, her family story was much bigger than that.

For Sarah's dad, the act of moving out was the dividing line.

Before, her dad lived some of the time as a woman. After, she moved into the new place as a woman and all the neighbors knew her as a woman. The most dramatic change in lifestyle, though, happened for Sarah's mom. She had been living for years in a beautiful house with a husband and kids, and almost overnight ended up living in a... "We'll call it a mobile home community—a trailer park," Sarah said. "All of a sudden she was not married and not in her house anymore and in her mind, she hadn't done anything—this had happened to her." Sarah felt for both of her parents. She saw how hard it was for her dad to take this leap, and she also saw her mother's world turned upside down. "I have a lot more compassion for my dad now," Sarah said. "But I also have a lot of compassion for the fact that my mom just had her whole life upended." Sarah wasn't living with her parents anymore. They started their lives over separately, and she navigated between them. "My dad would have liked to stay closer to my mom, but my mom was not having it for quite a while." Now, the two have reconnected on friendlier terms.

When Danielle's stepmom came out, her first question was, "Are you and mom staying together?" The answer was, and continued to be, "Yes." While her family structure was staying the same, it was also changing at the same time. "What does that mean?" she said. "Are my parents now a lesbian couple?" Out on the street, like my parents, people might see them that way. When they went out together, that was how they looked to the world. "Well they're certainly seen that way," Danielle said. "Even though my mom still identifies as straight and my stepmom identifies as a lesbian." How they were perceived didn't necessarily match who they were. This shift can also shake up how we see our parents. "What does that mean exactly? I don't know. It's a big question mark," Danielle said. Who she saw her parents as was changing, too, as their relationship changed.

Justin grew up with a single parent. The parent he knew changed, but the family structure stayed the same. Leila and her younger brother were adopted by her uncle, who was already in a partnership with Carson. Their family grew when one of her dads had a baby. Monica and Christy's parents were both already apart when their parents came out.

The question is, where do you land in all of this? Whether your parents are together or apart, you get to define your relationship with each. Noelle H. described growing up with a parent who was gruff and distant. Though her parents split up during the transition, she grew closer to her dad after that.

Whatever shape our family takes, it can leave us with more questions than answers. Who are our parents, together and apart? Who are we? Who is our family in the world? How does this shape our parents' identities going forward? How does this impact us?

As our families continue to morph and change, so will we. We have a chance to understand our parents and ourselves from a new perspective.

GENDER AND THE SHAPE OF FAMILY

What if one partner is only attracted to the gender their partner once was? This came up in several families, but didn't always lead to a split. Sometimes it led to the partner in transition yielding some part of their new identity while the cisgender partner yielded a part of their sense of gender and attraction. It felt like both were offering a gift to each other, and the gift came with a certain degree of sacrifice.

In Sharon S.'s family, her parents found a compromise. "It's the realest struggle," Sharon said. "What do you do?" If her parent, Trish, fully transitioned to being a woman, "then she would definitely lose Marsha as a partner." If asked to make that trade, what would you do? For Trish, the partnership is a part of her identity, too. "She has such great love for Marsha—that is more important."

Sharon made a film about her family, *From This Day Forward*, in which she explores some of these themes. There's a scene in the film (spoiler alert!) at Sharon's wedding where Trish steps out on the field in a tuxedo with Marsha on her arm in a full-length gown. For months, Trish debated what to wear, eying the same gowns herself. Yet she understood that Marsha wanted that moment of appearing with her husband at her daughter's wedding. She gave up her own vision of the day to give that to Marsha. In the background, the music has a sad, wistful tone, underscoring the tension in that dilemma. How can they be together while being true to themselves? "It's this tension that is always going to be there for them," Sharon said. Both of them share in the dilemma, and both of them are working to be true to themselves while maintaining the bond they share. "This idea of sacrificing to be with the person you love—not sacrificing, but definitely compromising," Sharon said. In this way, family bonds shape our identities too.

While filming the documentary, *Alt Om Min Far* (*All About My Father*), Even shot a scene in the bathroom. His father looks in the mirror and comments, "I've grown bigger boobs." It came out in that moment that his father was taking hormones, something the family didn't know about. "We learned that he was transforming his body so he would be more female," Even said. Before, the family only knew that this was his father's preferred identity. The news about the hormones strained his father's relationship with his stepmother. She didn't want him to change his body. "It almost ended in a divorce between them." The two also came to a compromise, though, and stayed together. He made some changes, like removing all his hair, but didn't go forward with other treatments. He lives some of the time as a man and some of the time as a woman, some of the time in between. Not quite non-binary but more switching from one binary to another. Still, Even said, "He's always a little bit woman even when he's a man."

There's a scene in *Alt Om Min Far* when Even and his father are dancing, and his father switches from man to woman as they dance. Tom L.'s dad, now Jessica, dated another trans woman for a time, and Tom noticed a tension in the relationship because Jessica's partner wanted her to take on more of a male role. Tom's mom had wanted the same, but Jessica didn't identify with those roles. One partner might adopt certain roles, even if they don't feel completely right in them, just because it's easier or comes automatically. In any partnership, gendered negotiations come into play. As much as we challenge our own assumptions about gender, we come up against them in our intimate relationships and daily lives.

Once, when I was dating someone and we talked about the future, he immediately assumed that I would be the one to stay home with the kids. I felt boxed in by that assumption, and eventually the relationship ended. Since all of us have aspects of all genders, it's a dance in any relationship. Our ideas of gender can play a part in the roles we play in our lives, and the roles we ask others to play.

In any relationship, at some point, one person will ask, "Who am I now?" The answer can bring the couple closer together or further apart. The answer can become the question for the other partner. One parent I spoke with, Kate, said, "We're evolving—it doesn't mean 'Oh, I am this and that's it for your life.'" Our answers are not complete and done once. They're continually changing. For the kids, they watch the shifts and learn about negotiation and partnership. Sometimes the changes come as a surprise, and other times they seem inevitable.

In many ways, my dad fit traditional gender roles more than my mom, who hated make-up and thought high heels were torture. On parents' night at school, it was my dad who fit the part in his tweed jacket and loafers. My mom preferred faded jeans and T-shirts to skirts. I wanted her to fit more with the other moms in their bright lipstick, perfume, and heels. At the same time, my dad related more to the moms and shied away from the circles of dads. Sometimes my mom got jealous of how well my dad got along with the other women at work. She would never have thought that my dad was one of them.

A trans identity didn't fit my dad, either, because she landed on the flip side of the binary so absolutely. I didn't think of her as trans. I thought of her as now man, now woman, like a switch that flipped. One life, two people. Still, I had to get to know her as Dana, switching from the way I used to know her to a completely new way. As she aligned her body and personality with herself on the inside, she seemed at first like a stranger.

Before the transition, my parents sometimes talked about how it might bring them closer together. The differences that seemed to pop up from gender and sex would now be erased. My dad might understand my mom better. The gaps between them would disappear. Instead, though, they grew apart after the transition. There was a part of my father as a man that my mother cared for and didn't want to let go of. The same was true for me and my sister on some level. It felt sometimes like a stranger appeared—someone I didn't understand. All of us were on our own satellite journeys of understanding. Our family was changing, but we didn't know how or why.

We might confront our own ideas about gender as our family changes. "We have this deep-seated idea that gender is just part of us and doesn't change, and that's something that we have to come to terms with," Danielle said. When we watch our parents out in the world, we come up against our own biases, too. Riley's mom has an open and loving personality and has always loved connecting with kids in the world. Now that he's out in the world as a man, though, this has changed for Riley. "Even though I know how...much he just wants to uplift other people, I'm like, 'Stop—that's making me uncomfortable to watch you interact with these children on the street.'" He acknowledges that this is his "own bias coming out." We're given a chance to question the assumptions we make about gender in the world.

The mystery of attraction is another layer, and especially with our parents, we don't want to know all the details. With my parents, I assumed there was no physical intimacy whatsoever. They were both instant nuns in my mind. Both dated other people, but at one point, they did get involved romantically again, briefly. When I heard this, I felt uncomfortable about it. It didn't fit with my idea of my parents. When Dana dated a woman more seriously, I was confused. Wasn't the whole idea that she liked men to begin with, and also felt like a woman? Her sexuality was more fluid than that, though. We make assumptions based on appearance. I had to question my own bias, too.

DIVORCE AND REMARRIAGE

The "D" word is one I used for years to stop unwanted questions from friends. "My parents are divorced," I said. That stopped the conversation. It was only true on paper, because in real life, they stayed close, talking every day, even when they were miles apart.

The split happened years after the change, and it was mostly about money. Sometimes the kids see it first, before the parents.

We can see the places where the relationship is fraying at the seams. We pick up on the tension just under the surface. On the last Christmas we spent together as a family, we went over to Dana's place on Christmas Eve. As the night went on, I could see the exhaustion in my mother's face. She was tired of trying to make it work. Dana was working hard, too, trying to keep it afloat. The two of them were working, working, working, and getting nowhere.

From my perspective, I had watched my parents and saw them as two sailboats tied together in the middle of the ocean. I felt like they needed to be split up in order to fully find their own course. We didn't know how, behind the scenes, our mother was holding everything together. Dana started to unravel, the ground beneath her feet turned to quicksand. For Dana, all of her security and sense of connection was built around our mom. Her source of support in the world was now gone.

For years, my mother had been financially supporting Dana, but when she abruptly stopped just as Dana approached 50, Dana didn't know what to do. She struggled to find work. She dealt with both age and gender discrimination. She'd been writing for years but hadn't found a publisher. For a while, she supported herself by buying and flipping homes, but when the housing crisis hit, she couldn't do that anymore.

Now, my sister and I had to establish our own relationship with Dana—one apart from our mother, who for years had made sure we spent time with Dana. At the same time, Dana looked to us more for support, and we hadn't played that role as much before.

I wish I could say there was a happy ending, but there were years of struggle after that split. My sister and I tried not to carry the anger back and forth between them. We tried to build our own relationships.

Thirty-eight years. I spoke with one parent and child who hadn't talked for 38 years. They reconnected a few weeks before I reached out to the parent. They were in the process of rebuilding a relationship, but it was a rocky road.

"There's a 12-year-old in me that wants my father back," Elsa said. When she told her children about their grandparent, their response was "Cool!" The next generation hasn't grown up in the same world permeated with transphobia.

Elsa and her parent are starting slow, exchanging e-mails, getting to know each other again. When they stopped talking, it was a different world full of many silences about trans topics. Her parents split up, and after a few years of trying, Elsa decided she needed more distance. Now, the world is more open, but they still have to find their own place of understanding. What we know in our heads about equality and justice and identity can take a while to travel to our hearts, especially when it comes to our own parents changing. Elsa felt like "part of the equation" that was forgotten along the way. She found it frustrating that it's "looked down on if we're not accepting 100 percent." Her parent wants to fast-forward through the misunderstanding, but it's taking time.

When Amy's parents went into divorce counseling, she was eight years old—15 years before her parent came out to her. "There [were] a lot of issues there, so it just bubbled over." At first, when her dad came out, her parents tried to make it work.

"If you don't want me to dress like a woman out in public," Amy's dad said, "then I won't—maybe I can just do this at home where I feel comfortable."

Her dad tried this and other ways to be herself. "My mom was trying to force my dad to not dress the way that she was comfortable—even around her," Amy said. Amy looked back on this in between time when her parents were trying to negotiate themselves and their relationship, and when her dad was trying to change to fit into the relationship. "That's really honestly not a good thing to promise, because you don't want to do that," she said, reflecting on that time. "That doesn't help anybody." Her parents separated, and then went through a slow process of divorce. From Amy's perspective "it was just really, really super messy." Sometimes we watch our parents do the dance between their own desires and what the other person wants, and sometimes they don't find a compromise. At the same time, our parents and guardians are part of our compass for the world. We might want them to stay together, but it doesn't always happen. My sister and I used to watch the movie *The Parent Trap* and think of ways to bring our parents back together. We didn't wish that as much after the change. We had some idea of what a family looked like, and our parents didn't look like that anymore.

At the base of the conflict lies more than gender. Each of our parents has complex personalities and while the conflict may seem on the surface to be about gender, other dynamics are likely at play. Sandra P. talked about how the hormones made her dad more emotional, which impacted the whole family. Her mother didn't want to be "judged in the community." Her dad wanted "a chance to live on her own as herself." There's never one reason. From Sandra's perspective, though, "her family shrank." She was the only one of her siblings to support her dad's transition initially. Over time, her family "grew back together, in a way." She watched her family make peace. "My sister reconciled with my dad." Fast forward to her nephew's graduation, where Sandra sat between both parents. "That," she said, "was a triumph."

Right now, Jay's parents have split up, but she doesn't know why. She's nine years old, and she knows that her parents have some disagreements and aren't living together anymore, but that's all. She doesn't know that KC, her dad, is non-binary. KC spoke of feeling blamed for the split, though other reasons came into play. When parents split up, it's often about other issues that were below the surface all along.

KC is waiting for the right time to tell her daughter. "I'm always juggling the balance of trying to be authentically me, but then lying to my daughter—lying by omission by not saying who I am," KC said. KC did a lot of research to try to find out the best time to tell. She found that it's best to approach the topic "before they're in second grade or after they're 18 years old." Up until second grade, they can adopt these new ideas easily. From second grade through 18, "that's when their hormonal changes are going on, and things are more cut and dry." After 18, "they become more of an adult and they can understand the concept." KC was looking for a time to bring it up with her daughter before she started second grade. She wanted Jay's mother to be part of it, too, but she resisted. It never felt like the right time. As KC wrestled with this, one of Jay's cousins came out as trans. Jay ended up being the one to correct KC when KC told her they were going to pay a visit.

"We're going to see Allie tomorrow," KC said.

"Didn't you hear?" Jay said. "Allie's a boy now. Allie's Johnny."

"Oh really? Wonderful! What do you think about that?"

"Ah—it's cool."

KC saw first-hand how kids can go with it. "They don't have the stigma and everything else." It was a weight off KC's shoulders, but now the question is when to share her own identity. She also needs to find the words. Being non-binary is often misunderstood. "When I present myself female, it's because I feel female inside. I never felt like I'm a woman and I'm in a man's body. I'm in between, and it's been the hardest thing in the world for me to describe and understand for myself, let alone describe to someone else. I'm matching my outer identity with my inner identity." KC looked for books to share with her daughter, but there were more about being transgender within a binary structure than about being non-binary. The closest book she found was *Bunnybear*, about a bear who feels more like a bunny. She hopes more stories like hers will appear.

KC wants her daughter to know that it's okay to be who she is, no matter what, but she's struggling for herself to find that place. That is the greatest gift our parents can give us—seeing them be themselves completely. It's not just about gender. Sharon described the gift of having Trish as a parent: "She's very creative and wacky and funny and has a great sense of humor and is a fantastic painter." She watches Trish live her own creative life fully. "I think that has been really nice just to have a creative person like that in my life; someone to show how you can just really march to the beat of your own drum and you don't need to conform. So that's been a great lesson."

Your family might return to a place of peace after it splits and recombines. New partners appear and half-siblings and in-laws join the family. Your family might continue to grow in new and unexpected ways.

HOW DO YOU AVOID GETTING STUCK IN THE MIDDLE?

You might be torn between a sense of loyalty to each of your parents or torn between your own feelings and the hope of maintaining your relationship with each parent. If your parents had already split or you have a single parent, you might be torn about any struggles your parent is facing.

After Sarah W.'s parents split up, her mom watched the difficulties in her relationship with her dad.

"Why do you keep in touch with him? Why do you still talk to him?" Sarah's mom wanted to know.

"It's tough," Sarah said. "But she's my dad."

Though our parents have cut ties, we need to shape our own relationships.

Danielle's parents stayed together, but she found herself in a new support role as her stepmom transitioned. "It went from having a parent–child relationship where they were supportive of me, to then being a reversal where I had to be a support person for her as she was dealing with mental health stuff." This new role was one she hadn't expected. "Me supporting them had never been a thing before."

What do we do when our parents need us to support them? First, know that you need support, too. You might have reached a level of independence that makes you think that you don't, but you do. After going away to boarding school, I had this idea that I could operate on my own, without the input of my parents. But I still needed them and others in my life to help me find my way. Find support for yourself first.

Take time for yourself. Danielle wasn't living with her parents when her stepmom came out. "I could just say, alright, I need a few days to process and take that time, because I wasn't there all the time, I wasn't steeped in it." You can do this, too, by taking time with your friends and other activities, and even asking for some space. You can say, "I love you, and I support you, but I need a few days to get used to some ideas, here. I need some time to myself." That's okay, to take that time for yourself.

What if your friends don't fully understand? Sometimes all that's needed is a listening ear. You can say that. You're navigating something about which there's a lot of silence and misinformation. Not everyone will understand right away. They might need to educate themselves or open their own perspective.

At times, Dana's ex-partners helped me and my sister. They

knew some of the issues at play but were able to have enough distance. As tempting as it may be to vent your frustration with siblings or other parents, it helps to have someone outside the family to give perspective.

If there's no one in your family or immediate circle, try to find a group like COLAGE. You'd be surprised how many people share what you're going through. In COLAGE's Facebook group for People with Trans Parents, people post their good news and their struggles. People they've never met before often offer solutions. You might have to weed through the responses until you find the one that helps. Someone might post something awkward or off-base. Look for the helpful ideas and ignore the rest.

On your own, you can make a list of all the things that have influenced who you are today: the places you've lived, the people you've known, the jobs and school subjects you've mastered. It's not just about your parents. They're a part of you, but not all.

WHAT WE DON'T WANT TO TALK ABOUT

The part I don't always talk about is the part where Dana is angry and full of despair, and where that anger lands on me or my sister. The anger inside her sometimes comes out by lashing out at us. The sadness she feels sometimes pours out at us because with strangers she keeps up a good front.

Sometimes I've wanted to cut off contact with her. Sometimes I've wanted her to die. Then I could say, "My dad is dead," and I wouldn't have to explain anything. It's terrible to admit that, but it did come up as I struggled to understand. No one in the world asked me to accept this, but as a child, I kept reaching back for my father and trying to make sense of what had happened and where he had gone. I wanted him back, but that didn't feel like an option, so I wished her dead. I wished her gone from my life so I wouldn't have to tell anyone, so I wouldn't have to be separate from my peers and held at arm's length, asked, "What was that like for you?" as if the person asking the question never had anything they had to go through in their own lives, as if they never had to explain something that people just didn't seem to understand.

I was often mean and spiteful, pushing her away. I didn't want to be seen with her. I was often embarrassed by who she was, so I didn't treat her with kindness and respect. In many ways, we are still trying to repair the distance created by those years.

These are the stories we don't want to tell so they don't feed the fuel of transphobia in larger society. Yet, like any family, trans families are human. We have conflict, anger, dysfunction, alcoholism, abuse, and neglect—just like any family. As kids, we aren't always perfectly accepting and loving. We don't have to paint a perfect picture of our families for the sake of the LGBTQ+ movement. We can share the whole story for ourselves and for each other. We can be imperfect, too.

Sarah W.'s dad, Tricia, is a widely known public figure in the trans community in her area. Tricia also had a high-profile job at a tech company when she first came out. "My sister and I have been interviewed in the press for articles about my dad, and we feel this compulsion to put on this very positive face in public: 'Oh—no, having a transgender dad is just the best, and she's wonderful and she's amazing.'" The truth is more complicated. "Inside, I'm like, 'She's kind of crap at this, but just like any parent can be kind of a crappy parent.'" She added, "I could never say that in public." We often feel the need to present a particular image of our parent, our family, or ourselves so people won't judge us or our families. We deny any flaws because we don't want it to be picked up by someone and turned into a transphobic rant. It's this inborn desire to say everything's great while there are these difficult things going on.

Rachel's dad struggled with addiction to drugs a few years before coming out. She often left out that part of the story, not wanting people to draw a line between drug use and being trans. Fiona B.'s dad had been diagnosed with bipolar disorder and she described how "there was a lot of trauma going on in my family." Her dad took himself off his medication and then made a series of "uncharacteristic decisions." One day, he walked into the hospital where he'd worked for over 25 years and quit his job. His marriage was splitting up. A lot of pieces of his life came apart, and then Fiona got the phone call about his decision to transition. The sequence made her question the whole story. "For a long time, it was a real question for me of how crazy is this person? What is mental illness? How does it manifest itself?" The stigma around mental illness can keep us from sharing these parts of our stories or finding a community of support. Since Fiona's parent's coming out was wrapped up in a diagnosis of mental illness, she didn't feel like she could claim a place in the community of kids of trans parents.

Dana struggled with major depression both before and after the change; and after the change, it got worse for a while, not better. That didn't fit into the larger cultural narrative of "now that I'm my true self, I'm finally happy," so I kept that part of the story to myself.

The truth is that families are complicated. Part of why Dana grew more depressed after the change was that my mother started dating someone, and the emotional bond they shared was fraying. Both my parents thought that maybe the change would bring them closer. The opposite was true, though. My mother didn't know where to go with the sense of loss she felt about Daniel; and Dana felt misunderstood, isolated, and left out.

I thought of the year of the transition as a good year—one when my family was back together again. Later, though, my mother told me that she used to climb into the closet with a bottle of vodka and drink it alone. She drank on a daily basis to feel okay. I thought drinking was what you did when you grew up, along with wearing high heels and make-up—something to look forward to. This was different, though. This was another part of the story I didn't want to tell, because some might take it as cause and effect. Cue: transition. Cue: heavy drinking. My mother's drinking did become a problem, and she ended up getting help and turning her whole life around. That changed my parents' relationship, too. None of us had a road map for these changes.

People sometimes mix up our struggles with our parent with the fact that they're trans. They automatically assume that this is the underlying cause. "My mom's not a great parent," Brian L. said, "and happens to be trans." When he feels anger toward her, though, people assume it's because of that one part of her identity. "No," he said, "I'm mad because my mom didn't care about what I did in school." It's also important to remember that, as Danielle C. said, "Just because your parent is trans doesn't mean that everything they're doing is helpful for themselves and for you."

Becca's friends saw her pushing her dad away. "You were so mean to your dad," her friends said. On the inside, she saw it differently. "I didn't even look at it as me being mean to him, I just looked at it as 'Just get away... I can't deal with it right now... It's too much...too much mental space.'" She needed time apart from her family to do her own thing. What her friends saw as rejection was her claiming her own independence and understanding. "It's just part of it. People really don't get it." We are finding our own way, and sometimes push our parents away in the process.

No family is perfect, though sometimes as children with trans parents who struggle, we envision a perfect family—one that has it all together. That's a myth, of course, and no one wants their parent to struggle, but it's part of any family. "Every family has something," Even B. said. "Our family struggles haven't been about him being trans—it's been about all this other stuff that families usually have problems with, because every family has problems."

As a teen, I looked at other people's families and envied the shape they had: moms and dads who went to work in business suits and drove shiny cars; two-story homes with extra rooms; two cars parked outside by the garage. "Every family has something," said Even B. But looking at those families on the outside, I didn't believe it. It felt like those families had the answers. I didn't know of any internal struggles going on behind the walls of those homes. I only knew the ones in my family.

Sometimes, when I share my story with people who grew up with cisgender, straight parents, I think they couldn't possibly understand. And then they surprise me. They get it, too. They face things that the rest of the world doesn't always understand. I thought my family needed changing, that we had to fit into the rest of the world, not the other way around. I didn't know enough to think that the rest of the world was what needed to be changed.

Anger and conflict happen in all families. Sometimes in trans families we want to keep quiet about it because we don't want to add fuel to the fire of prejudice, but it's important to acknowledge that these things exist and to look at resources and tools for responding.

Toolbox for Approaching Conflict in the Family

Here's a start to your toolbox. Other tools will come up later, to add into the mix.

1. Therapy...with your parent: Amy and her dad did intensive, joint therapy, which helped them to find their own blind spots of understanding. When there are a lot of emotions involved, it can help to have a third party and professional give each of you perspective.
2. Family meetings: Becca's family held weekly meetings with donuts to entice the kids. These were open forums for discussion.
3. Time out with friends: Even when there isn't conflict, but especially when there is, it helps to have time out doing other things to distract yourself and remind yourself of the rest of your life, of which your family is a part, but not all.
4. Take a pause: In times of heated debate or arguments, or when you're confused, it helps to take a break, go for a walk, and not respond in the heat of the moment. This pause can be extended when you need time to reflect on any changes or questions you might be having overall. You might just need a break.
5. Talk to each other: Find a way to start the conversation in a way that's low stakes and comfortable for everyone. I probably wouldn't have been caught anywhere near a family meeting or therapy as a teenager, but I might have been willing to talk.

THE GOOD TIMES IN OUR FAMILIES

We don't see news stories of the quiet contentment in trans families: going to church, ordinary school days, walks in the woods. Sharon's parents share a love of hiking and mushrooming. The two set off into the woods in search of a mushroom called a morel. They set a broad path, an arc, making their way through the thick band of trees in search of these morels. They have a clear purpose, but wandering is also a part of that purpose, and being together. Sometimes Sharon goes with them and they shift formation, walking in pairs or single file, or sometimes with Sharon between them. They disappear between the trunks and branches, wearing colors that blend into the forest.

In my art class in sixth grade, we made decoupage boxes about ourselves with copies of our class pictures mixed in. To mine, I stuck a gold mascara box and pictures of lipstick to show some of my favorite things. When I got home, I showed my project to Dana and she beamed with outsized pride. Everything I brought home was a work of art, a masterpiece. She shone her light of pride on all of it. I felt like I could do anything. She didn't come to my school that year, but I shared all my projects with her. She must have a felt a loss in how her role was marginalized and confined to the home, to the role of "aunt," but she didn't show it. She only showed excitement and pride in my work, encouragement of what I was doing, and sheer delight in my raggedy attempts at art.

When Jonathan goes to visit Paula, they go to church together. Theirs is a church that is open to everyone who believes. The two sit side by side, sharing the act of worship. Becca told of going to church with her family, too, her dad's hair back in a ponytail, dressed in neutral clothes. An ordinary Sunday at church. She could tell, though, that people knew something had changed.

"How are you doing?" people asked. "How is your family doing?"

They were going to church just as they had before. As time went on, the church community distanced themselves, but they kept going. Some of the judgment seemed to be about the fact that her parents stayed together. "My mom was looked at differently because she was still with my dad. They're still married." People faded away, but her family kept going, doing what they'd always done on an ordinary Sunday. The community reaction didn't faze Becca. "Everyone needs to get over themselves at this point," she said. She takes other people's opinions with a grain of salt. All of us can learn a lesson from that.

Harmony and peace also play a role in trans families. After all that time of hiding, telling the truth can have a powerfully positive impact on our families, whether they stay together or split up.

THE FUTURE SHAPES OF FAMILIES

"My dad is having a baby," Leila announced to her classmates at school. Her friends went home to talk to their parents, and the next day came back with their own news. One of her friends, Amanda, approached her.

"That's not even possible—my parents said so," Amanda said.

"Yes, it is," Leila said.

Later she said that it was possible *because* her Dad is trans.

"My trans dad can do anything!" Leila announced proudly. Her parent could be a dad and have a baby, and create a family through adoption and birth.

Leila made a rainbow cape for her school's rainbow day. We talked about her favorite superheroes. She could be a super hero, too, one representing LGBTQ+ families. She could show her friends that they didn't know everything about how families are formed.

Mya and Kennedy Power got together to create a family.

They also transitioned together. "In any household, there are challenges with parenting," Mya told *The Gay Star News*, "but don't allow being transgender to scare you from creating a family of your own. Lots of stigma comes with it, but don't get upset with the world—educate!"

Our families are changing shape by the minute. There are shapes of families we might not even know about yet, ones that are still forming. What's possible now with the advancing of reproductive technologies wasn't possible 30 years ago. The shape of our families continues to change. We've come a long way and we still have discoveries to come. Kids who grow up with parents who already live in the identities that fit know that their family is a gift.

As Leila said, we are "special because not that many people have transgender parents."

In the future, this just might be the response you get about your family; or your class might be filled with other people with trans parents, too!

Prompts for the Shape of Family

1. Do you like the current shape of your family? In your mind, what is an ideal shape for a family?
2. How did the transition impact the shape of your family? Has it brought your parents closer together or pushed them further apart?
3. Do you try to hide any conflict in your family because of the pressures in society to look a certain way?
4. How was your family made? How do you think technology and changing ideas about the roles of moms and dads will impact the future shapes of families?

Chapter 6

Grief and Loss, Gifts and Gains

"In the process, I somehow lost the old, reliable parent/mentor that I came to know in the course of my life."

—DOUG S., AGE 29

"[It feels] very strange.... like a loss which can't be fully mourned."

—STEVE VINAY G., AGE 48

You might find yourself missing your old parent. At the same time, they're still there in your life, so why would you miss them? How can you miss someone who's still there? And if you sometimes wish your old parent would come back, does that mean you aren't being supportive of your parent as they are now? Where can you go with these feelings?

When Sarah W. found herself struggling with a mix of feelings, a few people she talked to said, "That sounds a lot like grief." But grief is what happens when you lose someone completely, right? We don't always know how to name what we're feeling.

I didn't register the grief for a long time, since I was caught up in the stories we were telling. I missed the dad who I could introduce my friends to with such pride. "This is my dad," I used to say, parading someone around who, I later learned, was not who my dad was through and through. Still, I missed that. I didn't want to parade Dana around, and I wasn't sure why.

Some of us might not feel grief or loss at all. We might see our parent happier or more content, and feel a sense of relief at this change. If we do feel grief, other people might not recognize it. Our friends' efforts to be supportive might not leave room for the complexity of our feelings.

If we open up the door to grief, it can feel like a kind of rejection: *I wish you were who you used to be.* But if we try to keep the door shut, if we close it up and build a wall, then the grief comes out sideways, upside down, and backwards. It will come out as anger, fear, or confusion. It will appear as rejection when our parent asks a simple question about school. If, instead, we open the door, then we have a chance to ride it through to the other side.

On the other side of grief is the place where we start to see the gifts and gains. You might see those gifts right away or it might take a while to uncover them. Sharon talked about gaining a new worldview. "I'm really grateful to have a trans parent, because I always felt like I sort of related to outsiders, and I felt like I have this compassion for people." If we try to skip over the grief, we might not see the parts we've gained.

For a long time, I tried to skip over the feelings, to find a way around them, but they followed me. They were there all the time just under the surface. There's no shortcut with grief. You might struggle with parts of your relationship with your parent still, and you might have to adjust to big changes, but you'll also have a chance to see things differently. That's what you just might find on the flip side of grief.

DEALING WITH GRIEF OVER THE LOSS OF YOUR PARENT AS YOU KNEW THEM

When I was little, my dad and I were peas in a pod. We went on long walks in upstate New York. The winding roads led us through the hills and back to our driveway. We went to bookstores and movies, libraries and candy stores. Sometimes the two of us stayed up at night talking right until my mother sent me to bed. He acted like what I said mattered, and never talked down to me or made me feel stupid for not knowing.

I wanted to read all the books my dad read, and it seemed to me that he knew about everything under the sun. He had the answer to almost any question I had. I idealized him a lot, too, since he wasn't always there. When he came, he brought presents and treats, he made homemade cookie dough and cakes, seven minute frosting on my birthday, and perfectly crisp chocolate chip cookies.

The day I met Dana, I didn't think much of the change. She was my dad just in disguise to the outside world and we couldn't say "Dad" anymore. So what? To my ten-year-old self, it was no big deal. This is the part that is sometimes hard for people to understand—how ordinary it was. They think it must have been a struggle from the start. It wasn't, but when we stepped into the outside world, I had to give up having a dad. It was primarily a social loss at first. Inside our house, it didn't feel like anything was going to change, so we acted like everything was the same.

There was the in between time when she was both/and,

when she was adding Dana to Daniel, and before Daniel was gone. It's hard to describe, how someone can disappear right in front of you. They are changing, changing, changing, until they're just different. The change happens so gradually, though, that you don't question it or think of it as a loss. Since it's a gradual evolution, it doesn't register right away. And since it was a social loss first, it simply felt like my life was divided. I still had both parts—Dad and Dana—just not all the time. Later, Dad was gone completely. When he was gone-gone, I couldn't hit a rewind button to bring him back, and Dana couldn't take his place. She had a new place in our family, in the margins.

At first, I didn't feel grief as much as disappointment. That she couldn't dress as my "dad" anymore and talk to the principal of my school. That she couldn't be there for the Father and Daughter Dance because people would ask, "Who's that? What's she doing here?" That she couldn't flip back and forth between these two roles. I didn't realize I would have to stop saying "Dad" forever. Forever was a long time.

The gradual changes were like *going, going, gone*. He was there and then each part of him faded away. For a long time, Dana wore scarves to cover her Adam's apple. It became part of her style. She seemed so formal compared to my dad, who wore comfy jeans and any old shirt.

The two were just different to me. Maybe it was because my dad got good at playing a part or maybe it was everything that happened in between, but it felt like Daniel was gone, the one I knew as Dad. Like he slipped out the back door and Dana came in to take his place.

Who are you? I got to know this woman who had little pieces of my dad mixed in. The parts of him I missed: the silly, goofy parts, the horse-around parts; the parts that made me laugh for no reason. Dana didn't have those parts. She loved books in the same way, and loved animals, especially horses, which was something she shared with my sister. She loved us, and that showed for a while, and then went underground when she got sad.

Since the change was gradual, it was like my dad was still there under a layer, and then disappeared more and more. At the time, I thought it was a good thing, and my dad was still accessible behind that one layer. It kept being a good thing for a while, and we still shared books and movies and dinner around the table as a family. But then she was Dana, and dad was mostly gone, and I had to say, "aunt," but I didn't want an "aunt." That's when it changed. No one gave me another option. It was aunt or nobody, so sometimes I just chose "nobody," acting like she wasn't there.

I thought if my dad, as Daniel, were around, everything would be easier. I didn't have a way to articulate that, though. To my parents, my dad still was around, just in a different form. To the rest of the world, he was completely gone. That was when I knew things would be different, but I still didn't understand fully the impact it would have on my life.

No one told me that I might be sad about this. At the time, my parents thought that if they didn't make a big deal about it, it wouldn't be a big deal, but as I moved out into the world and met other peoples' families, I noticed a gap in mine. Maybe everyone has that gap in some form, but mine seemed to be like a blinking sign on the door of our house: "Dad doesn't live here anymore."

In our house, the "Dana is still the same person" story felt a bit wrong. But I wasn't going to tell the professional woman behind the big desk with her shelves of books and plaques on the wall that she was wrong. All that telling us that nothing had really changed wasn't true, because I woke up one day and everything had changed completely. None of us knew how to make it go back to how things were.

For a long time, she was always *over there*, on the outside of the family. On the other side of the fence. Left out. Forgotten. We made plans without her. It felt different with her than with him.

Maybe all of us missed him a little bit. Did Dana miss the parts of herself that were silly and goofy? Maybe. All of us had to trade something in. And then we weren't the same family anymore. Even living apart as we had before, something had changed. It didn't feel like we needed Dana the way that we needed our dad. It felt like she was added onto our family instead of inside it.

We stopped planning things to do, just the two of us. This wasn't on purpose, but in time, we grew apart. As I entered junior high, I became aware of her difference, and I didn't want her anywhere near. I didn't want either of my parents nearby, but with her, I pushed her away.

If she was always there, just buried under layers, then who was he? Was he just a made-up person she played on the side? A part-time person? A part-time dad? I still don't know, but whoever he was, I knew him well. We were peas in a pod going on walks near our house in upstate New York. He delighted in all that I said and did, and then he exited stage left without warning or advance notice.

"I look back at my baby pictures and my childhood pictures," Sarah said. "And a video of me riding a bike with this guy, with this man, and that man just does not exist, and if you talk to my dad—never existed. And I'm like, 'That can't be true.' The cognitive dissonance around that is very hard to navigate."

It's almost as if he left. That funny, silly, doting dad who brought me the *Wizard of Oz* and picked out all the right books. And then I didn't know him. The woman in tailored suits who he became. This year marks 32 years, and I think I understood better back then, when I was 11 years old and thought that anything was possible.

The grief came up first in the form of rejection. As my "aunt," she didn't hold the same social currency as a dad in my school life. She was just there, off to the side, saying "hello" in a raspy voice. The grief came out in disguise. I wrote about missing my dad because of the divorce, but the truth was more complicated than that. I missed the one who could make people laugh and charm a whole room. I didn't know that behind that laughing sat a great and profound sadness, one that cut deep below the surface. To us, as children, it seemed that he could make everything okay. He was slender, handsome, and silly, crossing his eyes and singing funny songs. Dana and I didn't share the same connection we once did. When she hugged me, I sometimes shrugged her away.

I don't remember the first time I registered missing my dad, and I know it didn't feel possible to have him back. I just remember the discomfort when the subject of parents came up, and the gymnastics of avoiding pronouns. I didn't have a name for the grief. My dad was still there in some ways, but he was also gone. How could someone be there and be gone all at the same time? It was something that came up under the surface, this sense of missing someone, of missing the dad I knew then.

When we can't name the feelings and our parent is still there, we might skip over saying goodbye. How can we say goodbye to someone who's still there? "I feel like I don't allow myself to grieve because it's not like they're dead," Olivia said. "Like, one day I will grieve. That blocked my grief process." She found herself stumbling upon the grief instead at random moments. "My grief would come out unexpectedly, like looking at pictures or just memories." The memories appeared and she pushed them away. "I couldn't really revisit them. It was like I wouldn't let myself go back, and kind of like erasing my whole childhood of these memories." The memories are of another part of our parent, one our parent may no longer recognize. In a way, the family follows suit. "For the first few years," Olivia said, "it was as if my dad did not exist anymore. It's weird—no one talks about it, so it feels like they're really gone." Her parents had split up, and her mom and brother didn't talk about her father at all. Even if your family is together, though, it can feel like a member of the family is gone.

We boxed up everything connected to Daniel. All the pictures of Daniel were gone. His clothes were gone. He used to shave with Bic razors that left little nicks that he dabbed with tissues. Now, our mother used the razors to shave her legs, and I did, too, the first time I shaved my legs. When mail arrived addressed to Daniel, we knew it was junk mail or someone in his family who missed the memo: *Daniel doesn't live here anymore.* We rolled our eyes and tossed the junk mail in the trash.

I have a Polaroid of him in a cable-knit sweater and jeans, looking sternly at me sideways since he didn't want me to take another picture with the bright white flash. His hair is cropped close, and I can see the dimple in his chin, which went away later with electrolysis. I remember him sitting on the screened-in porch in upstate New York, foot crossed over his knee, a yellow legal pad propped on his lap or a lap desk balanced on his knee. My mom lit up when my dad walked into the room. The two of them together made sense.

To our parent, it may seem like they haven't changed or that the change is closer to who they really are. This can contradict our grief in losing the "old parent." Sarah talked about missing her "old dad" and said, "I know my dad wouldn't see it that way—to my dad, 'I'm the same person,' but to me, not at all."

At the same time, as her dad changed, she wanted to leave her old self behind. Sarah mentioned things that her dad said, such as: "I was never that person" and "I was never him" and "I hated being that person."

Our parent is leaving behind someone we planted as a permanent part of our landscape. Our feelings might clash with our parent's feelings for a while.

If my parent stayed more in the in between, would I still feel this sense of a loss? I don't know. Maybe if there were more flashes of who she was, it would be easier. "It's very difficult to watch your parent transition," said Chelsea W. from Nebraska, "and knowing you will never see that parent the way you remember them again."

I could see that Dana felt more comfortable like this, that there was an inner ease that came with inhabiting her new body. She slipped into the role overnight and it fit her. She landed in the right place for her. Her smile came easily at times. She struggled with depression after the change, too, but she still looked at ease. She had the quiet comfort of content even if she seemed sad at times. Still, there were times when I missed my "dad" as I once knew her. This didn't mean I wanted to go back, though sometimes, in my teenage years, I thought that I did. At the same time, I didn't have a name for this feeling or a space to talk about it.

A DIFFERENT KIND OF GRIEF

We often think of grief as something connected to funerals. Long trails of cars following behind a hearse. When my dad started to take hormones, and the edges of the body I knew as

"Dad" changed, I didn't think of it as a loss at first. It was more like sliding sideways into another reality.

I related sometimes to friends who had lost parents, but this wasn't the same as that. At the same time, the grief was real. No one said, as they do when a parent dies, "You must really miss him." But I did. He was gone.

Here is what the grief looked like: It lived on the edge of things, the borders, just outside the lines, always out of reach. If I looked, it went away, hiding itself. It was always there. It was a vague off-to-the-side feeling. It was under the surface all the time. The grief came out in pieces. Not all at once. It was this vague sense of missing someone who technically was still there. I didn't have a name for the feeling, but it was no less real. When I heard about girls whose dads were taking them to parties or important school events, I would just feel left out. It was more of a feeling of being left out of the world of people with dads.

It felt like a missing piece, one I couldn't talk about. Dana was there, but she couldn't play that role anymore, even if she wanted to; and sometimes I knew that she wanted to, if only for me and my sister. If she could snap her fingers and switch into that role when we needed her, she would have. She wanted to be that person who we wanted.

It's a funny kind of loss since the person's still there. And there are new parts of them that weren't there before, so there are gains, too; but in high school, I wasn't looking for a funny, feminist intellectual in my life. I just wanted a dad to stand in like a paper doll at school events. I wanted my parents to show up the way I wanted them, and then to disappear like smoke when I didn't.

There were other parts of the grief, too: the grief that my family didn't look the way I wanted it to look; that we had to keep the truth a secret for so long; that we didn't fit into the picture of a family that I saw in the larger society; that we belonged on the outside; that my father had to go through so much just to be who she felt she was; that it took so long to answer people's questions, which sometimes felt endless; that I couldn't just say, "Oh yeah, my dad..." and that when I did, it felt like I was hiding something, like I was lying, when all along, all I wanted was to be like everyone else, to fit in. It felt like everyone else had a shortcut because they had families that looked a certain way on the outside. Nicola Bass has a mom and dad, so why can't I have parents like hers?

What do we do with this loss? It's not one that anyone recognizes officially. There are no funerals. No memorial services full of flowers. No trains of cars with hearses in front, flags waving on the hood. Someone shared in the COLAGE Facebook Group for People with Transgender Parents about having a memorial of their own to recognize the loss. I didn't even know it was a loss for a while because everyone told me Dana was the same person on the inside, that only the outside changed. Also, a lot of the energy in my family went into keeping it hidden. There wasn't time to say, "I miss who my dad used to be," when I had to keep up with the story.

When no one around you knows or thinks of this as a loss, it's hard to know what to do. "People don't generally recognize it as a loss," Olivia said. "It wasn't marked by anything. There's no memorial service." There are no set rituals. People don't show up on your doorstep, bringing food or flowers. "When there is a loss in people's lives, their support systems rally around them, but there's none of that." Asking for support can feel strange, because you don't quite know what you need. You're feeling your way around in the dark. "Even trying to explain it to people feels weird or not right, so it's a weird experience,

I think." You may not even know what you're going through, let alone how to describe it to anyone.

Without a built-in social structure for recognizing the loss, it gets pushed aside. "People with a transgender parent suffer a huge loss which is socially unacceptable for them to grieve," said Sadie T. from Australia, "and for which there is virtually no support." Nothing has been set up to account for this loss. You might also feel a push to be supportive, which adds another layer of guilt about grieving.

That feeling of missing someone, wanting them to come back, that feeling of "Where did that person go?" Yes, it was a kind of grief, one I carried with me, one that represented this loss. One I never really let myself feel—not completely.

I didn't even see that I missed my dad until my senior year in high school. I wrote about my parents being divorced, and about missing my dad. It was supposed to be a memoir, but I left out most of what really happened.

I felt different from my peers. My dad was gone, but not in the way of some friends where their dads were somewhere else and now they had a stepdad. Or the ones whose dads died and everyone felt sad all together. It was like having someone missing, but you weren't supposed to be sad, because now they were who they wanted to be, even if you didn't know who that was. To them, they were the selves they'd been all along, only now they matched, inside and outside. To you, you're meeting them for the first time.

It's like a giant etch-a-sketch came in and erased everything you knew. So you're looking at your dad and thinking, "That's not my dad." It was like when my mom died, years after the change, and when I looked around, all I could see was that everyone was not-my-mom. The world was full of people who were not-my-mom. The brain doesn't know what to do with an absence of someone who was there from when you first opened your eyes. Before you even formed memories, they were there, so their absence is baffling.

"It changes everything you thought you knew," Jonathan said. "My dad's my hero, so I felt like I was losing my dad... You've lost them, but they're here, so what do you do with that? There's a tension there, and so it's really trying to figure out what to do with that tension."

Sometimes we don't even know that it's an option to be sad. Everyone is urging us to say yes to our new parent without thinking we might need time to say goodbye. I didn't even think I could be sad. And part of me was truly happy to see my parent happy about becoming Dana (because she was happy for a while). It didn't seem too bad to do a trade-in for an underground dad instead of one who was sad all the time.

Everyone said my dad was still there, that she was the same person, so why didn't it feel like that? I missed someone who people said hadn't gone anywhere. But if he wasn't here, then where was he? Where did he go? I don't have answers for these questions. I may never know. I may never fully understand. As Even said, "I stopped trying to understand it, because I can't; because you have to be transgender to understand it. I just learned that some people are different, so it doesn't really matter what they are... Don't analyze it, just accept it."

Grief came out sideways, dressed up as other things. Anger, rejection, fear.

"Where did you go?" I want to ask.

I imagine Dana saying, "I'm right here, I'm still here, it's me—I've been here all along."

Maybe if I squint, I can see that. If I look past all those layers of Dana. I can see the person who was there all along. I can see all those times Dana was trying to reach me, when I wasn't there, because I was looking for someone else.

I never had a word for this kind of loss, but recently I learned that it's often described as "ambiguous loss."

Olivia C. discovered this term after her own experience propelled her to look into it further. "When I first started reading about ambiguous loss," she said, "it was helpful to me because the idea is that it's a type of loss that occurs when the person is lost—gone in body, but not in mind, like people who went out to war and never came back... The same term is used when people are present in body but not mind—[like] people with dementia so the person's still there, but they're kind of not." It's a loss without closure or recognition. "You can see the parallels," Olivia said. "It's sort of a similar concept, except that they are there both in body and mind." The change is in gender, and so the absence is more of an evolution, but we often see two different people. We look back in our memories at someone who is no longer physically present to us.

Ambiguous loss can lead to a sense of unfinished grief—one that is unresolved, under the surface. It lives with you in a kind of hibernation all the time. It's this sense of someone who is there, but not there at the same time.

"I didn't know what I was feeling for a long time," Sarah said.

Justin described it as "almost like a phantom limb—it's like this thing that existed and no longer exists, but kind of exists." He didn't find himself missing his old parent, because as Trevor she was "just sad all the time." Whatever faults his parent may have, she's a better parent now than before the change. "Those memories feel in this far, distant past and I miss them," but Justin wouldn't wish it were otherwise. One of the memories that stands out was "peeing together," which "is a thing" with boys and their fathers. He said, "It's one of the memories that looms largest, probably because of what happened, but also it's a common memory." He remembers throwing a ball around with his dad and sharing a "closeness," but he still doesn't want to go back.

As kids, my sister and I idealized our dad because he wasn't there all the time. He popped up with presents and treats, trips to the movies. When we moved back in together, he had already started the slow metamorphosis: the sharp angles softening, the beard and stubble disappearing hair by hair. When we were little, it felt like he easily solved things through his presence. People acted differently toward our mom when he was with her. He was like a human shield. He felt this, too. That people paraded him around like an object.

If my father felt like a solution, then Dana felt like a puzzle, like she was adding to the problems instead of taking them away. "Who are you?" people wanted to know. We had an answer ready, but our own questions stayed unresolved.

When "Dad" was gone, when she didn't want to be a dad at all, I wasn't sure who we were to each other. I couldn't say "Dad" or "Daddy" anymore. It seems like a small thing, but it felt significant. Something started to change between us, but I wasn't sure what.

At age ten, I fully accepted the idea of transitioning. I saw it as part of an expanding world. Dana was the underground part of our dad coming out. Like turning inside out. It made sense to me. One by one, though, important things came up that Dana couldn't do: come on class trips; meet with my teachers to talk about my work. Here, again, is a place where the rest of the world could have been different. Would the loss have been the same if the world said, "Hey, great! We can't wait to meet your dad as Dana!"? I still think the loss would have been there in some form.

No one told me that I would miss the part of her that was Daniel; that I would miss running to jump up monkey-style on his tall skinny body; that I would miss peeling off the little bits of skin when he got burnt in the sun (Dana always covered her arms and legs, even after all the hair was gone); that I would miss who she was before.

"I'm right here!" she kept trying to say, but I couldn't find the one I knew best, I couldn't see that person anymore.

The sadness built up over time, bit by bit. Celebrations, trips, plays, readings, meet-the-parents with boyfriends, birthdays, parties. All the times she missed such events. At first, the reason was because we kept her a secret and our extended family didn't know. Later, it was because we had gotten used to the distance. The dad who wasn't there became the parent who wasn't there. Dana retreated. She also didn't want to be set apart. She didn't want to feel different, either.

She must have felt her own sense of loss, too. The complex grief happens for everyone in the family. Her brothers and sisters felt it, too.

You may get more sad about other losses, with this one buried underneath it. In sixth grade, I had an English teacher, Mr. Courage, who was my sun, moon, and stars. He used to recommend books to me, grown-up books, not the little kid books we read in class. He encouraged my writing. Each week, I wrote extra credit essays for his class. I thought he knew everything about the world and books and everything in it. In the middle of the school year, the school fired him. They wouldn't tell us why. I was devastated and angry at the school. I felt like I'd lost a friend and teacher. All this sadness came out. Would everyone I loved most disappear? The teacher who took his place was nice enough, but it wasn't the same. All my sense of loss poured into this teacher. He was a stand-in for the complex loss going on in my family, the one I couldn't name.

"The same person," Dana's therapist said, but it didn't feel that way at all. I was never embarrassed to walk up the street with my dad, though I'm sure I would have found a reason in my teen years. He felt like the glue, the solution, and Dana felt like the one breaking things apart.

Hiding made it more complex, but it also gave me a reason to feel like I missed my dad, since we told people that he lived far, far away. Coming out of my own silence, the shock and awe that came from different people displaced any feelings I had. I felt most at ease with the ones who had always known, the ones who did not act like I just bought a one-way ticket to the circus through my family. Dana's ex-partners, both gay men now living with their own long-term partners, treated it like part of the background. They also told me that much of what I saw as Dana was part of Daniel all along—I just didn't see it as a kid. That didn't change me missing my dad, but it did show me my own blind spot in any case. And it gave me a place to go where I wasn't seen as different.

At the same time, I needed room to grieve, to go through the mix of feelings inside, the part of me that missed my dad and the one that was getting to know Dana. Some would say that Daniel wasn't gone since I could access him in memories. In that way, he and Dana can both exist at the same time. That is where the ability to hold two ideas at once comes into play. That we can have this person we remember and also the one just now emerging both at the same time. That both are true aspects of this person from different times.

Later, it can change again. As my dad gets older, the parts

that I remember as Daniel are coming back again. I see more of that part of her. It's comforting and familiar, like returning to someone I knew a long time ago. It can be like a pendulum, swinging out until it returns to the middle. Your parent might change a lot in a short time, and then return back to another place in between.

GRIEF? WHAT GRIEF?

Jordan L. said that his dad is pretty much the same before and after the change. Same interests, same personality, same life. His parents stayed together, and though they sleep in separate bedrooms, their relationship hasn't changed much otherwise. The gradual slipping away of a dad as he knew him isn't something Jordan experienced. Jordan was the one to change, letting go of old ideas about gender and identity

Leila has only known her parent as trans. She looks to him as a hero, as special, as someone who can do anything.

What if Dad as Daniel had never been a part of my life? Would I still shrug away when we hugged? Would I cave my shoulders to keep my distance? Would I look at her thin legs and arms so critically?

If my dad came back as Daniel, it's likely that we would have many of the same difficulties in our relationship. It's likely that the anger and depression would get in the way. For now, I only have my dad as Daniel frozen in time, so it's easy to idealize her like that, and to think that if my dad were back, everything would be different, everything would be okay.

"Some people transition and stay very similar," Sarah said. "Maybe it's just some physical appearance and maybe they're just happier, and that's great, but I've seen a lot of people—especially those who are older when they transition—who seem very different." Maybe they've travelled further away from themselves, so they have farther to go to get back. At that point, we might not recognize them, but inside, to them it may feel like a huge relief. Finally, they match who they feel on the inside.

MAKING MEANING

"Does this mean that my dad's gonna die?" Maya, age nine, wanted to know. I can tell her that her dad's body will not die—that is a fact. The heart, the lungs, the brain. At the same time, there is a new life coming, and with any new life comes the shedding of the old. It's like taking a leap over six decades of change in a week. It's like nothing else.

As Sarah said, "My dad's still alive, she's still here, I can still talk to her, but it is not the same person—it's a very different person now. I think that's a very unique thing to people who have a loved one that transitions in general."

A part of your parent does die. A false part, one that was a stand-in for themselves. Her question made me see how we can sometimes get at the truth sideways. While the physical body doesn't die, some parts—like personality, appearance, and who they are in the world—does. It's a second life contained in one, like the Native American word for this—"Two-Spirit."

I told Maya that her parent has a chance to live more than a lot of people do. Admitting difficult truths about herself. The second life eclipses the first, and as kids, we say goodbye to who our parents once were.

Since it's not a grief that's recognized, we might hide it under the guise of our feelings about divorce or distance. You won't get flooded with cards or flowers, reminders that you have memories to keep. People won't share with you their own memories of that parent unless you ask. Sometimes I think I would like to travel back in time and know Daniel better, too; but if all along he was Dana, then the best chance I have to know him is now.

Remember, just because there's grief doesn't mean that this is wrong. That's the part that's sometimes hard to see. If something is painful or difficult, we sometimes wish it wasn't happening. Add to that a part of the world that says it's wrong, and you get a big pile of confusion.

If you feel grief or sadness, don't skip over this part. Don't try to fast forward through. I didn't even know that I felt it, since it came wrapped up in confusion and "What is going on?" and rejection, all bundled together.

No one gives us a map with signposts to follow. When it comes to grief, there are no rules. It's okay to miss your old parent. No one told me I could. Letting yourself miss them is how you get to the other side. Forced acceptance doesn't work. It's useless. You can miss them while getting to know who they are now.

You might also feel relief that something hidden is now out in the open. Or, like Jordan L., you might see your parent as pretty much the same without any loss except your own old ideas about gender.

For a while, I thought that if I missed my dad as Daniel, then I wasn't being understanding or supportive; that it was anti-trans to say that I sometimes wanted my silly, goofy dad back. There's still part of me that thinks this. As if one day I'll wake up not missing my dad, and that will be the right thing, when I can see Dana as the one who was there all along.

"Every grief brings up grief over the loss of your father," my mother said to me once. At the time, I hadn't thought about how grief can live in layers. And that what I felt about my father was, in fact, a sense of grief or loss.

It doesn't mean that Dana shouldn't be here. I get to miss Daniel and see how lucky it is to have a second chance, to leave behind the body that doesn't fit anymore like some awkward old jumpsuit. It sounds strange, but by missing her as Daniel, I make room for her as Dana. If I skip the missing part, then there might not be room for anyone else to come in.

RESOURCES FOR GRIEF AND LOSS

How do we approach this grief? What tools can we use to work through it? Where can we find support? We might not even know where to start when it comes to looking for support. One family I talked to said that they looked everywhere for some resource or help. Where can you go?

Talking to other people who went through the same thing helped me a lot. Peer support can be formally structured or shaped informally with a group of friends. I found a shared language. We got what each other had experienced without too much explanation. We could fill in the blanks. Some of us had gone through grief and some of us hadn't, but we still shared an understanding and could give space for whatever came up.

In studying ambiguous loss, Olivia found methods for working through it. "There are a lot of guidelines for how to work through ambiguous loss, like learning how to tolerate ambiguity and how to hold multiple things at once." The whole idea of gender plays a big role in applying ambiguous loss to trans families. "It's very tied to your expectations of gender. The more you hold onto gender roles and stereotypes in your mind, the harder time you have with the grief. If you really hold this person who used to be my dad [and] who's now like my mom—that's a complete replacement of the person." If, instead of replacement, we think in terms of evolution or coexistence, then we can have a different understanding and hold onto more of who our parent was. Olivia talked about her own process. "That piece...helped me look at my own gender expectations and how they played out… Why did it matter that my parent was my dad? And why is it sad? And what parts am I really grieving?" Some of the questions might not have answers right away. You might have to live inside the question, to accept the ambiguity.

It might also surprise you how fixed your ideas of gender are. I thought I had pretty flexible notions of gender, but when it came to my own family, it was different. Olivia found her ideas of gender surprising, too. "Before all this I thought, 'I don't subscribe to gender norms,' but then looking at it, I'm like, actually, there's a lot that I have. So I think just noticing it. Because I didn't notice it at first, I couldn't explore it." Once we're aware, we can consider our ideas of gender. We can see what we might take for granted and what can change.

Finding some continuity or through-line helps, too. When Riley's parent said, "I'm still your mom," it gave him a reference point through all the changes. "Being able to hold onto that conversation and have that as a baseline was so important for me and for my relationship with my mom." He was Riley's mom and a man in the world all at the same time. As a family, they talked through the changes in a way that helped them claim their relationship. Riley experienced some sense of loss with the changes of his parent's physical body, but not an overwhelming grief.

If I could go back in time, I would ask Dana, "How can I come with you?" It sounds funny, but with misunderstanding and grief, gaps can form. You can grow distant from each other. If I'd known ways to go along for the ride and be a part of it somehow, that is what I would do. Sharon said, "It's funny how—as much as transitioning is a personal thing—your whole family—everyone is either coming along for the ride or being dragged along and denying it every step of the way." Finding a way to be part of it by talking to your parent is one way to come along for the ride instead of being dragged.

If we feel like we're being dragged along for the ride, we might resent having to process any grief at all. Sadie from Australia talked about how she sometimes feels like "the collateral damage in my parent's decision to transition. For me it has been a major grief to process with basically no support."

Toolbox for Grief and Loss

Here are a few steps to try out for moving through the grief. We'll talk about professional support in greater detail in the next chapter, but here are some initial steps.

1. Even if it's not socially recognized, you can set up your own memorial to recognize the part of your parent you miss.
2. Talk to your friends and peer support networks, especially people who can relate.
3. Find a counselor or religious or spiritual mentor who you trust and who is willing to educate themselves on these subjects. If you don't feel comfortable or feel like you are being given suggestions that aren't helpful, try someone else.
4. Keep a journal, writing letters to your parent. You don't have to show it to anyone, but you can use it as a place to express feelings that you can't quite name.
5. Keep a picture of your parent as you remember them, and write down memories as they occur to you or as you look at the picture. Those memories are a part of you, too. You don't have to erase part of your childhood or experiences with this change.

A GUIDE TO AMBIGUOUS LOSS

Olivia Chen

Olivia's experience as a PTP inspired her to pursue her Master's degree in Counseling Psychology (LGBT emphasis), working toward licensure as a Marriage and Family Therapist. She researched ambiguous loss to make sense of her own experience with grief when her parent transitioned.

> *"My dad's still alive, she's still here, I can still talk to her, but it is not the same person—it's a very different person now. I think that's a very unique thing to people who have a loved one that transitions in general." —Sarah*

People with trans parents sometimes feel a unique experience of loss. Acknowledging these feelings can help your family move forward as a whole. Seeking support for yourself has been linked to the quality of support your trans parent receives.

Ambiguous losses occur when people are unclear about the absence or presence of a loved one. In the case of transition, your parent is still present in both body and mind, but you may feel that something has been lost.

What is being grieved?

- Loss of gendered identity of your parent.
- Loss of gendered expectations you may have had for your parent.
- Loss of your gendered relationship with your parent.
- Loss of your own gendered identity.
- Loss of past—you may feel that the gendered past you have with your parent was not authentic.
- Loss of assumptive world—you may feel that you've lost the "world as you knew it."

Guidelines for working through ambiguous loss

- Label the ambiguity.
  - Identify and validate your feelings (both positive and negative ones).
  - Acknowledge that feelings of presence/absence or sameness/difference can coexist.
- Reduce the ambiguity.
  - Engage in intentional meaning-making. Consider: How does your family's transition fit into the story of who you are?
  - Clarify ways your parent's identity, your relationship, and your family are still the same and still present.
  - Explore how your own ideas of gender may impact the degree of loss you are experiencing.
- Tolerate the ambiguity.
  - Learn to accept that you and your family may hold multiple "truths" that can all coexist.
  - Connect with others in the same situation.
- Recognize that the journey of transition—and the journey of your grief—may never be done, and that both are different for everyone.

We might grieve the loss of our family, the loss of our parent as they once were, or the loss of other family members who don't understand. We might not grieve at all. If we do grieve, it doesn't mean an end to the relationship. It's just part of coming to understand the new reality. There are layers to the grief, but on the other side of that grief, and sometimes intertwined with it, lie the gifts and the gains.

GIFTS AND GAINS

Dana has seen both sides. She has an insider's view of the lives of men and women. She knows the privilege that comes with living the life of a white, cisgender male. She left that privilege behind. Jonathan told a story of being on a plane with Paula. Someone near them started to talk about the kind of plane it was and what it was going to do. Paula stepped in. "She said, 'No, this plane's this kind and it's not going to do what you said it's going to do.'" The person looked at Paula, and then turned around to ask someone else. Now, Paula gives talks about gender in the workplace, because she knows first-hand about this bias. Dana got it when I told her about the sexism in my high school. She knew it was real because she'd been on both sides. She went from the whole world nodding and saying "yes," catering to everything she did, to the whole world shaking their head and saying "no," dismissing most of what she did. She understood because she'd experienced both perspectives and knew that it was real.

Danielle felt like her relationship with her stepmom improved alongside the change. "That was a major shift in our relationship for the better. It was already moving in a better direction, but if you were going to look at a graph, it would be a sharp turn." They are much closer now than they were before. She gained a whole new relationship with her parent, and a closer connection than she ever experienced growing up.

Sandra described it as a do-over in a way. "Having a transgender parent is honestly like having the chance to do it all over again." She didn't discount the loss at all, but she felt like they had a chance to build their relationship further. "My father as I knew him in so many ways is gone, but he didn't die. I get the gift of true appreciation of having my father as a parent, and having my father present in my life." In some ways, it's almost as if the change made this presence possible. She also felt inspired by watching the change happen. "My father is living her best life and that inspires me to do the same thing."

Watching her parents be themselves fully gave the same gift to Morgan. "Coming from two parents who very much were themselves, it is easier for me to be myself in this world." She described her "dad's commitment to authenticity and expression," not only in gender, but in his way of being in the world. "I think that that is useful for kids to see their parents role model." Our sense of self can strengthen by watching our parents claim their own.

What if we watch our parent struggle even more? What are the gifts then? Noelle H. watched her dad reinvent herself more than once career-wise. She got to see how to start over and move in a new direction. Amy saw how finding a trans roommate gave her parent the solidarity and community she needed. In my family, Dana has moved both by choice and by necessity. Each time, she builds a new community with friends of all ages and transforms her homes from dim, dull spaces into bright, shining jewels. She regained the voice she'd lost in surgery, and found her voice again in her writing, too. Our parents' struggles don't mean they aren't living their true lives and identities. We can still learn from them and be proud of the courage it takes to change your life.

Like Sharon, I've always related to outsiders. Having been on the outside with my family gave me a wider perspective. It gave me an understanding of what it means to feel you have to hide a part of yourself. Even though we're the kids, and may feel like we're going along for the ride, we experience the sense of feeling different, too. Justin described it as "this enormous empathy and understanding of 'the other' in American society. The feeling of oppression and the feeling of having to hide. The feeling of looking at a TV or looking out in the world and not seeing your story and not seeing yourself." It brings about another way of looking at things and a sense of being set apart, but also fosters understanding.

Even a handful of years ago, I felt pretty unique about having a transgender parent. When I stepped into rooms with people with LGBTQ+ parents, I could relate. All of us had faced some kind of bullying or misunderstanding with our peers. All of us had felt different in ways both good and bad. The first time I stood in front of a group of people to tell my story at a transphobia workshop, I knew that this story could be a bridge. We get to say that this is a part of our lives. To show how ordinary it can be to have someone you love take a U-turn in their lives and start over. That we don't have to be set apart. That our families are like any family, with a twist. Sometimes we get to be a bridge between those who get it and those who don't. Maybe you get to tell other people that they can live a life outside the coloring lines, too. Sarah described how: "It helped me have a voice. I found a voice in feeling comfortable standing up and talking about what I believe in." She found her own voice, her own convictions.

One of the things you might get on the other side of grief is you. Sarah talked about reconciling her parent's identity with her own. "My dad is not the person I thought he was, so my whole life is not what I thought it was. I'm not who I thought I was." It felt to her like a rupture of solid ground. "It can feel like your whole foundation shakes—when your parent isn't who you thought they were, you question everything about your life and who you are." As she came back to steady ground, she woke up one day to this realization: "Wait a minute, I am exactly who I think I am, and whatever my dad does has no bearing on me." It was a moment of claiming her own identity and sense of self. "I still got to decide who I was." You get to choose your direction. Sarah was challenged to confront her sense of self and claim what was hers. She was her own reward at the tail-end of grief.

Your overall perspective might widen. Olivia described how "I don't have those assumptions anymore that you can know a person or that you could know what's gonna happen in your life, and I feel like that has been quite freeing." She let go of old ideas about how life unfolds. Riley also described a sense of freedom, saying, "I feel a lot more open—life happens a bit. My sense of self is a bit more malleable and fluid. My vision of my family in the future is a bit more fluid." He doesn't feel fixed into one way of being.

My parents never expected me to be anyone other than who I was. They didn't expect me to conform to any standards or fit into any roles. They expected me to live a life outside the box. They gave me a glimpse of the different shapes a life could take, and they left the doors and windows open for me to find out for myself.

Jordan felt that his experience of his parent changing later in his life was overwhelmingly positive. "I think it's just made me a better person in a really big sense in my capacity to relate to other people's perspectives or experience, and also just to step out of myself more." He also found he had a new way of approaching other things that came up in the world, too. "It gave me the capacity to go head-on at stuff that's really challenging."

Some of this growth might have happened anyway. Even said, "I learned something about being open and not being prejudiced against things. It's very difficult to say, as maybe I would have learned those anyway." These parts of ourselves are intertwined with other experiences, but a lot of people shared this feeling. He also touched on the idea of accepting what we might not fully understand. "We have so much trouble understanding ourselves, you know, trying to understand everyone, we would have a really hard time, so acceptance is a much better way to go."

Another gain is being part of a community that shows you

more about where you fit in with all these changes. In 2015, when marriage equality passed in the U.S. Supreme Court, the voices of the kids were part of what made a difference. It's tough for us if our parents aren't out in the community or if we ourselves aren't out, but even if you tell one person, that's one less person who sees "trans" as something separate or other—"over there." It's one less person who makes a sweeping judgment about a whole community because they don't know someone inside it. We're inside it, too. When I marched in the New York City Pride Parade in 2011, wearing a "Kids of Trans" sign, most people looked at me with curiosity like, "What is that?" It felt good to be out there, though, claiming my space in a community that's mine, too—one I grew up in, one that is a part of me.

When I went to the Trans Wellness conference in Philadelphia for the first time, it was a relief to be around a huge community of trans-identified people. It helped me to know in my bones what I knew at age ten—that this is just part of the world. This bigger community is part of the gain. We get to see people claim their lives at any age, and step into the in between where all of us live at some point, whether we wear it on the outside or not.

Prompts for Grief and Loss, Gifts and Gains

1. Write a letter: Write a letter saying goodbye to your parent as you once knew them. Then, write what you think they would say in response.
2. Has grief been a part of your experience?
3. If so, how have you addressed this grief? What resources have you sought out?
4. What have been the gifts and gains?

Chapter 7

Finding Community

For the first time in my life, I don't feel like a unicorn. At my first-ever meeting of the New York chapter of COLAGE, I'm in a room full of people with families like mine in a two-floor apartment tucked between Avenues B and C in the East Village. I can tell my story here without feeling like anyone will give me weird looks or act like my family is a Jerry Springer sideshow or exotic creature at the zoo. I don't have to answer uncomfortable questions about my parent's anatomy. No one here puts me under a microscope.

I have some meeting-people-for-the-first-time jitters. I topple a plate of crackers and veggies. A curly-haired guy sits on the floor and a cute carrot-top college student sits next to him. We're there to plan a screening of Ed Webb-Ingall's film, *Raising Hell*, about people with gay and lesbian parents. When I tell my story, people act amazing, not shocked or weirded out. I can say, "This is my family," without feeling like I should hide out under a rock.

When I found COLAGE in 2010, I felt like I'd finally found a place where I could share my story and have it be just another part of who I was. I found people who understood. Even if they didn't all have trans parents, they still got what it meant to have a family with a unique shape.

The strength of community also helped me to share my story more openly in my wider community and with more friends. I knew I had my COLAGE friends supporting me, and when I heard others share stories about families like mine, I felt less alone. Community gave me the courage to share my truth, and to come out of the silence that had been the norm in my family for so many years.

FIND YOUR PEOPLE!

It might not even occur to you that you might need a community, too. Or your parents might usher you to events where you feel like you don't relate to the other kids. Your parent might jump into a new community right away in the process of transitioning. It can take a while to find your own community.

On the way to finding your community, you will come across people who don't fully understand. Once you find your community, though, those other voices won't matter so much. The people who don't get it. The people who are confused. You'll let it roll off more.

Once you have a community, you can bring it with you wherever you go. Take it along to the awkward family picnic or the first day at a new school. It's kind of like having invisible armor around you all the time. That's what having a community can be.

COLAGE AND OTHER GROUPS

Around the time of my dad's transition, COLAGE formed across the Bay in San Francisco. Still, it took me 20 more years to find it. When I did, I was living in New York, and I discovered the

New York chapter. Sometimes I wonder if it would have been different for me if I'd found COLAGE back then, if I'd had a strong community around me, saying, "Yeah, we get it, we've been there, too." At the time, we didn't know about COLAGE, and we didn't think we needed anything like it. We felt somewhat unique in that my dad disappeared and quickly moved away from trans spaces. We were just living in a new reality. Why would we need other people to talk to?

The trans community at the time didn't feel like a community as much as a fragmented constellation of people. My sister went to a pool party hosted by Dana's therapist, a gathering of trans families. That didn't help either. There was still a sense of shame and secrets, of each family going through this on their own. We had a few families over to our house. One of the families had little kids, much younger than me and my sister. Other than that, we didn't know any other families going through this.

I remember going to the Castro in San Francisco and feeling the difference of this place with rainbow flags and men dressed in leather. In many ways, my family was less a part of that community when the transition started. There wasn't a place for the "T." The gay community had pockets of strong community. The trans community didn't have a place just for us. At the time, I almost didn't realize or recognize that I needed the resources, but I did.

When I found the Kids of Trans (now People with Trans Parents) group at COLAGE, I felt like I found a place where I fit. Though each of us have different experiences and shapes to our families, we share the misunderstandings that can come with telling people, the zig-zagging journey to acceptance, and the awareness of an expanded world and that what most people think they know about gender is only a part of the story.

We need more spaces like these where we can gather to share our stories, or even just talk about our lives without our families being a focal point. One of my closest friends from COLAGE is a woman who grew up with two moms. We talk about our families sometimes, but mostly we talk about our lives and adventures in dating. Our families are part of the background, and that's a good thing. They are not the focus, but we can still talk about them openly. There's nothing to hide.

Sarah talked about the first time she met up with people who shared her experience. She went with her parents to a weekend conference for cross-dressers, where they organized a panel of the kids. "That was the first time I had met other people like me and seen other people like my dad in one place. It was empowering in a lot of ways to talk to the other kids." She also had a chance to tell her story without filtering it through the lens of her parents. It was the start of finding her own voice.

Early on, she also looked into starting her own chapter of COLAGE. "I tried to start a COLAGE chapter—I was 16 and desperate for local connection. Through the COLAGE website I met a lesbian mom who was trying to get a COLAGE chapter going for kids, and we connected for a while, but nothing ever panned out there." She knew from that first experience the power of community. Though she didn't form the chapter, she started to get connected. If there isn't a group in your area, you could start your own. You might be surprised by the people who will turn up at the meetings: your nemesis from fourth grade or your future best friend. All you need is an e-mail and a willingness to reach out.

There might be a group that already exists in your area. You can try PFLAG (Parents, Families, and Friends of Lesbians and Gays), Family Equality Council, or your local LGBTQ+ center, too. You could start something at your school. Just see who else is out there, wanting to start up a similar group, and join forces to support each other as you get started.

THE INVISIBLE "T"

What about the "T" that for so long felt like a last-minute add-on to LGB? Even the name "COLAGE" first came as an acronym for "Children of Lesbian and Gay parents Everywhere." Adding in the "T" would make the word sound clunky, but it also reflected this absence. As Sarah said, "It just felt like even with the acronym COLAGE—oh, and there's an invisible 'T' for 'transgender'—it's very invisible isn't it? Not a lot of resources out there." Now, many more letters can be added into the acronym as the larger LGBTQ+ movement continues to expand. Yet it's only in recent years that the "T" was really inside the movement, so the resources for families and children were limited, too.

At the time when my parent transitioned, there were so many silences around it that I tried to hide in the silence for so long. I didn't even think that I needed anything in terms of community. It didn't occur to me to try to find this community. I tried really hard to fit into cisgender straight spaces. I tried to act like my family was this certain way, and I spent a lot of time hiding.

We didn't have a built-in community, either. The gay community wasn't ours anymore. I didn't fully know what this meant at the time, but for me, it felt like I went from having dozens of uncles to maybe two or three. Sometimes it felt like all of us were in hiding. I wanted to lift up the roof of our house and say, "Come out, come out, wherever you are," and we could all come out and say, "Hey, this is where we were all along."

In the early days of my dad's transition, her therapist tried to create a community of sorts. She sent over other people in transition to visit like it would help us to all mix together. Some of the parents in transition had beards with long, long hair. One came over in a navy-blue stewardess suit and a little Dutch girl wig, with feet squeezed into navy-blue flats. "Don't stare," I told myself. I still stared even though I tried really hard not to.

The community didn't stick. There weren't kids our ages and our parents didn't connect with the ones transitioning or their partners. It was like mis-matched puzzle pieces. We tried to force them together, but it didn't work. Another issue was that Dana didn't relate to people who wanted to disappear into their chosen gender, but couldn't. Before she started the full transition, she went to support groups at a place called "The Center for Special Problems." She gathered information that started her on her way. There, she met someone who was still together with her family as a "sister-in-law," which might have inspired our own story.

Once she was on her way, though, she didn't fit into that community, either. She fit more simply in communities of women, which meant erasing her past for her and for us. It meant living as our aunt and skipping over the community. We struck out on our own with a few people along for the ride in our pact of silence.

During the year of the transition, we might as well have been living on an island. I didn't bring friends home for sleepovers and our neighbors didn't know. They met Dana as Daniel's sister, and we lived outside of town, so we didn't run into people too often. My sister and I went to school across the Bay, far enough away that it made sense for us to go to our friends' houses when we had playdates. Our friends had moms and dads, and at least on the surface looked like all the families on TV. We didn't fit into the community the therapist thrust at us, or this one, so we kept going on our own like a satellite family floating through space, breaking through barriers that we didn't even know existed.

All the messages from movies, books, and shows told me that anyone who stepped outside the gender lines was different and somehow strange. When I went to my friends' families' houses, no one was trans. I learned that this wasn't happening in other homes. Maybe somewhere far away it was, but I didn't see it around me.

People are often surprised when they hear that my family lived in the San Francisco Bay Area and still we didn't find a big, accepting community. At the time, in the late '80s, there were still silences about being gay. Being trans was like no man's land. You can be in an area that's known as open and still feel far removed from other people like you. Also, since we moved there right before the change, we morphed into this new family with few traces of who we were. Justin related to this idea of reinvention from the moves he made with his mom from East Tennessee out to Colorado and elsewhere. We could say we were whoever we wanted. "We're not daisies—we're tulips," he said. This reinvention continued wherever we went.

"The kids are fine—they're doing great," my parents told their friends, which was true. We were fine. We didn't think we needed anyone outside our family and the handful of people who knew. We were just busy fitting in. There was a lot of misunderstanding and lack of awareness at the time, so it felt like we were protecting our parent. Even just from someone staring and staring.

Justin echoed this idea of keeping his parent safe. "When she transitioned and came back from surgery, I had been living with that secret for really formative years, and nobody thought to tell me that it wasn't a secret." They moved after the surgery, and the secret settled in even more. He thought, "I can never tell anyone that my mom is trans, so this has to be a secret forever." Later when he left home, this continued. "I can keep her a secret," he thought. "I can keep her safe forever now."

Fast forward 15 years, and the isolation hadn't gone away. "The biggest challenges were in the early days," Sandra P. said. "It was 2005, and the transgender community was small. Facebook, etcetera weren't nearly as pervasive and I felt so isolated. There was literally no one to talk to about it and how I felt." By then, more people were transitioning, but there was still a sense of isolation. Sarah W.'s parent came out around the same time. "All through the early 2000s, there was all this LGB discussion and acceptance and progress, [yet] there was still not [as] much [awareness]—transgender still seemed pretty out there in terms of the public perception." She was living inside the silent "T" with her family, finding their own way.

When Noelle Howey's book *Dress Codes* came out in 2002, I was excited to find someone who had a parent like mine. As I read her book, I felt a sense of kinship through the shared experience. "You're not the only one," she seemed to be saying. That was my start of finding community: in the pages of a book.

Now, Noelle lives in a neighborhood with more than one family with trans kids. It's a different time in terms of finding community. You might find it right on your block. Jordan worked up to telling one of his business partners, not sure about how he would react. When he did, the partner said, "Oh yeah, my daughter's trans." He realized as he was telling people that nearly everyone "had one degree of separation from somebody who was trans." He thought he was sharing something unique, but he found that his family wasn't so special after all.

When I talked to families living further out in rural areas, though, they often searched for a community for their kids and didn't find one. Trans support groups didn't always have parents with kids. Their local LGBTQ+ center didn't host family-friendly events. Sometimes it's a lack of resources or funding or a lack of awareness about what's needed. Until we vault ahead into a time when people everywhere understand implicitly, we need to seek out the community.

One of the challenges to finding community was how invisible this was. It wasn't an identity that showed on the outside, so a lot of times, we were the ones keeping ourselves from a larger community by choosing not to say anything. There was a culture of silence, too, that kept us separate.

ONLINE AND IN PERSON

When Sarah first went looking for COLAGE, she found a much smaller group, and the Kids of Trans group was even smaller. "In 1999, when I first googled COLAGE, the Kids of Trans corner was extraordinarily small. We had this little Yahoo group—nothing was really going on in it for years."

Lara had a similar experience. "I ended up as part of an Indiana Yahoo group—a Yahoo message board." More recently, she found the COLAGE Facebook Group for People with Trans Parents. "I just figured out that there was support for it."

The Facebook Group—then the "Kids of Trans" Facebook Group—wasn't as active in those days, but it was a start. "Every once in a while, there would be a brief flurry of posts," Sarah said, "and you felt like, 'Okay there's at least some people out there that understand this.'" Facebook had a wider reach, and people could stumble upon the group.

Lily, Jeremy's Ema, posted pictures of her own transition on Facebook. A friend of hers from school reached out recently to say, "If it weren't for you, I would still be hiding." Had she stayed hidden herself, Lily might not have reached that one person. That doesn't mean we must be visible or share our story more widely, but this shows how one person can have an impact. A community can be two people across a million wires on two screens late at night.

The online group may be all you have for a while, but think

of it as a window into in-person groups rather than a substitute. As much as these online spaces are helpful, the physical space of conferences and gatherings gives more of a chance to connect. There's the Trans Wellness conference, First Event in New England, and Family Week in Provincetown. For young kids, there's also Camp Highlight, where young adults work as counselors.

Even if you don't think you need a community or support, try reaching out and widening your circle, whether online or in person. Try some conferences or local events. Start where you are and go from there.

IF OUR PARENTS AREN'T OUT

How do we as trans families show pride if our parents don't want to be out in their communities? We can start with spaces that accept our families, ones like Family Week or gatherings for LGBTQ+ families. Even if our parents don't want to go, we can.

If our parents don't want to be out in the community, they might not want to connect with other families. It might be something we seek out for ourselves. Mostly, it's about finding people who say, "Yeah, I've been there and this is how I got through."

Before I found COLAGE, I had a friend whose dad came out after her parents had been married for a long time. The two of us had a mini-community for a while. I remember the time she said to me, "It's not something to be ashamed of." Somehow, the shame had grown in me until I didn't know that there was any other way. If, as a family, we carry some shame, it is part of us, too. It's a shame both inherited and grown on its own from feeling different. It wasn't a matter of simply saying, "Go away, shame." But almost like a ripple effect, the more I met people with families like mine or with families in the larger queer community, the more the feeling got diluted. It's the antidote to looking out in the world and seeing no one with your story. To one by one find stories closer to yours, ones that show that your family is not so different after all. Even if they aren't being broadcast yet, they are out there.

We might also choose not to seek out community for the time being. "In some ways I think there are a lot of reasons why I haven't sought out the Kids of Trans community," Fiona said. She was cautious about sharing her story because of the thread about mental illness. "As the daughter of a trans person, as a gay woman myself, and just sort of as a human, I don't want trans people to be pathologized." Stepping into the community could also mean opening up this part of the story that she protected. "There's enough in the world of this is about mental illness and not about truth, and I don't want to contribute to that in any way." A wish to protect our family and others can keep us from community, too.

Had someone tossed me into a roomful of kids with trans parents back in the day, I would have felt exposed. "My family's different," I might have said. "We're fitting in." I might not have wanted the community, even if it was offered to me. Only later did I see that the shame that led me to push it away was the whole reason I needed it in the first place.

THE POWER OF COMMUNITY

On a beach in Provincetown, Massachusetts, people set up tents and clusters of towels. They light a bonfire inside a pit of sand. The kids on one side, the parents on the other. People wade into the water, which is shallow, though the tide is coming in. From far away, it looks like any bonfire at the beach. Close up, you might see two dads in the water with their toddler or a trans parent talking to one of the camp leaders. Every year, families come from all over for a single week in Provincetown, Massachusetts. At the end of the week, the families parade across the town, rainbow flags waving. For the rest of the year, they might be in towns where there are no families like theirs. This one week fuels them for the rest of the year.

The power of community can exist between as few as two people. In 2011, I met a woman at the COLAGE Northeast Regional Retreat who had a trans parent. We were the only two with trans parents. We immediately bonded and shared our stories. That's where I learned that a community can be two people saying, "Yes, I understand." We were the only two in a retreat of many, but it didn't matter. When we went out in the larger group, the two of us had a tiny bubble around us. She was only there for the weekend, and I wanted to soak up every minute together sharing our stories. The whole group had a shared language, and ours was our own sub-language. We got what the other was saying before we even said it.

Even if your community is only one other person, try to find that person and share some pieces of your story. It's tempting to try to keep this within the walls of our family. For us, we often felt it was private. It was our story and should stay there. So we kept it just between us. It helped to have my sister to talk to, but having someone outside your family to relate to can help even more.

At the Trans Wellness conference, it felt good to be in spaces filled with trans folks. It made my experience as a child feel widespread as it was, though we were taught to be silent and kept apart.

We have a unique perspective born of a life where the

uncertainty was woven into the fabric of our families. We can share this perspective and build on each other's strengths.

COMMUNITY? WHO NEEDS COMMUNITY?

In the lunch chat for people with trans parents, there are two people: an eight-year-old boy, whose parents dropped him off in this room, and me. He's not sure why he's here, and he doesn't have a lot to talk about. He unzips his lunch sack and pulls out a neatly wrapped sandwich, some chips, and a bag of carrots. For him, the fact that he has a trans parent is part of the background of his life. He barely notices it until his parents drop him off at a group like this. This is the future, where kids don't need this community, where they don't feel different because of their families.

In New York City, parents drop their kids off at events hosted by COLAGE, and the kids mostly say, "We're good." If the kids are alright, then why bother gathering? The ones who are good, who don't need a community, can blaze a trail for the ones who do. There might be someone in the room who doesn't feel a-okay about their family, so they get to show them another way.

Maybe you like being a unicorn, the one in your class with the cool trans parent. You get to show what it's like to be comfortable with your family and yourself. That's no small thing.

THERAPY AND PROFESSIONAL SUPPORT

"[I suggest] family therapy, to support everyone in the transition."

—STEVE VINAY G., AGE 48

For grief and other more complex emotions that come up, some Kids of Trans and trans families might seek out therapy and professional support. How can we find someone who can help us as a family and as individuals?

Olivia's family went to a family therapist soon after her father came out and once her brother knew. "We ended up... deciding to do family therapy to navigate the whole crisis situation, but in a really condensed time period." She went home for two weeks and did a marathon of family therapy with her whole family. "It was way too much," she said. They could only address so much in that timeframe. Also, the therapist wasn't well versed in this area. "I'm sure she's a great family therapist, but I don't think she really was well equipped to handle trans issues." The therapist doesn't need to specialize in the area, but some familiarity or a willingness to educate themselves is important.

My family saw Dana's individual therapist, who specialized in gender reassignment. She had seen many people and families going through the transition. We only went a few times, however, and it didn't feel like she listened to me or my sister.

Dr. Green had an office in her house, a ranch-style house in a sunny part of Northern California with palm trees and outdoor pools. She led us down the cool corridor to her office. Dana and my mom sat on one couch, and my sister and I sat on the other with our arms folded. Dr. Green sat behind a large desk with her name stenciled on a plaque at the front. On both walls, there were shelves full of books. I didn't know why we were even there.

Dr. Green wanted us to talk about how things were going. I wasn't sure how that was going to help. It wouldn't stop the world from thinking my parents were lesbians when they walked down the street. That was my big fear at the time. I was so mortified by this. In my class at school, the girls made fun of Ms. Cameron who had short spiked hair and wore parachute pants. She rode on a motorcycle to school. They called her, "Lesbo." I didn't want any association with that.

"People think they're lesbians," I said in one session with Dr. Green. It didn't seem like there was anything worse than that. Dr. Green tittered when I aired my concern. "Oh, no, no, no," she said, waving her hand as if to brush my fear aside with a quick sweep. It didn't work. The fear lingered, but I felt foolish for saying it out loud, so I didn't share anything else. She was dismissive of that, but I think that hid a lot of other things that she didn't really unpack. She also seemed to be trying to usher us toward acceptance in not-so-subtle ways, and we weren't entirely ready for that.

In another session, when my sister or I started to talk about something, Dana's face crumpled and she hunched over, starting to cry. This also stopped us from being fully honest in these sessions. We didn't want to make Dana cry, so we didn't say anything more.

Dr. Green knew a lot about trans topics at the time, but since she had been working one-on-one with Dana for so long, she didn't have a broader perspective for all of us. My family had taken away the stigma inside the walls of our house, as if this happened every day. At the same time, we kept a secret, and this grew bigger over time; and as I started to see my own family as different or set apart, I sought to make sense of where we fit in, and what this meant for me. My own struggles with anxiety and depression also led me to seek out help for myself later on, to find my own balance and sense of self in my family and as I made my way out into the world.

When I sought out individual therapy, it was difficult to find people who didn't have their own preconceived notions.

"I thought it just made you more interesting these days," one therapist said wearily during a consultation when I confided my struggles with sharing the truth with my friends.

"All transgender people are narcissists—let me tell you," another said angrily, her own story scripted before I even started telling mine.

They had certain lenses they were seeing through and strong feelings about the subject. Sometimes they made it all about that instead of seeing the whole big picture. In the end, it was the ones who saw this as a part of my story and not the only important piece, who I trusted. It's essential to find someone who understands. They don't necessarily have to have a specialty in this area to be helpful. They just need to be open to the topic and willing to listen.

What if you don't accept your parent? What then? Is the goal perfect acceptance? The way the therapist used to nudge me and my sister toward acceptance always felt wrong, like she had her own agenda and there wasn't room for our complicated feelings. The closer we got to acceptance, the better. Ideally, a therapist doesn't have a particular agenda or end goal in mind.

Amy and her dad did therapy some years after the transition to make sense of their relationship. "My dad and I recently have been through a lot of therapy together, which has really illuminated a lot about that transitional time." The therapist helped them to listen to each other and make sense of a time full of much confusion. "I think one of the major similarities in all of our stories is that it was really sloppy and messy and difficult for everyone, and it was no exception for my family." Going to therapy together gave them a way to understand the transition from each other's perspective, too.

Not every family can afford therapy, and it might not be the ideal model for everyone either. In some cases, a trusted religious or spiritual person can be helpful.

Lily went to see her rabbi when she was starting the process of transitioning. She wanted to know whether she was offending God by doing this. Her rabbi said, "In Judaism in the Bible, there aren't two sexes, there are nine different sexes. It's something that should be celebrated and not questioned." That was a big relief for her. She could also share that new knowledge with her sons if needed. It gave her a sense of permission to move forward.

Sarah started out at a pastoral care counseling service at a church. The counselor came recommended for having experience with these subjects. "He was used to talking to adults who were questioning whether they might be gay," she said. "So when a 16-year-old girl comes in completely messed up about her dad wearing dresses, he had no clue what to do with me—absolutely none." She went for a couple of sessions and then told her mom, "This is absolutely useless. He doesn't know anything about anything about anything." After that, she went to a few sessions with a couple of other people, but found that they were equally clueless. She told her mother, "They don't know anything to help me. They know zero things about what I'm going through, and they keep giving me this advice that feels just wrong." The lack of awareness at the time may have made it hard to find someone who could help, even if they wanted to.

Becca started seeing her therapist before her dad came out. "She went through the whole process with me, so that really helped. Just going through the whole process of my dad transitioning with the same person who knew every single little detail was so refreshing, because you never had to tell the story from the beginning. So once you find someone that just actually pays attention to you and listens to you..." The two built up a sense of trust and a strong relationship. "Therapy helped a lot," she said. "My therapist either validated my feelings or told me, 'You're acting stupid,' because sometimes I would just react to things and I would just be so mad. I really got over my anger going to therapy. That really helped." The therapist also educated herself. "She really did try to get educated solely for me, which was nice. She went to a conference and actually found COLAGE, and that's how I found out about COLAGE. She came back with this packet of definitions of 'agender' and being 'cisgender' and all this gender stuff and helped educate me." Now there are more resources out there, so even therapists who don't have a specialty can find additional support and information.

When choosing the right person to see, be aware that therapists don't necessarily have to have a background in trans families or gender. It's enough to find someone who, as Becca said, is "a really dedicated therapist and really open-minded who's not afraid to tell you when you're either acting stupid or it's okay how you feel—someone who's honest with you." For your family or for yourself, the key is finding someone you trust who will do the work to educate themselves and you.

WHERE YOU FIT IN THE LARGER QUEER COMMUNITY

I used to dread being different in any way at all. I was appalled by any suggestion my parents made to watch a movie with a trans character or align myself with anything different. "That's not me," I thought. Even as I supported LGBTQ+ friends and thought of myself as an ally, even as I bought the bumper sticker, "I'm straight but not narrow," I still rejected my own family, and in a way, myself. It took me a while to admit that I had a place in the community. I had a trans parent with two gay ex-partners who played a huge role in my life, and I felt comfortable in queer spaces, but I didn't know where I fit.

I grew up with a group of gay men who adopted me as their own, taught me what they knew about style and fashion, and gave me gifts of dolls, jewelry, and beautiful things. As I grew older, and my own cisgender identity emerged, I wondered where I fit in the community. I didn't want to kiss girls or be a boy, but I knew I fit into the larger LGBTQ+ community, even as I pushed it away through high school and college.

In high school, I went to a couple of meetings of the Gay Straight Alliance, but I didn't fit there, either. That was my first effort, though, the first awareness that this was a part of me. That I could travel far away from my family and still feel an affinity to queer spaces.

"Being a person who identifies primarily as straight..." Sarah said, "It can feel a little bit awkward sometimes to be part of the LGBT community. Where's my place in that?" While her parent is part of why she belongs, she feels connected to the community for her own reasons. "The LGBT community being such a wonderful community—I would want to be part of it anyway." Wherever she fits, she feels lucky to be there. "Getting to be a part of it, I feel privileged to be allowed even into a little corner of the LGBT community—I'm profoundly grateful for that."

In college at a training session for a battered women's shelter, one of the participants came out as trans. Once, we were on the same weekend shift together and I wanted so much to say something to her about my family, like "I have a parent who's trans," but something held me back. She never knew anything about the connection we shared, and I never told her.

We are part of the invisible rainbow, the ones who were raised in that world, but don't always show it on the outside. We can play a key role in bridging the gap in understanding. We know both sides. We've gone through our own journeys and landed somewhere on the spectrum between confusion and understanding. We can help people to see. We can be guides and ambassadors, joining both perspectives.

If we identify as queer, too, we can carry our parents' perspectives with our own, bringing a kaleidoscope view into the larger conversation.

RAINBOW KIDS

Monica had been dating someone in high school around the time her dad came out. When she told her boyfriend, he told her about his own family, too. "Oh well, you know, my mom is kind of a lesbian or something—I don't really know." His mom had dated a woman after his parents split up when he was in middle school. He hadn't mentioned it before, but this was now something they shared. She had a friend with a gay uncle, too. "It's that LGBT umbrella," she said. "Even if it's a different experience, we can kind of relate around this."

Some people use the term "queerspawn" or "rainbow kids." We are joined together by a shared experience of growing up in a culture that doesn't always embrace our families. We navigate in spaces often biased toward the straight or cisgender world.

One of my friends in COLAGE told of how she would pair off her two gay dads and gay moms for her soccer games. She wanted only one mom and one dad to come. Never mind it might be a different dad or mom on any given week. She only thought of fitting into the family models she saw around her.

Many of us experience shifts in our family's structure when our parents come out. We may go through a time when our relationship with our parent changes or shifts. This can be true for all, too.

We often watch our parents change as they slide into their new identity. That can happen for all of us, but sometimes feels more pronounced as we watch our parents' shift in gender expression. When my dad came out as gay, it was mostly invisible to me. He was very good at fitting into straight spaces. In the years when Dana lived as a gay man, our family got bigger. Two men, who continued to play an important role in my life, joined our family. Friends gathered at our place. We went to parties full of people who worked in the arts and lived lives as part of a counter-cultural movement at the time. AIDS changed the community we belonged to. Our family friends started to get sick. Still, when I went out with my dad, it didn't feel much different.

Later, when she came out as Dana, it felt like watching another side of my parent emerge. And yet, it did feel like an emergence of something new. It wasn't an adding on or acting as if, or layering over. It was the coming to the surface of something deeply held inside. And maybe that emergence happens for gay parents, too. Finally, they can slip into the skins of the selves they claim as true. All of us go through transformations and emergence in our lives.

Our experience is unique. It's not the same as those who grew up with gay parents. Having grown up with both, I felt a difference.

We get to see how gender can be blurred or changed, how it can emerge in our parents, and in that way, how it can be shaped rather than given. We know that gender is something that lies under the surface, waiting to come out.

While it didn't lead me to question my own gender or sexuality, it did make me aware of the way genders are treated in society. It made me aware of the differences. As a man, my father claimed a space of authority that wasn't there when she came out as a woman.

We are impacted by the larger society's transphobia. In our

silences and fear, we hold some of that transphobia inside of us. Also, when we share about our families, we often feel isolated in the sharing as people wonder out loud or ask questions. Those who haven't been through it can sometimes unintentionally "other" us through their responses.

We know from watching our parents that the feeling of disconnect is real in someone whose body doesn't match their felt experience.

We are unique. "You are special for having a trans parent," Leila said. We are part of the rainbow kids, but we also have our own unique perspective to share.

SUPER-SOFFAS: HOW YOU CAN BE AN ALLY TO THE TRANS COMMUNITY

What does it mean to be an ally in the trans community? What role do "SOFFAs" (Significant Others, Friends, Family, and Allies of trans people) play in the trans community?

Leila spun around in her rainbow cape. She was getting ready for her school's "rainbow day," a day recognizing and celebrating LGBTQ+ culture. She waved a rainbow flag in front of her face. She was showing how to be an ally by celebrating the culture, by claiming it as her own.

In the summer of 2011, I marched for the first time in the New York Gay Pride march as part of a float for COLAGE. I wore a "Kids of Trans" sign and saw people reading the sign as we passed, maybe seeing this phrase for the first time. We wore "Queerspawn" shirts and "COLAGE" shirts. Someone carried a sign that said, "turkey baster baby."

We joined the river of people on 5th Avenue. We marched from the East 50s all the way down to Christopher Street. My mother marched with me. She was a part of this community, too. All of us are. We belong.

At the end of the Pride march, we scattered, our feet sore, our faces soaked with the sun. We were filled up by this day of marching, by the power of the collective, the force of people gathered in one place.

The float of "Queerspawn" and "Turkey Baster Babies" had its own message about the shape of families. We offer people a glimpse into another way of being. We are part of the movement, too.

Monica got involved in Kids of Trans advocacy a year or so after her parent came out. "I remember having this moment of seeing my dad as a person—I was probably 18 or 19 at the time, and I just remember having this moment of being like, 'Wow, this must be so hard,' and really seeing that." In turn, she wished there were more resources out there for her and for kids like her. That was why she ended up working to expand the resources for Kids of Trans at COLAGE, and in the process, connecting with the larger trans community. "I was really wishing there was something for people like me." She shared her perspective widely, forming that bridge of understanding as a "SOFFA," one who shares in the experience and can shed light for those who don't.

You don't need to go from zero to SOFFA overnight. Sadie talked about the "pressure to become a super trans ally or otherwise cut off contact with the transgender parent, both of which are not generally speaking emotionally healthy for the child. It is very complicated." The two extremes don't give us room to come to our own understanding and take the action that feels right for us.

Taking an action helps move you forward to claim your own identity as your parent has claimed theirs. Taking an action takes you out of yourself and into the world. You get to see where you belong. It doesn't have to be in the LGBTQ+ community. For me, that is a part of my world, but I also feel at home in communities of writers and artists, book-lovers and librarians, people who want to make the world a better place. In those spaces, I can tell my family story too, until more of our stories fill the bookshelves and movie screens, until we see our families in toothpaste commercials and on billboards. Until then, we can gather to build up and recognize our strength.

These spaces where we gather and gain strength give us back the gift of community. We can seek it out or it can find us. We are a part of this, something bigger than ourselves, writing history the more we come out.

Prompts for Finding Community

1. Have you found a community where you can share your experience?
2. Do you have any friends with trans parents?
3. Have you or your family sought out therapy? What has been helpful? What wasn't helpful?
4. How can you expand your community of peers with trans parents based on where you are? Would an online or in-person community make the most sense for you?
5. Where do you fit in the trans community? In the larger queer community?

Chapter 8

Dating and Family Ties

Dating is awkward for everyone. Who you date and how you date is your choice, but we don't choose our families. You might connect with a neighbor who lives up the block, but if your parent isn't "out" yet, what do you do? The person you're dating is someone you're going to spend a lot of time with and share many things, so leaving out this stuff about your parent can feel like a big omission.

"It's definitely a first date conversation," a friend of mine with two moms in COLAGE said.

"No way," I thought. "It's a three-month serious relationship-only talk." For each of us, when and what we choose to share about our families in dating is a very personal choice.

At one point, Dana asked that I not share the truth with a significant other unless I planned to marry them. This raised the dilemma—am I leaving out a big part of my own experience by not telling? Or should I respect my parent's wishes? Ultimately, it led me to be more cautious in sharing, so I generally waited until I'd built up a level of trust before telling. Recently, though, I was messaging with someone online, and I told them directly.

It felt freeing to say it out loud, to tell someone and not hide or wait.

When it comes to dating, there's no definitive rulebook, though sometimes it feels like it would be nice if there were one. We're all figuring it out as we go along.

LOVE WHO YOU WANT TO LOVE

Riley was in middle school when he sat down with his family for dinner one night before a night out at a Broadway musical. His mom and cousin were talking about the sexuality of a kid they knew, when his mom said, "Oh well, Riley might be gay."

At the time, Riley didn't want anyone saying this. "My immediate reaction was you can't say anything about me until I'm ready to say it." He was at "the height of the 'do-not-look-at-me' phase, so even though it was innocuous and the intention was 'any door's open—be who you want to be—be free—love who you want to love—whatever—it's all good,'" he still didn't want her bringing it up. Though he had a family open to all ways of being, he didn't want a lamp shone on his own becoming.

He feels differently about it now. "The special amazing gift that I got out of that in the end was, as much as I wanted to ignore that earlier on, it's awesome now to have that freedom." It gives him a sense of options as his own life takes shape. "On the other side—having come out, I know I can have a family—I don't know what it will look like, but I know I can make it work."

How do we come to our own understanding of what Riley called "the difference between friendship and love and sex and all those different things"? Even as we watch our parents, we have to find our own way. "I could project sexuality into these relationships that my parents were having," Riley said, "but I was focused on it so externally." Our family gives us one view of gender and sexuality, but ours grows on its own. "As I grew, because I'm gay myself, that was an interesting dynamic, too. I knew intellectually this is what gay means, but I think it was all kind of in a weird soup of different queer straight gender ingredients that I'm still parsing."

Having parents who are more open doesn't necessarily give us a shortcut or secret code. Riley still had to find his own way. It might give us a different way of looking at things, but we still have to come into our own identity.

Having a dad who's gay and trans didn't make me a boy-crazy girl who dressed as Marilyn Monroe for fourth grade Halloween. That was who I was. My sister and I went to a girls' school, and when she went to her first boy–girl dance in sixth grade, I was so jealous. I wanted to hear all about it. I wanted to fast forward to sixth grade, so I could go too. I sent fan letters to George Michael, Ricky Schroeder, and the lead singer of A-Ha, spraying the envelope with perfume and sealing it with a kiss. SWAK! I stuffed my bikini top with tissues, impatient for my body to grow, and insisted on buying a tube top though my mother had to take it in to fit the size of a pole. I was so flat-chested that boys called me "The Plank" during my first year in high school. Why couldn't I fast forward until my body had the shape I wanted? I never thought that I was on a parallel journey with my parent, our bodies changing at the same time. Everything my parents did felt like it was happening on another planet—the planet of adults, one I had yet to arrive on.

It never crossed my mind that I would date anyone other than boys. At dancing school, we paired off boy–girl–boy–girl. We looked across the room, counting down the line to see who we would be matched up with, sometimes shuffling ourselves in line to get matched up with a crush.

At school dances, we dip our toes into the world of dating. Sharon's parent used to chaperone some of her school dances. Sharon said, "I'd be like, 'Are you kidding me? I do not need this.'"

Trisha liked being involved with the school community, but for Sharon it crossed a line. "It's important for kids as you get into middle and high school to have more of your own independence." They didn't have a conversation about this. She said it could be as simple as saying, "Let's talk about boundaries and what you need to do to respect me as a person who's becoming a young adult and what's okay." If it's steering clear of the dances or your cross-country meet, that's not about rejection as much as finding your own spaces and creating that independence.

Fast forward 20 years, and when Carter had a concert at his school, his parent said, "I'd like to come to your concert, but I'm going to be coming straight from work and I'm probably going to be wearing a dress and I don't want to embarrass you."

"Why would that embarrass me?" Carter said. "That's what women do—they wear dresses."

It was simply a matter of checking in, and of a time now when parts of the world have opened up to our families.

Our own understanding of sex and gender is a bit of trial and error. When I was younger, we had a book called *Love and Sex in Plain Language*. Inside, there were drawings of naked people that I was curious to look at. I smuggled it over to my friend's house one day for a collective study. There was nothing in there about being trans. You were this way or that way and that was it.

I had my first boyfriend, Nick, in fifth grade. Our relationship lasted approximately three days. A combination of his new haircut and my unwillingness to kiss on the lips brought it crashing down. Over the course of our relationship, he suggested that I shave my legs, which was my first experience of trying to change myself for someone else. I did, and he promptly forgot that he'd said anything. He looked at my clean-shaven legs with indifference. We didn't date long enough for him to meet my family.

The advice my mother gave me when I announced that I had a boyfriend was, "Keep him away from your zipper." What did that mean? Boys were a total mystery to me.

Donnie, one of Dana's exes, was one of us—boy-crazy and fun to be with. We taught him the words we said if someone was cute—"hella fine"—and he said them too. He was our go-to chaperone for concerts or other fun things.

In eighth grade, I dated a boy who played football at the local high school. I was too young to go on dates with him alone, so my sister went with me. My sister was ahead of me, and the two of us shared everything about dating and boys. Dana was always a little nicer to guys we dated than our mom, who held them at a cool, appraising distance. The meet-the-parents moment was changed, because guys thought they were meeting our mom and our aunt. Really, they were meeting both our parents. My college boyfriend was the first to meet Dana as my parent. The two of them got along well. I felt a little different, but his extra-friendliness put Dana at ease.

What if you identify as a part of the rainbow with your parent? Does having parents who are trans or queer make it easier to come out? According to Jennifer, a lot of people think that. They would say things like "Oh, you must have had the best coming-out experience. It must have been so much fun, because your parents are all women."

Before she came out, though, it didn't occur to her parent that Jennifer shared parts of her own story. Mem, her parent, would say things like "You can't understand what this is like—this is a whole other level—you can't understand homophobia. You don't get this stuff."

Meanwhile, Jennifer sat there, thinking, "Well I do though, because I'm bisexual—I'm in the community."

Jennifer added, "It was kind of a weird thing, because I didn't know how to tell her—it hurt my feelings to hear that stuff."

Jennifer came out to herself at 16 and to her family at 18. The day she came out, Mem picked her up on campus, and she had just been at a bi+ support group. She started the conversation by saying, "Do you want to know where I was?"

After she came out, they talked about it more and Mem said, "I'm so sorry—I never would have thought about that being a thing."

After that, Jennifer said, "It definitely got a lot more fun, because then there are two of us in the community who get it."

She's still not out to her mom, though, who she was living with when she first came out to herself. The messages she was getting from her mom at home brought up a lot of internal conflict. "Christian guilt is real." The main reason she hasn't come out to her mom is because "If I come out to her, then she's going to blame my parent." Her mom might not understand that we are who we are. Having a trans parent can help open some doors and windows, but it doesn't make us become one way or another in terms of gender and sexuality.

As Even said, "I had this period where I was thinking about whether I ever had the urge to dress up as a woman, and I felt, 'no.'" It might not have crossed his mind in another family, but if the urge was there, having a different family wouldn't make it go away.

I never questioned my gender except to know that never in a million years would I switch places with a boy. My parents didn't tell me anything about how I should be. That was a gift, and the subtle open doors and windows were a gift, too, though I didn't see that at the time.

In seventh grade, my friend and I declared to Dana that we were bored, and she said, "Why don't you have a lesbian affair?"

I was struck dumb in the moment, not knowing what to say. My friend, who didn't take it as seriously, just said, "That's okay. I like guys." I was relieved when she spoke up.

At the same time, I always felt like in my family I could be anything. I felt like the door was open, which is nice in retrospect. My parents encouraged me not to have to fit into a box.

It's pretty deeply ingrained—who I like and who I am. It feels woven in on a deeper level. It's not a choice. It's not something I pick off the menu. It's built into who I am on the inside, which makes me see why my parent went the route she did. If I woke up tomorrow in a boy's body, I would do anything under the sun to get back.

SHAPING IDENTITY

When Olivia's parent came out, it raised for her some fundamental questions about truly knowing another person: "The fact that someone so close to me could be hiding something so pervasive." Looking back, she saw moments where she glimpsed the truth. "I was so close—so many times in *my* life, I was so close to the truth." She looked back in her journal, and found an entry that said, "Oh—went to lunch with Mom and Dad the waiter thought Dad was a woman, and was like, 'Hey ladies!' and Mom was super upset for some reason."

Living with that secret for so long and not seeing it, Olivia wondered how you could be sure about anything. "Really questioning if you can know a person... Just what it means to be a person and what it means to know someone loves you—all that kind of existential stuff." She found herself questioning everything. Even ordinary arguments would turn into these bigger questions. "Something small would happen when you disagree with someone about what you said, and then I would be like—did I say that? I don't know. What is real?"

If we know that things can come apart, that the unexpected can appear at any time, then how do we go forward? How do we call up our own sense of trust? How does love work?

It's possible that who our parents are and who they love is not imprinted on us as much as how they love and how they are who they are. We learn patterns and actions. Who we are and who we love is as unique to each of us as our thumb prints. Having a trans parent won't change that. My own gender was written on the inside and who I wanted to date was, too.

I used to think that my parents were an example of what not to do. Getting married young and then trying to keep things together, no matter what. Now, I know that none of us get a rulebook. None of us gets the perfect script.

When my mother married my father, she told me that she believed she was marrying her soul mate and best friend. If someone had told her the rest of the story, would she have gone forward? I recently found a pile of cards given to them on their engagement, and ones they wrote, too. "I think we have a great thing going," my mother wrote to my dad at the time.

Each of us has our own route to take when it comes to dating and feeling at home in our bodies. No one else can tell us how to do it. That's the good news and the bad news. No one decides for us. No one knows. We get to find out what works for us, making mistakes along the way. And maybe it's that uncertainty that we get to embrace—the sense that no matter what happens, we'll be okay.

Even growing up in a family that breaks the rules, we still learn the rules in subtle ways. "Growing up in that environment," Olivia said, "even though they're presenting as male when you're growing up, there must be something about the messaging you're getting about what it means to be a woman." We discover our own sense of gender as we go.

Justin sometimes wears high heel boots or scoop-neck shirts, but he doesn't think of it in terms of changing his body. He's just bending the gender lines. "That's my jam," he said.

The woman he's with noticed this change of clothes and asked him, "Do you want to be a woman?"

He was surprised by her question. "I would tell you!" he said. For him, it was just a part of his expression. It didn't mean he wanted to change anything else. People pick up on gender cues and read them along a binary, but maybe we already know that this binary exists only in our minds.

Sometimes I had these old ideas about gender: that if I still had a dad, my dad would stand up for me if a guy was a jerk. What was I thinking? Like he'd be standing on the porch with a shotgun or something? Riley confirmed that this was unlikely to be the case. "My dad is still a man," he said, "and he would never do that. We all have different kinds of dads."

After his parent came out, Jordan looked closely at the ways he kept himself closed off from the world, the ways in which he wasn't being authentic—not necessarily in terms of gender and sexuality, but in general. "Being able to identify ways in which I keep myself in the closet...the process I learned from my dad about keeping self behind a façade at all times, so it's been helpful for me to attack and deconstruct the armor that I build around myself—always insulate myself from the world kind-of-thing." His parent coming out has helped him challenge those habits of keeping parts of himself hidden—the things that keep him from living an authentic life.

Having a trans parent doesn't change the outcome, but it can make it easier to say, "This is who I am."

MEET THE PARENTS

The first time I told someone I was dating about my family, I sat on the floor of my dorm room across from Alex, my serious boyfriend at the time. Another friend was there, Julie, one who knew about Dana. Our families had known each other since we were little. She knew my whole family story. She was encouraging me to tell. This wasn't something I told people about at the time. I was fine with keeping it buried until the end of the earth. Even very close friends didn't know, but in a way, it felt like the right time to tell Alex. How would I tell him? What should I say?

I started, then stopped, not knowing how to explain it. Every part of me said, "Noooooo."

If you've never said something out loud, how do you find the right words? What do you say? I started the story and then I couldn't even finish it. Julie helped me out.

I'd only gotten as far as saying that my dad had come out as gay. That felt like far enough. It was the mid-'90s. *Will and Grace*, one of the first shows with an openly gay character, wasn't even on TV yet.

Here is what Julie said, more or less: "Her dad lived as a gay man for a few more years, but was still struggling, and after a while her dad saw that all along the struggle was about gender, not about attraction. That was when her dad started to change."

She made it sound so simple, like it happened every day. The whole time she talked, Alex was listening, holding my hand. This was the same friend who'd said, "It's not something to be ashamed of." If that were true, at age 18 I thought: Why did I only see people presenting as the opposite sex as jokes or freaks in movies? Why were there no strong examples of trans folks in politics or the news? I hid the truth about my family because there were no spaces in the larger social or political sphere that said otherwise.

A huge fear sat in me while Julie revealed the truth out loud. I don't know what I thought would happen—perhaps that Alex would judge me or want nothing to do with me. Neither of these worst-case scenarios came true.

"Wow," Alex said. He was from Southern California and had grown up in a gated suburban community. The world he grew up in, though, didn't fit who he was. He wanted something more, something bigger than that closed world. He was open to the wide range of experiences in the world, but this still came as a surprise. He didn't treat me any differently, though. It was my first lesson in the strange truth about dating—that when we share the hidden parts of ourselves, the parts that are most different, we are brought closer together.

It felt like a gift he was giving to me—not turning away when I shared about my family. Of course, now I know that this is a given—that the people in our inner circle should support all of us—but at the time, I didn't know that in my bones, so it felt like an unexpected grace.

After my friend left that day, Alex held me in his arms. He didn't run a mile or ask stupid questions, like I thought he would. Instead, he just held me. Telling him felt like tearing off my skin. In a way, I was, since I took down a big cover over part of my life. I won't say I felt relieved, because I still felt exposed. I was okay, though. The world didn't implode.

"You can tell me anything," he said. People can say a lot of things, but he showed me that this was true because he didn't go anywhere. And then he knew. That was it.

For a long time, I defended my decision to wait until I told. "This is such a big thing!" I thought. "I can't say it right away." In some ways, I made it a big thing by not saying anything. It became this big, looming thing. Sort of like when I told one of my friends from high school.

"Oh, that's all?" she said. "I thought it was going to be something way more serious with the way you started to tell it."

How we tell does have an impact. It doesn't have to be dropped in out of nowhere like a non-sequitur:

"Do you want to get coffee?"

"My parent's transgender."

It can come out naturally, easily, part of getting to know someone bit by bit.

Like anything you hold close, this can be a litmus test for who you trust. For a while, I saw it as a measure of who I could get close to romantically. If I trusted them with this, I could probably share more and build something that could last.

Isn't it better to find out sooner rather than later if the person you're sitting across from is transphobic? In the best cases, the revelation will bring you closer. For me, it never led to the exit door, but in the worst cases, there might have been an uncomfortable moment or two. Like when one guy I dated blurted out that he liked the movie *Normal* with Jessica Lange and Tom Wilkinson, an early HBO movie about a family with a trans parent; or when another man, who I was with for three years, asked me Inappropriate Question #472:

"What did your dad do with his balls?"

Ew. Who asks that? I never asked him about his parents' anatomy. Yet, instead of justified rage or refusal, I actually tried to answer the question.

"I don't know," I said, instead of, "Why the f*** are you asking me that?" Instead of "None of your g** d*** business!"

In a parallel world, there is a sassy version of me that says these things. In the real world, there's me navigating the confusion of other people. The conversation lurched on to other topics not related to my parent's anatomy. *Thank you!*

"One thing I didn't have then that I have now is boundary setting," Olivia said. "I would just answer all the questions." Learning to be your own advocate means that when someone asks a question, you get to pause and say, "Hmmm... Let me think about that." Then you get to decide whether you want to answer.

"What was that like for you?" people sometimes asked.

That one is not so easy to answer because at the time, a lot of other things were going on. I was ten going on eleven, taking acting lessons, reading books, making friends in a new school, and my parent was transitioning. It was happening off to the side, in the periphery. So my first answer to this is something like: "It was like life. An everyday change, a shift, but the biggest change was switching to be an underground family, telling people my dad was my aunt, being one family in the house and another outside."

After dating someone for a few months, we were at my place when he said, "You talk a lot about your mother, but do you have a father?" I hadn't even noticed that I'd been erasing my other parent in our conversations. Again, I played the pronoun game.

"Yes," I said. "We'll see each other in Colorado."

I had a feeling that the relationship wouldn't last, and it didn't. Whenever I told someone, it felt like I was giving them a part of myself. I was glad I kept it to myself.

With dating, we're thrown into other people's families. At a meet-the-parents dinner with my boyfriend Chris and his family, I sat next to his dad, a tall, soft-spoken man with white hair and glasses. I was explaining about an organization my mother ran for teen literacy.

"What about your father?" his dad asked. I had the moment of panic that usually came up with this question.

"My dad works at a gallery," I said, avoiding pronouns.

"That's nice," he said, folding the napkin on his lap.

I tried to steer the conversation in another direction. Chris's dad must have seen that I was nervous, but did not understand why.

Chris was the one to tell his parents. He sat them down one night and said, "Her dad's a woman." His parents were shocked. It sometimes felt like there was this thing about me that they had to get around, that they were going to accept me nevertheless:

"We love her in spite of that." It felt like this piece of my history that they were keeping boxed up *over there* so it wouldn't get in the way. As the relationship continued, I had this feeling that we were supposed to idealize and emulate his parents' relationship, not mine; that my parents were the example of what not to do. That felt somehow wrong to me. Our families should be on an equal footing, but his felt like the model and mine the one with a blinking sign over it saying, "Do Not Repeat." I was supposed to learn some new, "right" way to be in a relationship, to adopt the values of his family, not mine. I was supposed to try to be someone else. It felt like I was being put into a box.

Jordan talked about questioning the models we're given. "More and more I'm looking at my definition of love or relationship built not by me but by society," he said. In some ways, his parent coming out brought that into relief. How much are we given and how much is built on our own sense of what is right for us?

It's important to be able to share our family story with the people we're dating, and also with their families, but we should never feel like ours are somehow "less than." We should be on an equal footing with our partners and their families. If it doesn't feel that way, then it's time to look at the assumptions and biases that are getting in the way of an equal view of both families and lives.

"With all things—choose honesty," Sandra P. said. "Choose honesty with your transgender parent, as well. Speak your truth to them about what you need, and be willing to accept their truth."

For Jennifer, coming out as bi made it easier to tell people about her family, too. "It definitely changed when I came out," Jennifer said, "because now everything is so much easier. I really don't even think about it because, like, I don't have any straight friends. It's not a problem, because I'm like, 'Oh, I have a trans parent,' and they're like, 'That's so cool!' It's not really a big thing at all."

Having a queer community of her own changed her experience of telling. "Definitely when I was younger and didn't have that community around me, it was a lot more difficult—not that I was embarrassed, but more that I was scared of what people's reactions would be."

Try acting like the world has already given space for our families, like people get it, and bit by bit, more and more that will be the case.

WE ARE FAMILY

At weddings and big family gatherings, the truth comes out, whether you want it to or not. My sister's wedding was the day many members of my extended family found out the truth about my family. Nearly 20 years later. My sister and mom talked about it for months leading up to the wedding. Do we tell the family? How should we tell them? They didn't want the news to eclipse her big day. So they didn't tell anyone. They thought that was going to work. *We just won't say anything.*

They didn't count on the flurry of questions.

"Where's Daniel? How could he skip his own daughter's wedding?"

At a party the night before the wedding, my grandmother turned to my great aunt, Dana's Aunt Lucy, who had had a couple of Scotches by then.

"Where's Daniel?" my grandmother asked. The question echoed through the hallways. "He's not coming to his daughter's wedding? Where is he? Is he coming?"

My Aunt Lucy, who was not one to waver over the truth, especially after a few glasses of Scotch, clarified the whole misunderstanding.

"Of course Daniel is here," she said, gesturing to Dana. "As Dana Victoria Brown."

And just like that, the secret we'd built for 18 years came out in an instant.

At the party, it spread to a circle of my mother's friends. From there, it rippled through acquaintances and across the whole family.

On the day of the wedding, we walked down the center aisle between the rows of chairs, and lined up in front in an outdoor garden. My sister walked herself down the aisle. I could see Dana in the back row, hiding in plain sight. She wore a tan suit, almost like camouflage, trying to disappear. She sat between Donnie and his partner. She'd been erased from the day. No one was supposed to know she was there. At the same time, we looked so much alike that, when we were standing side by side, people said, "You must be related."

"Yes," we said, offering no further explanation. By then, though, people knew, but in this roundabout way.

In the women's bathroom partway through the wedding, Dana and I waited for the stalls to empty out.

"Who knows?" she said, once we were alone. I told her the people I knew for sure, but even I didn't know how the news was spreading. "I feel like I'm in a hall of mirrors," she said.

At the end of the reception, when the photographer gathered groups of the family for pictures, I overheard my grandmother trying to point Dana out to my grandfather.

"He's right there," she said, pointing to the tall, lithe woman standing in the back of the Bryant family photo.

"Where?" my grandfather said. He couldn't see. I stood there, just a few feet away, saying nothing. I didn't step in to defend Dana or anything. I just stood there, following my grandmother's pointed finger.

"Right there," she said, and still my grandfather didn't see. He had Daniel fixed in his mind. He didn't recognize Dana at all.

Maybe he was looking for the boy he knew years before, the one who first married my mother. At my parents' own wedding, the two of them were children, just starting out, not even graduated from college yet. My grandmother thought they should wait, but my mother was determined. My grandfather declared at the engagement party that she was ruining her life. They knew my father for a few years after that, and then he just disappeared. They hadn't seen him since. Maybe, for them, or for my grandfather in particular, he was frozen in time. He couldn't see the woman in front of him as related to Daniel at all.

"You must be very proud," one of my great uncles said to Dana at the reception. He didn't ask questions or show any surprise, he simply said without saying it, "I know, and it's okay."

Some people didn't find out through the grapevine, and they were sorry not to have a chance to say congratulations to Dana. Telling them before might have made it easier.

It took a long time for Dana to recover from that day. She felt exposed, wrenched out into the open. She wanted to go back into the safety of no one knowing. That was how we had lived for years, and that was where she felt safe. I felt safe there, too. I'd learned the same thing: that keeping it secret kept us safe.

In the months after my sister's wedding, the rest of my extended family found out the truth, but no one talked about it. It was as if it went from being a secret to being a taboo. I wanted to talk about it, but everyone acted like it didn't happen, like we could brush it under the carpet and pretend it wasn't there. That wasn't helpful either. Acting like it wasn't there was another way to teach about shame. *Let's just not talk about it.* But if it's part of my life and we act like it's not there, how am

I supposed to understand it? Silence can take a long time to unlearn. It can become a habit in your family, in your life.

"No one knew at my wedding," Olivia said, "so it was extraordinarily uncomfortable." Her dad had just come out, but came to the wedding dressed as male, so there were layers between the truth and what was presented on the outside. "Both my parents were pretty much like, 'Whatever you want to do.' My dad was like, 'If you don't want me to come, I don't have to come.'" Olivia kept the ceremony very focused on her and her husband. "The hardest part was the Father and Daughter Dance. It was very, very difficult. I didn't want to feel all the grief and sadness during that moment. I just kind of dissociated from all the emotions, so it was hard to enjoy. I ended up kind of forgetting a lot." It was almost an out-of-body experience for her. She was both there and not there, splitting off from the moment in her mind.

When Sarah called her dad to say she got engaged, her dad took the news in briefly, then went on to talk about other things. "Wait, this is big news," she wanted to say. When it came to her wedding, she was surprised by what came up. "I've never been a very traditional person and I'm feminist and all that, but boy, some of these traditional father–daughter archetypes that you have in your head," she said. "I didn't want my dad to walk me down the aisle, because that just feels really weird—I'll walk myself down, it's cool." At the same time, it made her reflect. "It's these little moments where you're just like, what is the role of my dad in my life now? If it's not this traditional father–daughter relationship, then what are we? We're not mother–daughter—you're not my mother, so what is this thing between us? I'm not quite sure anymore."

When Andrea got married, she and her husband sat down to tell his family before so that there wouldn't be "this elephant in the room about my trans parent." His family was fine with it, and the day went smoothly. At the wedding, all her moms dressed in blue. "My mom wore a blue dress and my stepmom wore a blue dress and my other stepmom wore a blue dress, and my dad said, 'If someone asks me which one my wife is, I'm just going to say it's the one in the blue dress.'"

For Sharon, the question wasn't about telling. "By the time I got married, I was very open with everybody about who Trisha was, so it wasn't a problem for me at all." It was her mom who had an ideal of the day in mind.

"I want to have my husband at the wedding," her mom said.

"I didn't care either way," Sharon said. "But I totally understood her point, too."

In the end, Trish wore a tuxedo. She knew how important it was to Marsha, and in that moment, family trumped all the rest.

Any time the whole family gathers, you're mixing up the people who get it with the ones who don't. Some of my family live in a parallel universe where my dad is still Daniel. To them, Dana is not real. They come up with reasons and explanations. My paternal grandmother once sent me a letter with a picture of my dad as a baby with curly blonde hair. She explained that when my grandfather broke my dad's arm on a swing when he was little, my dad decided it was too dangerous to be a man. The explanation was so clear and direct. This was why her "Daniel dear" was now Dana. It took her a long time to switch pronouns and names. She was still hoping it could be otherwise.

At a family picnic, someone introduced my dad to my cousins as "Your uncle who likes to wear women's clothes." This was humiliating for Dana. She didn't know what to say.

Jennifer's family has big family reunions every year on the coast of New Hampshire. When Mem came out, the extended family had different responses. Jennifer's aunt embraced Mem as her sister, while her grandparents disowned them. "It took a while for a lot of our extended family to come around—thankfully, a lot of them eventually did, except my grandparents." The first year after Mem came out, they went to the family reunion, but it was difficult, and Mem left early. "It wasn't necessarily bad intentions," Jennifer said, "but she was just being misgendered so much and it was just really hard for a lot of people in our family to grasp that. You could just feel this deep-seated uncomfortableness throughout everybody—there was definitely a lot."

Since then, though, things have gotten better. A number of people in her family have come out, too. Mem was the first, but now more family members have opened up about themselves. When her cousin C.J. came out as trans, Jennifer said, "His parents actually understand him because Mem had come out." C.J. could also look up to her dad as a role model. She described it as being "so cool, because then you have someone else older to look up to. It's pretty cool having that." Multiple generations of trans in one family gives others a chance to be free to be themselves.

As Jennifer said, "One person being like, 'This is who I am' can be freeing for everyone."

Prompts for Dating and Family Ties

1. Is it important to you that the person you date be supportive of your family?
2. Do you have any major family events or parties coming up? Do you have a plan in place?
3. Would you want to have a wedding or other ceremony to mark a long-term commitment? If so, how do you envision this? How would your parent play a role, if any?

Chapter 9

Transphobia and You

Why does this word even exist?

Dana and I talked about how the word itself sounds strange, like Transylvania. Something foreign and far away. If something is too far off and distant, then how do we raise awareness and change how people think?

What I witnessed that someone might call transphobia is actually ignorance, misinformation, and fear. If we call it what it is, then we can change it. If we name it something strange, then we won't know how to respond.

Transphobia comes in various guises. It appears in the question a boyfriend asks about your parent's anatomy. It appears in the expression on a stranger's face when they learn about your family. It can even seem well-meaning, but it often comes from a lack of understanding and fear.

Gender policing. Mis-pronouning. Calling someone out in public. Deliberately disrespecting who they are.

Our non-binary parents are asked to pick a side. We're given binary frames through which to view the world.

Transphobia can come in the form of silence. It can come up in the gay community, too. It can come up in our families.

Once, a great-uncle criticized Dana to her face, telling her the parts of her that didn't read as female to him: slender hips, wide shoulders, long arms. That is transphobia. He could have said the same about me. When I wear shoulder pads, I look like a linebacker. My arms reach down low, poking out of long-sleeved shirts. He didn't gender police me, though. Dana and I also wear the same size shoe, and both of us have small feet, which he failed to notice.

All of us will encounter transphobia at some point, and sometimes we encounter it within.

DEALING WITH TRANSPHOBIA FROM OTHERS

Sandra P. was out with her dad when an older woman who was pointing and staring at her dad nudged her husband. Sandra looked directly at her, forced a smile, and waved. "I made very clear I saw," she said. "And the woman was crestfallen. She clearly knew and saw that I noticed." Sandra gave her the benefit of the doubt. "Maybe she also has a trans family member and just thought she'd point it out."

Kim A., a healthcare student, took a shift at a psych unit. One of the people working there started to gossip about one of the patients.

"Is that person trying to be a woman or what?" they said. The patient had "tattooed on eyebrows and eyeliner" and used to sometimes "dress up 'in drag.'"

The co-worker might not know about Kim's parent, but she also felt like it was disrespectful not only to that patient, but to the other patients who might have heard.

When Chelsea W. had to take her parent to the E.R., she said,

"They kept using her deadname and got standoffish with her." Chelsea was there as an advocate. "I was there to stand up for her but I shouldn't have to." Her parent's voice still comes out at a deep register. On a regular basis, Chelsea said, "People will often call her by the wrong pronouns, even when corrected."

In Jennifer's community in New Hampshire, transphobia is more hidden. "You know you can't be outwardly homophobic here." When her parent came out, she worked as a teacher in the public school system. "When she transitioned, it became a hostile environment. It wasn't in the sense that people were being outwardly 'I hate you because you're trans,' but the way that people treated her was a complete 180." The other teachers excluded her and shut her out. "[It] was really, really hard and she ended up having to leave." She was unemployed for a while after that, having lost not only her job but her identity of many years as a teacher. She had to rebuild her sense of self. Even if she wasn't being recognized as a teacher by society, she still had that part of herself. Now, she works at a local Pride Center, bringing in her past as an educator alongside the issues that matter to her.

When transphobia is hidden, it's hard to call it out or advocate for yourself. "When it's covert, when it's not named," Morgan said, "there's a certain element to it where you kind of feel like you're losing your mind, because somebody could deny that it's there at all." More than one person's parent lost their job not too long after the transition, but there were other reasons tied into it that made it hard to pin down. Lay-offs, downsizing, budget cuts.

Lily noticed that when she went to her friends' house, the husband was usually out. She pressed about it one day, and finally found out that he was uncomfortable with the changes. He felt like Lily had more in common with his wife now than him. "People tell me I've changed a lot," she said. "I see little change." In areas where transphobia or homophobia aren't tolerated, the changes can be more subtle on the outside.

Some areas are more outwardly transphobic. "I don't want my kids around someone who had a sex change," Rachel's neighbor in Kansas said. That's transphobia, rooted in ignorance and fear, at its worst.

The subtle forms are more common. Simply not being recognized or acknowledged. Mis-gendering. Mis-pronouning. Mistaking someone for their old gender. At a local autobody shop, Lily was called "Sir" by the guy about to work on her car. She was standing there in a skirt suit and four-inch heels. "There are still a lot of uneducated people," she said.

Justin told of going to Target with his mom and her partner in Tennessee.

"Thank you, sir," the clerk said to his mom.

Justin, who was about ten at the time, looked at the clerk's nametag and nearly scream-shouted back,

"Thank you, Susan!"

He had all this energy in him, trapped with no place to go. These microaggressions brought it out in him. "These weird awkward reactions that are like, 'I don't know how to deal with this moment, but I know I should do something.' There's all this energy in me and I'm so terrified." It also came up with his friends. "I was running around with other boys and there were conversations about 'fags' and 'its' and 'he-shes' and all this stuff, and...those things—them saying that felt like violence. I would immediately get really quiet." Fear spread inside him. He felt vulnerable. "I wish that I'd been a warrior for that. I was really quiet and I would get really scared and say weird stuff to try and fit in with the conversations."

I related to blurting something out in an effort to fit in. I remember in high school a friend reading something from an advice column in a magazine: "Dear So and So, My boyfriend dresses in women's underwear sometimes. What should I do?" And I remember my friends laughing really loud, and I felt this immediate sinking in my stomach, but I was laughing too. It was an effort at protection from what felt wrong.

Justin understood this response. "That awkwardly loud laugh where you're like, 'I'm laughing too... Ha, ha, ha, it's so funny, look at that,' and everybody else is like, 'Yeah, it's funny, but why are you yelling at us?'" The way we try to fit in by laughing the loudest or being the one to point out difference first. "There were some scary moments and some awkward moments," Justin said.

Morgan was traveling with her dad in Ireland, and they were staying at a B & B in someone's house. Her dad had a sense that the situation could be potentially hostile and told Morgan, "Don't mention to our host here that I'm trans."

"He just felt unsafe in that situation," Morgan said. "They hadn't said anything, but we were staying in their home and he felt vulnerable." That was Morgan's experience of transphobia for the most part. Not something direct, but a feeling about a particular person or place. "I have encountered situations when either my intuition told me or somebody else told me not to talk about it," she said. "My experience of transphobia has been mostly walking on eggshells to avoid others' transphobic reactions."

What if transphobia happens inside your family? What then?

Amber's ex-husband, Peter, has decided that he doesn't want their boys to spend time with someone who is transgender. This means the boys haven't met Amber's dad, who is trans. They have one less grandparent. Peter's dad died, so the boys grew up with two grandmothers. Maybe they grew up thinking the world is full of grandmothers with no grandfathers.

When Amber's brother came to visit, one of the boys asked, "Do you have a dad?"

"Yes," her brother said. "Yes we do."

They were out to dinner with Amber's new in-laws. It didn't feel like the right time to tell them, and she didn't know how to tell them. Her brother didn't say anything, either. It felt like they were creating the same culture of silence and secrets that was part of their family. She lives in a part of Nebraska where few of their friends have divorced parents, let alone trans parents. But is making it a big deal or keeping it from them a form of transphobia, too?

Something similar is happening in Hannah's family, too. When her sister was still with her ex, he set up a wall that their parent, Stephanie, couldn't cross. The whole family had trouble crossing that wall at different points, but Stephanie most of all. Now, the boys don't know her, and her sister doesn't know how to tell the boys. The community they live in is silent on trans topics. Even the fact that she and her ex are divorced is slightly taboo where they live in Eastern Washington. It's almost as if different places exist in different timeframes. And it could be a matter of simply bringing this into daily life. If people knew more trans individuals in their community, it would be a start.

Morgan's mother-in-law has told her that her parents don't know about her dad being trans and that "it's best that they don't have that information." It's a giant "X" through a topic that is woven into her own identity. "I do feel this sense that I need to hide it, even when I wouldn't normally be talking about it anyway, and that does feel like a burden."

How can we change this? One neighbor. One friend. One teacher. One parent. One sister. One aunt. One person at a time.

Our families change, our communities change. Tiny steps, bit by bit.

When someone at Christy's church started to talk about someone trans in a way that said, "Can you believe it?" she piped up,

"Yeah, my dad's trans."

The woman wasn't expecting that. It stopped her short. It banished her "us-and-them" thinking. It woke her up to the reality that this was in her community all along.

INTERNALIZED TRANSPHOBIA

I don't know how it feels to be bullied or excluded because we went out of our way to fit the social mold. I didn't witness direct transphobia because we became a secret family. The only transphobia was within each of us. *No one can know. We can't let anyone find out. We can't say anything.* We carried inside us the larger fears that came through on television and in movies. Men could dress as women as jokes or in disguise, but not to change who they were. If they did, they were the villains, the criminals, the outcasts.

Living in the world, we absorb transphobia. It leaks into us. The fear and revulsion I felt at times was part of that. The shame. Where did this internal fear about being trans come from? I grew up with the fear all around me. I learned fear from the way that I learned it was important to hide. Why did I sometimes worry that people would think I was transgender? Why did I feel the need to emphasize that it was my parent and not me?

Two men came to build a desk in my apartment. I covered up the stack of trans books on my chair. Why? What is it in me that tries to distance myself from that identity, when it's part of my family?

Dana and I step into a bakery in Cherry Creek, Denver. I look around at the clerks and other customers. Is anyone watching us? Does anyone see? While Dana orders her food, I watch the clerk carefully to see if she's having any response. What's happening isn't in anyone else. It's in me. This is my transphobia. It was important to me that Dana "pass," that she would not give us away or stand out as different. I was the one policing her gender, the one who wanted her to be different than who she was.

It's internalized transphobia that can sometimes be the hardest to spot.

I once worked at an event in a space where the bathrooms had been switched to gender neutral. Instead of gender, the bathroom door indicated what was inside (i.e., stalls and toilets where the women's room once was, and stalls and urinals where the men's room once was). Someone was complaining about it.

"It's so confusing," she said. I found myself slipping into the familiar silence that I lived in in the past. Why wasn't I speaking up? Now, I felt more comfortable sharing about my family, but something kept me quiet that night. Somehow, I knew that if I said I had a transgender parent, the woman would stumble over herself to act correctly, to not offend me. I would be the bathroom expert and she would be the one who doesn't get it. It felt somehow like lecturing to bring up my parent, which is weird, because it's just part of my reality. That's a subtle form of transphobia, too.

Our parents carry their own internalized transphobia. "For a lot of my older friends," Lily said, "they have 44 years of hiding themselves—your mind is still stuck. This is why I'm visible. If I can be visible and have someone younger not get trapped, then they have the rest of their lives ahead of them to do anything else but be trapped in their own mind." Lily still finds herself being critical of how she appears when she looks in the mirror. People tell her that they see two completely different people, but she still sees only how she could be different, better. She's still stuck in a mind that resisted itself for a long time. "I question myself when I look in the mirror. It doesn't matter how much I change now, I'm always going to have this doubt in my mind, I'm always going to be trapped, thinking of the last 44 years of self-hatred, disgust, sadness." She thinks of how it might be different growing up today. "If I was ten years old today, feeling the way I felt when I was ten years old, I would just be like, 'Oh my god, maybe I'm trans.' There wouldn't be all this feeling ashamed, feeling disgusted."

Years of prejudice and lost friends have led Dana to keep her history to herself for the most part. She doesn't explain. I can't know what she has experienced. There's a lot I take for granted. At the same time, the kids get part of this, too, part of the being stuck in our heads. The questioning, the uncertainty that comes when the whole world says that's not what a family looks like. The precarious moments when we aren't sure what will happen.

Once, Monica was lost on the way to visit her parents in rural Vermont. She stopped at the country store because her navigation system wasn't working.

"Oh, who are you looking for?"

Since it was a small town, they knew almost everyone in town.

"Connor," she said tentatively.

"And then they started to ask me to describe the people, and so I had this moment of "Oh man, what's gonna happen right now? I don't even know how these people see my dad and her partner."

"Young couple? Older couple?" they asked.

"Older," Monica said.

"It never got weird," she said, but she thought it might. She eventually found the house.

Later, her dad said, "Oh you should have just asked where the village queers are. Everything's fine honey—they just think we're weirdos. It's fine."

It's those moments of feeling like we're walking on a tightrope until we look down and see that we're on solid ground.

Once, when I was 13, Dana brought me to a spa for my birthday. It felt like such a special treat, going to the spa. The aesthetician was faintly amused to be giving a facial to a 13-year-old. After, I got made up with a face full of make-up and off we went into the downtown crowds. When I spotted a girl I went to school with coming through the crowd with her mom, I wanted to hide. They were swinging bags of stuff they'd bought. The girl saw me and made her way through the crowd toward us. Dana and her mom chatted in a friendly way. Dana introduced herself as my aunt, and neither one said, "Really? Are you sure?" All they did was chat, and we went on our way, but it felt like a close call—phew! Just missed it. Most of the worst things that happened, happened in my mind.

I was a one-person gender police squad, enforcing as I went along. I remember going with Dana to a bookstore and trying to walk not next to her, but slightly in front or behind, watching her like a hawk to make sure she did nothing to make us stand out.

Our own internalized transphobia can shape-shift, slipping out of reach. It's the part of me that watched over Dana when she came to my shows at a local community theater. The part of me that didn't want her to come along on the first day at my new school. The part of me that wanted her to be someone else. It seeps in from all around us, the culture telling us that this is wrong.

My transphobia came on the tail-end of homophobia, which was also accepted at the time. I did a project on Virginia Woolf for my history class, and the teacher wanted me to say something about her relationships with women. On the day of my presentation, he asked me about it in front of the class, but I wouldn't say anything. It was as if I would be admitting difference to say that I chose a lesbian for my project. I refused. Later, when I told my parents about this, they were on my side.

"That's unfair," Dana said. They thought the teacher was wrong to put me on the spot. I felt vindicated. At the time, it felt like any association with gay was wrong, and trans was off the map, not even anywhere within sight.

I was afraid of her body, of how it had changed; of telling other people, wondering what they would say. It's an irrational fear with no grounding. Rachel talked about waking up in the middle of the night after a nightmare in which her parent appeared at the foot of her bed to kill her. The fear wasn't grounded in anything real, except for what permeates our culture. Trans villains on the big screen. No one teaches us otherwise.

Olivia said of her family, "My mom, my brother, and even myself, having not been exposed to a lot of trans people growing up, and the main exposure [being] through the media, which isn't great, there is a lot of transphobia to be worked out." They had to work to unpack the misconceptions they'd inherited from the culture around them. "Everyone's going to have some degree of it." The recognition comes first, before it can be confronted. "It has been hard with my mom. There's all this other stuff tied to the feelings she has toward my parent. That's been challenging. Same with my brother. My brother's sort of in the same place." False ideas can get mixed up with our emotions until they feel justified. It takes a lot of work to untangle them, to take them apart.

TRANSPHOBIA IN SOCIETY

The outrage and protest around transgender people in public restrooms flooded the news. It seemed absurd to me that people were so angry about a room full of toilets.

The bathroom itself was a side note—it was more about rights and truth and being yourself. The focus on the bathrooms distracted from that fact that this was about equal protection. What was really at stake: people's rights. The repercussions were felt across the country though, with trans folks reporting that they avoided eating or drinking so they would not have to use a public restroom.

Propaganda showed footage of bathrooms in the place of discussions of the laws being considered. This was the clearest view of transphobia in politics in recent years. This strange, irrational fear of who is in the bathroom, who is in the next stall, taking over what is really about public spaces and rights. During that time, I collected images of the bathrooms that said "Whoever" or "Everyone," the ones that stood out against the divide. The whole debate felt so incredibly absurd, but it also showed how strongly people feel about gender, how tied they are to their beliefs.

Amy had to cover for her parent in the bathroom once when she called out, "Pop" into the bathroom stall.

"Excuse me?" a woman nearby said. "Am I in the wrong bathroom?"

"No," Amy said. There was a long silence. "I call my mom 'Pop' for 'Poppy.' Is that okay with you?"

"Oh," the woman said. She continued on, but it felt like a close call.

The ban of trans people from the military has impacted families across the country. As Lily said, "They started taking the steps to be congruent with who they are inside, and that's being yanked out from them." A friend of hers is struggling with this now, risking the possibility of losing a long career because of this measure.

"When our parents are under attack politically, then the well-being of our family is under attack," Monica said.

Lily described her frustration with the prejudice she still encounters. She said, "It's like the '80s again, and it's frustrating because this year is 50 years [since] Stonewall[3] and we're 50 years from where we should be."

Across the news, we see trans people being targeted. The blurry picture next to the headline shows a woman. Another casualty. The story is all too common. It comes out again and again. The losses and violence are portrayed in numbers and percentages. Yet, this is our family. It's not a stranger anymore.

One day, Kim got a frantic text message from a friend: "Is your mom okay?"

It turned out that a trans woman was attacked and battered within two blocks of where Kim's mom lived. "It wasn't my mom," Kim said, "but it really easily could have been."

Monica's half-sister shared about her family with her class in elementary school, and somebody in the class said, "My dad's a cop who hates transgender people and he has a gun, so better watch out." As Monica said, this was "super-violent, threatening language" to her sister, who was around eight years old at the time. That kept her from sharing very much about her family.

Some of the fears are real. As Morgan pointed out, "Due to

---

3 Stonewall was the famous 1969 uprising when a gay club in the East Village was raided and people flooded the streets on behalf of the rights of the lesbian, gay, bisexual, transgender, and queer community.

stigma, trans people are at an increased risk of acquiring HIV, experiencing violence and other trauma, and attempting suicide. These risks can be amplified by racism, classism, sexism, and ableism." Our parents face job loss, harassment, inferior medical care, and issues with parental rights.

Jeremy hasn't seen Lily in two months. His mom managed to strip her of her parental rights, but Jeremy doesn't know this. He thinks that Lily is sick and needs some time to get better. While legal bills pile up on both sides, most of which Lily is responsible for, the kids are losing time with their parent. Also, when Lily goes to court with her ex, her ex's lawyer regularly uses the wrong pronouns, adding more frustration to an already difficult case.

The medical system has had transphobia woven into it for years. Being trans was considered a pathology. The fix was to send someone away from their family. Treatments encouraged the gender binary. The diagnostic literature had to be updated to eliminate transphobia. The *Diagnostic and Statistical Manual IV (DSM-IV)* for psychologists and psychiatrists, issued in 1994, listed "gender identity disorder" under "sexual disorders." Now, in the latest edition, *DSM-5* (2013), it's listed as "gender dysphoria" in its own category—not as a disorder.

Dana avoids going to the doctor because of mistreatment in the past. After she transitioned, she came close to attempting suicide. She had reached a place of having the body she wanted, but she found herself isolated and struggling. She has also struggled with joblessness. She struggled to find work, having erased a big part of her employment history. As a young, white, cisgender male, she had every opportunity handed to her. As an older, white woman with a limited employment history, fewer opportunities came up. She even tried once to get a job at Costco and was turned away. And few places were open to hearing her whole story.

One family I talked to was living in a homeless shelter. Parents lost jobs or left jobs that became unsustainable. It wasn't always due to direct discrimination that could be defended by law, but sometimes due to a more subtle discrimination and exclusion that became part of their daily lives.

Trans doesn't exist in a vacuum. Our parents' experiences are also informed by race, class, age, and many other factors. As Kim pointed out, "Trans does not exist by itself. I'm lucky in that my mom is white and had gender confirming surgeries. Without these, she would be in even more danger and get treated even worse." Dana told me once that she lived in fear on a daily basis because of potential violence. The fear was a veil draped over her daily life. Going shopping, going for walks, going on a trip.

There is so much transphobia out in the world and in the media. We have to unpack it in ourselves and in our families to understand what's being shown and what's real.

Going to the movies, we can find it laced into the plots. At the end of *Ace Ventura: Pet Detective*, a 1994 film, Jim Carrey's character realizes he kissed a trans woman and a dramatic sequence of showering and using a plunger on his face, all to the theme music of *The Crying Game*, follows. *The Crying Game* was an earlier movie from 1992 where a trans character turned out to be the villain. Transphobic humor and stories with trans villains were the stories being told.

Monica pointed out, "Transgender people are still the butt of the joke so much of the time. It's still pretty acceptable socially to make a joke about gender non-conformity—that's still funny." Jordan talked about going to see a comedian friend of his perform in New York, and how the jokes about race and politics were up to date, but he was making off-color jokes about Caitlyn Jenner and gender stuff.

The world teaches us a gender binary. We call out, "It's a boy!"

or "It's a girl!" on baby announcements, instead of, "It's a child!" or "We'll just have to wait and see."

Once, at a baby store, I picked up some diaper trash bags for my sister.

"Boy or girl?" the clerk asked as she led me across the store.

"Oh, it doesn't matter," I said. She insisted. She had blue bags for boys and pink bags for girls. As if the baby would look at the trash bags and have some kind of identity crisis.

We can also encounter transphobia dressed up as feminism. TERFs (Trans Exclusionary Radical Feminists), a group discussed in the social media section in Chapter 2, are radical feminists who reject the idea of being trans entirely. They think that gender is a construct, therefore, why play into gender norms by changing your own if you don't fit? Their perspective is a fundamental misunderstanding of aspects of trans experience.

I wish this chapter didn't exist, that this violence and ignorance was gone. I thought it would be mostly non-existent by now. There has been progress, but there's still further to go. Lily pointed out that in many places, where we are today with trans topics is where we were in the '80s with being gay. There are tiny pockets, which are growing bigger, of acceptance and understanding, but it does sometimes feel like stepping back in time.

What can we do with our fear and rage over what can or may have already happened to our trans parents at the hands of society?

We need to look with clear eyes at the issues being reported and acknowledge the risks, but at the same time we need to expand the stories that are out there. The next time trans rights are under attack, if voters have a friend or neighbor who is trans, or if they know that their friend has a trans parent, maybe—just maybe—they'll change how they vote. They'll see that we all deserve the same rights and protection, that we all deserve to use our public spaces equally, without fear.

Dana sometimes got frustrated that I lived in this alternate universe, this pink cloud, where everyone was accepting and open to our families. "That's not reality," she said to me. That wasn't where she lived on a daily basis. Friends fading away. Jobs turned down. People scrutinizing her for ways she didn't fit the female mold. The two of us lived in different worlds. How could we bring the two together? That's a question that's still unresolved. Once we have the answer, then our parents will be folded into the communities where they've been excluded. There won't be the same misunderstandings. People will just get it. In that alternate universe, we'll all just be people, like the time I was at the mall with my oldest nephew, at the time about five years old, when he leaned his face against the glass balcony, pointing down below. "Look!" he said. "People!" He was too young to see the divide or call it out. He just saw people. Maybe that is the future. We aren't there just yet. We're still learning and making mistakes, going step by step, alongside our families.

SPEAKING UP ABOUT TRANSPHOBIA

There have been many times when I've stood by silently when someone made fun of a gender code-breaking. Or when someone said "transgender" in a mocking tone, and I said nothing. In that silence is complicity: "Okay, you can say whatever you want."

Speaking up when someone is transphobic is hard, but it's a step in the direction of understanding. Otherwise, people land in a field of ignorance and stay there, fed by the silence of others.

A girl in my high school came out as trans. He had been living as Sara but wanted to be Seth. He asked a girl in my dorm to the junior dance. I didn't say anything when my friends were making fun of him. I laughed along with them. I laughed about how weird it was. I made fun of him, too. I think about that—the times when I stood by and said nothing, when I knew well that this was something that happened, that this was part of life. Why didn't I choose to speak up?

Standing to the side in silence isn't an option anymore. The next time someone says something that is misinformed, we can speak up. We can share our own perspective. We can offer up the truth. As a child of a trans parent, we have a unique opportunity to share our understanding in a way that people might hear.

The more people know someone with a relative or friend who's transgender, the more people can see it as something that happens every day.

If our parents don't want anyone to know, we can respect their wishes. We still have our part of the story to tell. There are ways to tell your story without outing your parent. Lara appeared on an anonymous podcast. I've written things without using my full name and I've used pseudonyms for my parent. You can use a pseudonym. There is a magic in dispelling myths and prejudices. Like zapping out the villains in a comic strip. You can share your story, too.

COMING TO AN UNDERSTANDING IN RELIGIOUS OR SPIRITUAL COMMUNITIES

On a visit to my grandmother near Washington DC, Dana went into the city to go to some museums. When she came back, she unlocked the front door and stepped inside to find a circle of my grandmother's friends from church. "Get thee behind ye, Satan," they chanted. The circle gathered to try to exorcize the evil my grandmother thought had taken over her child's body. She truly believed that this was some kind of evil force inhabiting her child, and that prayer could root it out.

Jonathan, a pastor at an LGBTQ+ inclusive church in Brooklyn and author of *She's My Dad*, found his church removed from the network of evangelical churches he'd been linked to for years when he decided to support LGBTQ+ members. When his dad, also a pastor, came out as trans, at first he kept quiet about it in his own church community. "When I did start to tell people in the church," he said. "It was like I expected—they said, 'We love you—are you on your dad's side or not?'"

He came to his own understanding over time.

"A year after, I said, 'Our church is going to follow suit, because I'm with my dad on this—we're going to be an affirming church.'" The community quickly withdrew, distancing themselves. "Everybody said, 'Okay, we love you, but obviously we're not going to fund you anymore and we're not going to be able to keep you on our roster of churches.' So it was like, 'Alright we're done with you.'"

Jonathan added, "For some religious people, they think that this is not how God designed you to be, so is that transphobia? Yeah, it is, but it's done with this guise of 'but, it's not how God designed you to be.'" In their church community, Jonathan disagrees with "all these people are praying for my dad and that she can turn around and become someone different. At my core, I believe she is who she says she is." He can't entirely dismiss the whole evangelical world, though. "Navigating that evangelical world—it's still hard. My whole extended family is in that world."

I used to wonder why any divine power would create this

kind of struggle for any person. Now, I see it as a part of the bigger picture. *This, too, is part of God's world.* As a child, that was how I saw it, before my peers influenced me to a narrower view. Perhaps we could all see differences as part of this larger tapestry. *This, too.*

In a documentary about a family with a trans parent, *The Joneses*, Jheri Jones talks about how her ex-wife couldn't understand her in her time on earth, but that she might find a "heavenly understanding" in the afterlife. Perhaps in divine form, all those obstacles to understanding would be removed. It's a nice idea to think of a way that our human limitations could be taken away. In this view, heaven is a place without transphobia, without any phobias. All fear of difference is removed.

TAKING ACTION

How do we banish transphobia from our lives and ourselves?

In the 1978 Pride march in San Francisco, Harvey Milk carried a sign that said, "I'm from Woodmere, NY." It sounds pretty quiet for a protest sign, but what he was saying was radical. He was saying, "I'm your next-door neighbor. I'm from a little town with yards and fences where the people gather in the town square—I'm no different from you."

We can say, "This is my family." We live in Little Rock, San Diego, Gettysburg, West Jordan, Madison, Haverhill, Storrs, Portland, Albuquerque, New York, Oslo, Sydney. You don't have to go on a one-person campaign to educate the world, but you can start small. Tell one or two people. Share it with a teacher. Tell someone you trust. Know the root cause: that many of these actions are coming from a lack of education and a lack of awareness.

When it comes to protecting our parents, there are times

when we can't. Jennifer couldn't go into the school where Mem taught and tell all the teachers to be different. We can be advocates, as when Chelsea brought her parent to the E.R. We can be there, but we can't stop the doctors and nurses from saying the wrong things. There are limits to what we can do.

As for violence, getting educated alongside our parent can dispel this fear. What are the situations that would put them at risk? Can you come up with a plan? Our parents who fit into the binary might avoid some harassment, but there are still areas of risk. Any parent can be placed at risk, but having a plan with our parents can ease some of the built-in stress that comes with those fears.

For all our families, the change needs to happen in the larger world. It's another case where we might mistakenly think that our families need to change. Does our parent need more gender confirming surgeries? Not if they don't want them. Do we need a better story? No—the world needs to catch up, to put on reality glasses, and see that the old stories about gender need a serious update. As Sharon said, "It was more the world was off—Trish wasn't wrong and Dana wasn't wrong—it was the way the world reacted to being transgender, and still does. That's what's wrong."

You may also need a plan for some of the emotional fallout of daily life or family gatherings where your parent feels put in the spotlight. Finding a therapist who gets it or a group support network can help. With family stuff, try to bring some humor into the mix. It doesn't have to be so serious. The wrong pronoun might pop out, but it's as simple as a brief apology and moving on.

One trans parent suggested moving if you encounter transphobia in your community. Find a place that accepts your family. Don't stay and fight. Just relocate. This depends a lot on having the resources to do that. Not every family has that option, but moving to a more accepting area can be one step.

The everyday stuff, the microaggressions can add up. Try to balance these with a broader view. This doesn't mean painting a silver lining around a giant black cloud. It's not a false grasping for the good. It's just looking at reality, which is not all one way or the other.

I grew up when people were still hiding being gay. The more people came out, the more they were visible, the more the perspective shifted. To this day, I have friends who hide it still. I hope we're moving toward a time when none of this is hidden. When none of us take for granted our pronouns and names.

I almost didn't want to grant any more air space to these stories about our families. But it's important to see the ways it can come wrapped up in a neat bow or hidden in other things that can seem well-meaning: *Who wants to argue with God? Maybe the feminist scholars have a point*. It comes in many disguises, so if you background and awareness yourself in one of these situations, now you'll have the background and awareness to see it for what it is and call it out.

CHANGE IS ON THE WAY

"I want to spell 'transgender'!" One of the kids in the COLAGE Sprouts camp at Family Week raises his hand. He holds the marker in his fist and proudly spells the word. T-R-A-... The kids know more than we do. They landed in a world where gender was not split in two. They can teach us more than we can teach them. They know the words and the names for what we are just learning.

Becca was excited to see that at her new college, people wore nametags that told their pronouns. It wasn't being taken for granted. These little changes in our daily lives add up to bigger changes over time.

Noelle talked about the changes that have happened since when she wrote her book, *Dress Codes*. "It was perceived as you couldn't possibly be okay." She appeared on a talk show when her book came out, and the host leaned over and patted her hand, wanting to know, "Are you okay?" People wondering how we turned out without a third eye or giant purple tail. Now, more people know that this happens in the family up the block.

The fact that Noelle's parent is trans "doesn't come up that often, and when it does, people don't have that much of a reaction or they're like, 'Oh, cool.' It doesn't precipitate a two-hour-long conversation. It used to be like, 'We have to stop everything else we're doing and talk about nothing else now.' That has changed a lot just in the last ten years. Everything about it has shifted."

We need to face the facts of the risks facing our families, but we also need to look for the gradual sea change that's happening around us. The trans kid living up the block. The trans politician in the news. Now, more people are visible. This is an asset, not something to hide.

Schools are introducing a gender expansive curriculum. Children are the educators of their parents. When you're living inside the change, it can sometimes be hard to see it. The bad news might be filling the newspapers, but we can look for the good news, too.

Monica talked about being at a trans conference at the University of Vermont. "It was just a day long, and by the end of the day, I wasn't clocking people's gender at all, because there were so many gender queer people there. It was the first experience in my life of being like, 'I'm not actually reading people's gender! What? This is freaking amazing.'" She was immersed in a space that taught her a new way of looking at gender. Her experience shows that this way of seeing is possible, too. The ripple effect of change in one person at a time.

Prompts for Transphobia and You

1. Has your family encountered transphobia? If so, how did you respond?
2. Do you have transphobia within yourself?
3. What are some changes you've noticed in your community to be more inclusive? Are there any changes you can initiate?

Chapter 10

I Saw It on TV

MOVIES, SHOWS AND MORE

Growing up, there were no movies that I knew of about transgender people and families. For my family, *Tootsie* and *Victor/Victoria* were our touchstones, the stories that we cheered on for telling of the way gender could be shaped and shifted, disguised and remade, molded according to our wishes or identity. Still, those told the story of passing, of going by unnoticed, which was what we tried to do. And there were no stories that told of full transitions. This made us feel more isolated without even realizing it. I didn't expect to see our story out in the world.

On television and in the movies, men who dressed as women were the butt of jokes. In *Bosom Buddies*, Tom Hanks disguises himself as a woman to live in a women's boarding house. Even then, I knew that what was shown on television was different from what I was witnessing. My father was no longer a man in the way I saw or knew men. He had crossed over into an in between territory, one for which I had no name or reference out in the world.

I never thought of the void of stories in the mainstream media when I was growing up. I simply soaked up the stories I could find. My parents more actively sought out the narratives of transition, of ambiguous gender. I just liked good stories, especially romances, and I didn't wait for the time when the stories would appear. I didn't expect them to, but when they did, I could see in a flash I wasn't alone, I wasn't the only one with a family like mine. I knew that from getting involved with the trans community and COLAGE, but now the larger world knew it, too.

IN SEARCH OF COMMON STORIES

When I was a child, the movie *Tootsie* was one of the few representations I knew of a man who stepped out of the gender line. I thought I was the only one who considered that movie as a reference point for the trans experience until I talked to filmmaker Even Benestad. "Maybe I thought that my father was the only one in the world that did this," Even said, "because there wasn't really anyone—well, there was *Tootsie* the movie. We saw that many times before I knew... I learned after why we saw that film all the time." He grew up in Norway. I grew up in the United States. Thousands of miles apart, our families were in search of common stories. At the time, they were few and far between.

In my family, we watched *Victor/Victoria*, too, in which Julie Andrews played a woman pretending to be a man pretending to be a woman. That gender could be bent I knew, but seeing it on the big screen somehow made it real. In the scene when Julie hits a high note and pulls off her wig to reveal a man underneath, I cheered at this twist and surprise.

For a long time, I had to settle for drag as the closest thing to my family that I saw. I loved the movie *La Cage aux Folles*, and thought I was very fancy for watching it in French with subtitles. Later, it was remade as *The Bird Cage*, and I loved that one, too. The message in the end was all about accepting your family and not trying to change them or make them fit in. Those were the stories that felt closest to mine.

In *Some Like It Hot*, Jack Lemmon and Tony Curtis witness a mafia murder and escape town by dressing as women and joining an all-female jazz band. Watching these stories, it felt like I knew that what they showed was possible, that someone could slide over and say, "Today, this is who I am." It felt like something I was in on—this rare knowledge of how the world really worked. Even the movies got it wrong, though, since the person underneath was revealed every time. What I knew was that the person underneath was sometimes the façade. I got it. It was a reverse of these stories in a way. "This is who I really am" got flipped.

Sometime in the in between point, before the transition, Dana was reading a book in an armchair facing the window. I walked up to her and peered over her shoulder. She was still dressed as Daniel. "What are you reading?" I wanted to know. She showed me. She never hid anything from me. The book was called *Second Serve* by Renée Richards.

"Oh." I looked at the dust jacket. On the back was a picture of a woman. On the inside was a picture of a man with the same features. I looked back and forth between the two pictures. My response was to think, "Oh, so that's something that happens in the world." It was this, "Huh, that's interesting" moment. And then I went on with my day.

We leaned on the culture of drag for a long time, even though it wasn't our story. When I went to visit one of Dana's exes, David, and his long-time partner, Noel, the drag bag was pulled into the middle of the room and dresses and necklaces came out. His partner and I dressed up in different combinations and took pictures.

Later on, we didn't seek out stories like our own as much. It was almost like we were so sure we were one of the only families, one of the very few, that we didn't even try. We quoted from movies—*Father of the Bride, What About Bob?* and *French Kiss*—ones that showed other kinds of families and lives, not ours.

In high school, I went to see a documentary about Harvey Milk. Watching the film, I knew I was connecting to a part of my history. I couldn't tell anyone why. I sat in the dark auditorium watching this man shaping history on the screen, knowing that I was linked to his legacy. It sat inside me, this knowledge of my family. I looked for connections like this, but didn't talk about it, and wouldn't admit the connection, either.

A few years later, a friend and I watched the movie *Ma Vie en Rose*, about a young child born a boy who is really a girl. The movie delighted me and Dana. We knew the story it told, the gap it filled. There's a dream sequence with the child's Barbie, Pam, larger than life, filling the screen. At one point we see Xs and Ys flying through the sky to make the child a boy or a girl, but one just misses the mark by mistake and they become a boy. It's clear, though, that they were meant to be a girl. That day with my friend, watching the movie, I felt what I knew to be true, but still wasn't saying out loud. The two of us sat in her room. What I wasn't saying felt like another giant presence in the room. The idea of the elephant in the room is exactly how it feels. My friend didn't know anything about it, though. Her room was elephant-free.

"He probably just doesn't know he's gay," my friend said. I remember feeling this strong conviction that she didn't understand, but not being able to tell her why. I knew from my own experience that it could be otherwise, but I didn't say anything. I held it inside. It felt important, this knowledge I was holding under my skin, just below the surface.

"He'll probably come out when he's older," she said.

Or maybe she'll get to be the girl she was meant to be all along, or land somewhere in between.

"Maybe he's a girl," I ventured.

She tilted her head as if to say "doubtful." It felt like she was tossing aside this character's deeply held wish. I wanted to protect that character.

I watched the films of Almodóvar, which had trans characters before they hit the mainstream. His life in bright colors was more like mine than the ones I saw in the blockbuster movie theaters. *All About My Mother* was a movie that told of loss and longing, and the trans character plays a key role. I collected these side references to trans stories, while still not saying anything out loud.

When Sarah's parent came out, she found no reference points on television, or in movies either. "*Will and Grace* was just barely a thing then, and transgender was definitely not remotely on anybody's radar, so I didn't even know what to tell people." The movie, *Normal*, aired on HBO around that time in the early 2000s, showing a family in transition, but it wasn't widely viewed. The parent transitioning works in a factory. When she starts to transition, she's bullied by co-workers. One of her kids is supportive and the other rejects her. Stories like that were still rare and mostly landed in the *drama* category. They were stories of struggle and challenge, which is part of the truth, yes, but they were missing some of the comedy, some of the light moments.

Danielle's parent came out to her around the time of the movie *Transamerica*, one of the first major motion pictures about a trans family. "*Transamerica* had just come out, but I feel like there wasn't a whole lot else in popular media that was positive. You look back at *Ace Ventura: Pet Detective* and how transphobic that was. I really never loved that movie, but

I don't have *any* interest in watching it now. There wasn't really anything, at least mainstream." Why were these stories so few and far between?

Transamerica was the first movie I saw that even touched my story a tiny bit. Seeing a main character who was trans facing some of the questions my parent did made me feel the wave of these stories coming. "I remember seeing it in the theater," Monica said, "and being like, 'Oh my god! This movie!' It was so exciting to me, because it probably came out six years after my dad transitioned, when it was 1998, when there was nothing in popular culture. It was mostly TV talk shows that were talking about it, and that was basically it." Around that time, she also found "*The Adventures of Sebastian Cole*, a story of a teenage boy whose stepdad transitions." The film tells about their relationship around the transition.

Each person I talked to searched for stories that fit. Christina M. found "several documentaries about gender through the years on HBO and other channels." She also found "a photography book years ago with photos of trans folks." Still, it was a while before these stories reached the mainstream.

AT THE DINNER TABLE

It wasn't until Caitlyn Jenner that the conversation was brought to the dinner table in the homes of families across the country. For the first time, I felt that I could share about my family without having to explain from the start what it means to be transgender.

When people started talking about Caitlyn Jenner, the first thing I felt was relief. Finally, people were talking about this. Before, only a handful of movies like *Transamerica* and *Normal* addressed being trans. It felt pushed to the side. Ignored. Even when people complained about Caitlyn Jenner, I was grateful. Finally, the conversation was open. The more people talked about it in the media, the less I felt I had to hide.

All the media outlets were in a frenzy, from magazine cover articles, to hour-long TV specials, to reality shows. I didn't follow too much of the day-to-day coverage. I just thought, "People are talking about it. People aren't acting like it doesn't ever happen." It felt like a step in the right direction.

Jordan's parent came out right around that time, maybe a month or two before the stream of stories came out. He was dropped into the middle of the conversation happening right then. "It's right at the same time that it's the most topical, most widespread talked-about thing, so I wasn't special. When I talked to people about it, it wasn't a big deal to most people and that was humbling, but in a good way."

To me, it was old news, but everyone around was acting like this was a revelation. "Can you believe it?" It became for some a spectacle and fascination, for others a target for their angry rants, and for others part of a page turning into a new chapter. *This is part of our world. It's not a secret anymore.*

Caitlyn Jenner was one view, a celebrity snapshot, a trans parent with a long train of celebrity kids. "She was kind of immediately put up as this representative of trans people," Danielle said. "No, her experience does not reflect most trans people, and she always said that—she was great about always saying that and acknowledging her privilege." Maybe she wasn't our parents, our families, our lives, but she marked the start of a time when this wasn't taking place behind closed doors. After living through whole decades that seemed to claim that this didn't exist, it felt like an important change.

Monica reflected on that time. "When Caitlyn Jenner came out, and was on the cover of *Vanity Fair* or whatever... That level of acceptance, but is it acceptance? I don't really know because there's so much backlash." There's a sense of acceptance because it's being talked about, but then the backlash feels like a step backwards.

For Danielle, it was a chance for people to "wrap their heads around" gender as a construct. The world saw that this Olympic decathlete who was "the quintessential masculine manly man…is actually a woman." It gave a sense of "how gender is not immutable—how…what we project might just be a projection based on how we feel we have to act." The story gave other people perspective on her own family. "I felt like it was helpful for other people to understand where I was coming from in saying, 'No I had no idea—nobody had any idea.'" When she was younger, her stepmom "was always the person that fixed things and she was an engineer. She was really into science. The whole half of our basement was her tools. She had a Land Rover and she would go off-roading, and I remember her coming home with the Land Rover totally covered in mud." Had someone told her she was a woman at the time, she might not have believed them.

This story led to stories of the extended family, too. "I was so desperate for any kind of connection with someone," Olivia said, "that I did watch the *Keeping Up with the Kardashians* episodes where they found out. There are four or five [of them] and they all had different reactions, which I felt mirrored different parts of me, like anger and sadness and confusion, and I thought that was actually really helpful. In my mind, I was like, 'Wow, this is really dire that this is the best resource I've found so far.' It speaks more to the lack of resources." She had searched and searched, and came up with nothing. She was looking for "stories where it's people who have been through it as an adult child who found out—there's not many that I found."

This story still marked the start of a shift. "Starting to see other trans celebrities," Danielle said, "and for people to be able to start to have those conversations, and for people to start to realize that being transphobic is not cool anymore—it's not okay anymore."

When *Transparent* swept the Emmies one year, again I felt relief and amazement. Here was a show that told the story of a whole family in transition, and it wasn't Jerry Springer or a reality exposé. I was late to watching *Transparent*—I didn't watch it right away. When I did, what I loved most was that the characters all came to life—it wasn't just a spotlight on the parent. I related to some of the emotions that came up—the grief, the humor, the confusion—but not all of them. It was the story of a family, and this was part of it.

More and more it felt like stories were moving in the direction of having the transition as one part of a bigger story.

Christina M. had the same family structure as the Pfeffermans. She found the show "funny, relatable but also far-fetched and entertaining."

"I relate so deeply to some parts of [*Transparent*]," Sharon said. "Obviously not everything, but it's just really cool to see that things like that are out there."

For Jonathan, he felt like his own family story was enough. "I don't even want to watch this—to get myself involved in another family's struggle?" he said. "I'm living that—I don't want to watch it."

Some found it overly dramatized and hard to connect with. "I think that's partly a criticism of how we tell stories in TV and movies where we feel like the stories can't be told with subtlety," Morgan said. Some of the everyday pieces are missing. Not that it isn't sometimes dramatic in our own lives. "It is a big thing," Morgan said, "and lots of emotions can be evoked."

The story captured one family, but was taken at times to be representative, which often happens when the stories are few and far between.

"Moira's character—her transition story is very classic, right. It's like, 'Oh she was at that cross-dresser's camp and the whole thing,'" Monica said, "and I totally can picture her at Southern Comfort conference in Atlanta with 16 suitcases there for the weekend." Some of the side stories and characters were more complex. "I do like some of the ways that they treated the other trans characters in the show," Monica said. "The way they handled the class aspect of it at different points." She connected more to the early parts of the show before "it just kind of spirals."

I never expected to see a show like *Transparent* on TV. I thought it would keep happening behind the scenes, not on televisions streaming in multiple languages.

"I'm glad that there are things like *Transparent* out there now," Sharon said. "I didn't have anything when I was younger. I'm sure that there were some little books or something, but at the time, I was also in deep denial, so I didn't want to read—I didn't want to talk about it." I related to this, too, to shying away from any references. Once I hit junior high, I didn't want anything to do with these stories. Had *Transparent* been out then, I would have probably pretended that it wasn't there.

"You should see *Transparent*," a friend of mine said recently. She didn't know about my family. She just thought it was a great show. Later, when I told her, she said, "If I'd known, I would never have recommended it." It comes up as a reference point with other friends now, though. It's part of a growing conversation.

In *Transparent*, the stories of the rest of the family held an equal weight to the story of the parent. "There just suddenly were these stories that featured trans people and also showed their family members," Danielle said. "There just wasn't any of that before. Having that—seeing some semblance of my family experience in a popular culture setting was good. It was helpful to see that."

Around the same time, *Orange Is the New Black* took over the screens across the country and world. On that show, a trans character played by trans actor Laverne Cox was one of the main characters. "I think if you have a trans character, that should be a trans actor," Jennifer said. "*Orange is the New Black* definitely did it in a more respectful way. They used her twin brother [for flashback scenes] so she wouldn't have to feel that gender dysphoria, which I thought was great."

Danielle remembered watching the show and seeing one of the episodes about Laverne Cox's character. "They show that really early time with her wife," Danielle said. "There's a scene where she's trying to figure out, and her wife is trying to figure out, how to do this." The show "brought in her twin brother—it was like, 'Oh Laverne Cox happens to have an identical twin brother? Bring him in!'" She could see the characters navigating some of the experience her family had come through.

"Some of it is so raw," Jonathan said. "*Orange is the New Black*—I'd watch these scenes. They have all these flashback scenes from when they're not in prison—and I was like, 'Oh my gosh, these are all so real—I don't want to watch this.'" He didn't find anything that spoke to him in terms of his own story. "I don't think TV-wise or media-wise there was anything that resonated with me."

Just a handful of years before, though, none of those stories were out there in the mainstream. "There just wasn't any of that in 2010," Danielle said. "[Or rather] there were, but they were very few and far between and definitely not in popular culture."

If I were growing up now under the umbrella of *Transparent* and similar shows, I wonder if I would have shared my story sooner with my friends at school. I wonder if I would have felt differently, understood more, felt less ashamed of the truth. What I found out is that people are still living with many of the same feelings, even with these stories out there. Most of our stories still haven't been told.

When Becca looked for her own story more recently, she didn't find much. "I noticed my parents started watching this show called *Transparent*—I've never watched it… I watched the trailer for *The Joneses* and I really liked it. I haven't found any books or anything like that. I found the basic, 'living with LGBT parents' [ones] and they just mostly talk about your parents being lesbian or gay, but nothing about your dad becoming a woman or your mother becoming a man—nothing honest and real and raw, and that's what I want." She was still looking for her own story. "There's literally nothing, there's literally nothing out there, and it's so weird, it's so weird." That void, the looking out in the world for your story and finding nothing, is what I felt, too, many years ago. I was surprised to find that this was still the case.

As people with trans parents, we often find ourselves in the role of educators to the people around us, whether we want to be or not. Shows and stories can take some of that burden off us, but at times it can increase the burden if we are misrepresented or our families are shown in a negative light. It can go both ways. More and more, we are moving toward seeing the stories that tell about our lives in all of their complexity, not over-simplified or reduced to a simple fairy tale or sensationalized view.

Other shows popped up about teens in transition—for example *I Am Jazz*—people in college, and more families. In the news, more people who were trans appeared. Each time I saw one, it felt like another bulb lighting up—blink! More stories to tell, more light shed on the subject. When I told people now, they had at least some reference points, some context for this part of my life.

Some TV shows brought in trans characters on one or two episodes. In *Veronica Mars*, one of the characters finds out his dad, who he thought was dead, is trans. Veronica talks him into reconnecting, into considering how precious that connection with our parents is. In *South Park*, one of the characters announces that she's "transginger" and wants to use the girls' bathroom. When it pops up, I notice it, but it never feels like, "Oh they're telling my story or my family's story."

"I look at the depiction of trans people on TV," Justin said, "and like you either have trans prostitutes getting murdered or you have this...idea of trans people who have made their money or made their families and their kids are old enough, and make these transitions that aren't super-smooth, but are also like at worst kind of funny and awkward." He craved a deeper, more complex narrative. He also found that the characters themselves were shown in the extreme. "They're either bad people or good people and they're never in between."

The way it's shown can also reinforce a gender binary. The character starts out as a man and then becomes a woman with high heels and lipstick. They show these very extreme binaries instead of the in between or the gray area. There's this pressure to be like, "Which box did you check?"

The movement between genders can be misrepresented, too. "There's always like a big sensationalized 'Oh, this person was a man and now they're a woman,'" Jennifer said, "but...they were always a woman—you just didn't always know." This is another misunderstanding that can come up. Jennifer felt frustrated because she knew her parent's experience. "My parent had told me about when she was very, very young—she was like, 'I knew since I was five years old, and had to keep it to myself for 50 years'—which is just awful." She hadn't found that story yet.

New shows like *Pose* are at the forefront of telling our family stories with trans actors playing trans characters and trans production teams bringing the stories to life. The show's by and for model puts the storytelling into the hands of the lives it portrays. *Pose* tells stories of finding family outside the lines of blood, which is one I relate to, as my family was made up of chosen members, too. I watched my own chosen family expand and shrink in the '80s when the AIDS crisis impacted our circle of friends. At the time, silences stole many stories. This show is claiming space in the silence to tell some of those untold stories from inside the community. It tells the story of "what it meant to be brown and black, to be trans and poor and femme in an era in New York City dictated by a series of ills, from HIV and gentrification to crack and greed." With over 100 trans people casted and employed by the show, the show marks the curve of the future for trans storytelling.

My touchstones for the experience are shows and films that tell the stories of ordinary lives that happen to include the transition. In *From This Day Forward*, Sharon Shattuck tells the story of a family in transition, of commitment, and of what it was like growing up with a transgender parent in northern Michigan in the days before people were talking about it.

I related to her emotions, to the desire to hide, to the wish to be independent and separate from my family from a young age. She told of the shift in her parents' relationship through the change, of her father's movement back and forth on the spectrum of gender, and of the relationship she built with a man who she decided to marry. The wedding is woven in as part of the story. The meaning of commitment, of compromise, and of family come through in the film. The story feels real not only because it happened, but because she shared the complexity of the experience. She didn't oversimplify.

Julie Anne Peters' *Luna* is one of my all-time favorite books. When she told of how the book came about, she said that the character appeared to her. "I'm Luna," the character said when she woke up one morning. "Write about me." When the character told her she was transgender, she hesitated. "I knew zip, zero, zilch about being transgender or gender variant. I should've known, but gender identity and sexual orientation are two different animals." She listened to the story and wrote it down. She took an imaginative leap, and also reached out to the trans community, so that she wasn't coming from an outsider's viewpoint. Living as a lesbian, she knew about a life outside the margins. Trans characters appear now on a regular basis in our stories, as the cis characters we took for granted once did. As writers, we must be willing to write down what they have to say and connect with the community we're writing about.

The book *Dress Codes* by Noelle Howey was one that I read eagerly. Parts of the story sounded like they were my own. The book articulated things that I felt or thought, but couldn't necessarily put into words. At the time of my parent's transition, my experience felt very much underground and separate from my friends and my world. Howey brought that reality to life. It was Dana who handed me the book at a bookstore. I looked at the cover and knew I wanted to read it. I was still trying to find a language and a way to talk about it.

Dress Codes also stood out for Monica. "I read Noelle Howey's memoir and the anthology she edited, *Out of the Ordinary*, which is also like...ah...it's so real, those stories are so real...those were really formative for me." *Out of the Ordinary* wove together the experiences of kids with gay parents, too. At the time, it didn't even feel like there would be enough of our stories to put in there. Now I know that there were—we just weren't visible.

When I read stories from the perspective of the children, like *Dress Codes* and *She's My Dad*, I'm surprised by how much I want to hear about the everyday lives of the kids. Who are they? Who did they become? In *Dress Codes*, Noelle told the story of her girlhood alongside her dad's transition. In *She's My Dad*, Jonathan Williams told of coming to a new understanding of his religion, but there was also a side story of falling in love with his wife. I was rooting for them as a couple as much as I was rooting for his dad, who also wrote short pieces interspersed between the chapters.

Leslie Steinberg's *Stone Butch Blues* helped me understand the experience from the inside out. *Conundrum* told of Jan Morris's transition, which happened years before my parent's. *True Selves* by Mildred Brown and Chloe Anne Rounsley gave a therapist's perspective, so it felt more distanced—not as personal. The documentary *Transgender Parents* puts the viewer in the shoes of both parents and children. I related to both sides, to all of the emotions that came up.

Jordan's dad gave him a book to read early on. "My dad recommended this book by Jennifer Finney Boylan, [*She's Not There*], and my dad was kind of like, 'This is my story.' I felt like ultimately the book was a sketch or a landscape, which is probably good, because it left a lot of room to fill in your own details." It told the story in a way where Jordan felt like he could step into the narrative. "I could inhabit in a more first-person way some of the experience. Being able to just inhabit a character and take on the experience in a meaningful way helped me to get through the first hurdle pretty quickly." The story was part of his bridge to understanding. "Once the first domino fell, once there was a certain amount of acceptance, everything else was just confronting things as they come up."

Your parent's experience won't be the same as these narratives, but you'll see pieces that they might not want to talk about. Not everything can be shared in conversation. Some of these stories can fill in the blanks.

I remember looking at the cover of *The Danish Girl* by David Ebershoff, a book that later became a movie, but when I saw that it was written by a guy, I didn't want to read it. Same with *Middlesex*, by Jeffrey Eugenides. And *Trans-Sister Radio* by Chris Bohjalian. I didn't want an outsider's perspective, which is funny, because how did I know they didn't have a trans parent or another strong connection with the trans community? Amy Bloom's *Normal* stayed on the shelf. I was skeptical of stories from what I considered the outside.

Another more recent book was Susan Faludi's *In the Darkroom*. "I did try starting to read *In the Darkroom*," Olivia said. "It was almost... It was so specific. There were parts that I kind of was like, 'Oh, this really does remind me of it.'" I related to trying to read that, too, along with other books people passed my way. Sometimes, though, I just needed a story that captured my experience in other ways. I needed to read a novel about a girl making her way in the world. That was part of my story, too.

KC looked for books to share with her daughter. She said, "None of them are quite there yet because I'm non-binary—I'm fluid, so I just have to make my own book is what it comes down to. They touch on the subject of transgender, but they don't do the non-binary part of it." The closest she came was the picture book *Bunnybear*. She described how the book had an impact on her: "Even though you feel like you're yourself, even though you don't match your outside, even you can still be fallible where you see someone that looks like they look and they act different. You can be like, 'No—you should be that!' And then of course you realize that they are who they are. I was in tears reading it at my daughter's house. When I saw that book—that just touched my soul so much, it was incredible."

BEHIND THE SCENES

"When I was 18 years old," Even B. said, "my father decided that he wanted to tell the world." A television program reached out to the family, wanting to tell the story. Even didn't want to be a part of it. "I didn't want to tell the world what I felt about it, although I didn't have any problems with it—I thought that was kind of strange." His father called him, upset. Instead, he proposed an alternative. "I told him that well, if he would just wait seven years, I would make the film, but I would make it the way I wanted it to be; [that I would] want to say the things I want to say about it." So he said, "Okay, I'll wait." It was set then: Even would make the film. "So then I just had to make the film—I didn't have any choice. Six years later, I started making the film."

In the meantime, they didn't talk about it much. It didn't feel like there was much to talk about. "I hadn't really talked to my father about anything, so it was all those years with a kind of silence in a way." While filming, they followed his dad all over. It came out through the filming that his dad "was transforming his body so that he would be more female." Hormones and other changes. Before the film, they didn't know this. "My stepmother says that in the movie—if he becomes too much woman and there is no man there, then she has to go. So he had to stop using those hormones." Even started out thinking he was simply telling the story of his father and his family to the world, but his family changed, too, over the course of the filming. His dad and stepmom stayed together, but new aspects of his family came to light.

When I watched the film, *Alt Om Min Far* (*All About My Father*), again I felt this moment of recognition and identification. Here, too, was my family in a slightly different form. Here was more of the language I was looking for.

During the making of the documentary film *The Joneses*, the family changed, too. The film tells the story of a family with a trans parent in Mississippi. *(Spoiler alert!)* One of the sons came out as gay and met someone while the film was being made. The grandkids, who didn't know about having a trans grandparent, found out the truth. Life unfolded and the story arc of the film changed in the making.

For Sharon Shattuck, the process of making the film *From This Day Forward* ended up being a way to reclaim the story for her family. "This film gave us a voice and a pride in who we are as a family in a way that we didn't have when we were growing up—we were very ashamed almost as a family, but this was a nice way to take that back."

Each of these stories shaped the families as much as the families shaped the stories. Through the telling, the families were changed.

OUR OWN STORIES

Our own family stories are both messier and quieter than the ones we see on TV. We might find our story without anything trans in it at all.

"*The Fosters*!" Leila cried out when I asked if she'd found any shows or stories like her family. This was a series about a foster family. That was part of her experience, too—being adopted.

We might find our stories in songs. "You know that Beatles song, 'Ob-La-Di, Ob-La-Da...life goes on'? Well, life goes on—that seems like a message that my own life resonates with,"

Morgan said. There's a tiny reference in the song where "I guess we're left to wonder if the person is trans of some sort," but it's told in passing and no big deal. Life goes on. "Not that that mirrors my own family story at all, but if I think about trans references, that's the one."

We look for pieces of our stories and put them together like that. Here and here and here and here. Put them all together and you have a mismatched collage that might come close to your family. There might be missing pieces still to come.

When I first started writing about my family, I told most people that it was pure fiction. "It's just what the characters are doing," I said, as if I were equally surprised. First, I fell in love with language and then I tried to learn to use it to describe the world. We need new words to encompass our families and ourselves, and we need new stories, too. All of us are waiting for these stories, the ones that tell about our families in an everyday way, like life.

Even our own efforts to tell the story can come out false at times. My first attempts to write about my family involved a lot of bullying and ostracization, and the *I-can't-believe-it* narrative that I saw out in the world, but I hadn't experienced any of that. I was telling the story as the world wanted to see it, not as it was.

I was interviewed once by Italian *Vanity Fair* for an article on kids with gay families. The interviewers didn't know my story before they did the interview. They had done some interviews already, all with kids with gay parents. They were expecting another kid with gay parents. When I told them, they were visibly surprised.

"We didn't know," they said, their eyes widening as if to say, "Whoa." For a moment, I felt like a zoo animal, a fascination, the child with a trans parent. I still had a lot of anxiety about sharing the story openly, and I didn't know how to respond. The interview continued, and they were very nice, chatting amicably with me, but it still felt strange. I can still see the strain in my smile in the photograph they took. "Say cheese!" This was in 2011. Fast forward 30 years, and hopefully that won't be the case. The girl in the article will be talking about her family, but for other reasons, just to say "This is who my family is." And then they'll go back to talking about something else, like farming or art.

The title of the article was "The Kids Are Alright," a play on the movie that came out around that time about kids with gay parents. What I felt like I couldn't express to the interviewers was how ordinary it was on some level. Most people don't believe it. How could this not tear the lid off of my world? It just didn't, not right away, not until we stepped out into the world. It was the other people's reactions that tore the lid off, not my family. It was the silence, the not talking that had the greater impact. Not talking about the change, too. Not talking about the loss. I do think that story still needs to be told.

Our own lives can sometimes feel like we're living inside a story bigger than us. "My life was literally like a movie," Olivia said. From finding out on an island in Southeast Asia to traveling with her fiancé and planning a wedding where no one knew, she was living on the stage of a set that was her own life. The story was unfolding around her, with plot twists and changes, only it was her life. "It's a unique experience," Jonathan said, "and so it's like, 'Nobody can quite identify with this because it's mine.'" Jonathan wrote his own book, *She's My Dad*, and he and his parent appear in a TED talk called "The story of a parent's transition and a son's redemption." When we don't see our stories out in the world, it sometimes brings us to tell our own.

"I just want to see more complicated trans narratives, you know?" Justin said. "I mean—yeah, still—I look to the trans narratives that are on TV and even some of the ones that are in literature right now, and I'm like, 'That still doesn't feel right—that doesn't speak to me.'" He's working on his own memoir. Even the best stories he found out in the world felt to him "like an adjacent story, so I'm like, 'I resonate with some of this, but at the same time, I don't see the story.' The queer white trash narrative is kind of hard to come by."

One of the few works that Justin related to was *To Survive on the Shore*, a compilation of stories of trans elders. "I found it and I looked at the website and just cried, and then got it and just cried, and will cry every time I look at it, because I'm just like, 'Mom.'" He found his own family in the pages of the book. Maybe that's what we're looking for—to see our own families not as fascinations, but as people living their lives. I think of times when Dana tried to give me books that expanded the gender narrative, and I pushed them away. I rejected them because they felt like a part of what was different about my family. That whole time, I could have found pieces of my story but I didn't want to.

Justin shared this resistance. "For so long in my life, the idea of looking felt like the idea of admitting or coming out, so I just shied away from so many resources or didn't look because I was like, 'If I start looking for this stuff, somebody's going to find out I'm looking,' which is really hard for me to admit. I feel a lot of shame about that," he said. One of the first trans narratives he read was Julia Serano's *Whipping Girl*, which is a mix of criticism and theory along with personal experience. The gaps in his reading were connected to the gaps in his own life.

One book Justin came across is *Paul Takes the Form of a Mortal Girl* by Andrea Lawlor. "It's weird and good," Justin said. "It's about a person who can change their gender and the shape of their gender at will, so trying to figure out what gender they are and what gender they're most comfortable with."

There have been so many shows and movies with gay characters over the years now. It has become part of the background, where it's almost like, "Oh yeah, no big deal." At this point, though, having a trans parent often becomes a focal point in the show, instead of "Oh, on the side, there's this trans parent." With mainstream media there's been a lot more representation [of having two moms/two dads]," Jennifer said, "but there's still like, when you say you have a trans parent, people just don't like it, don't get it, or don't even know how to approach getting it." She was still looking for that everyday portrayal. "I don't see it anywhere where it's at all portrayed as something normal," Jennifer said.

We need more stories about trans families where it is part of the background and it's no big deal. That's what we're still waiting for. That's the key, just having more stories out there, so people feel like "Oh yeah—that's my family, that's my experience."

Monica was approached by the film crew for 52 *Tuesdays* when she appeared on a transgender family panel at the LGBT center in San Francisco. "They came up to me afterwards and they were like, 'Oh my gosh, we are making a movie about a 17-year-old girl whose parent transitions.' And I was like, 'What?'" Monica was also 17 when her parent came out. The filmmakers were interspersing documentary pieces of real lives in the narrative. Monica appears in a part where the main character is sitting on her bed watching some videos her parent sent her. One of the videos shows Monica. "It's like me, telling my story and talking about what it was like to be 17." Other story lines weave into the main one, including one about teenage sexuality. As Monica watched it later, she found herself wishing for the narrative to be different somehow. "Why do I want it to be perfect? Why am I like, 'Why are they talking about teenage sexuality in this kind of edgy way in the same movie that has this thing.'" With so few portrayals out there, we don't want people to misunderstand. The more stories that are out there, the more we can show the mix of our real experiences as they are.

I thought that now that there are some more shows and more recognition in the media, it would be wildly different from when my parent came out when there was so little. But within each family, it's handled differently. It's not like the family pools all the articles and shows out there now and says, "Look! They're talking about us!" We still have to find our own way through our stories. There's only so much that the stories outside us can do when we're in the middle of our own.

As Stacey M. said, "All the explaining in the world doesn't change that I basically lost my mother... All the movies and books in the world won't change that for me."

When we're in it, an article or film can feel like extra noise, but we'll reach a point when we need them. The stories that help you might not come with the tag of trans. They might just be the ones that hit on an emotion that shifts something frozen inside you or that make you laugh and remind you of your family, just because.

FILLING THE GAP

There are still gaps to be filled in the stories about our families. There are still more stories to be told.

In the future, our stories will be in the background of stories about ordinary lives. Having a trans parent will be one part of a bigger story. It won't be the focus, but it will be part of our lives as portrayed on the screen or on the page. These are the stories that still need to be told, the ones where being trans is on the side. Like David Levithan's *Boy Meets Boy* for gay love, we need a story where we don't question that one character crosses the gender lines. It's just part of what happens. It's part of our lives. And we need stories that tell of our experiences in a way that's real and raw, not edited or laced with a laugh track.

In *Raising Hell*, a documentary by Ed Ingalls-Webb about kids with LGBTQ+ parents, they talk about wanting their families shown in toothpaste commercials. There are subtle ways we're told "This is the shape of families," and that's what needs to shift to reflect the truth. A lot of people said they had not found a story that reflected their own, which shows that there's still ground to cover. There are more stories to be told.

"I still think it's cool that we can talk about it now," Sharon said. "And the more we put out movies and TV shows where we have trans characters, I think it's just good—that's how things change. That's why we have gay marriage now, because people, allies, came out of the woodwork, so it's good to talk about it, and that's why I think it's good to be open about it with your friends. Then people are like, 'Oh my god, it's not just some random person on the news—my friend has a trans parent.'"

The more we tell our stories, the more the old portrayal of transgender people in the media will fade into the background. People will look back on how wrong and outdated those views were. We already do, but there will be a widespread understanding of this. *We were wrong*. Even the humor will be updated in terms of what's funny when it comes to gender. Our own families can bridge this gap.

We will open up the newspaper to stories of our families running soup kitchens and building landmarks and inventing gadgets. We get to tell our family stories, too. I thought with the rise of *Transparent* and shows with more trans characters, people would feel like their stories were out there, but they didn't. Most people felt like their stories weren't out there at all, that they were still looking for their stories. As Ann P. said, "No. Not at all. Wished there was. Every transgender situation is so unique."

Maybe since I grew up in a time of radio silence about my family, it feels like a big wave of stories to me. The fact that anyone, anywhere is talking about it feels huge. Still, each of us has our own story to tell. The more that our stories are out in the world, the more we get to see ourselves and our families all around us, and the more what we see on TV and in movies reflects the landscape of our lives.

Prompts for I Saw It on TV

1. What shows, movies, books or plays have you seen that reflect your family's experience?
2. Have you seen any shows that seem to misrepresent your family and/or the transgender experience as you have witnessed it?
3. What books have you connected with most that portray the trans experience?
4. What do you think of some of the high-profile stories about trans celebrities in the media?
5. What stories still need to be told?

Chapter 11

The Future Is Trans-Fabulous

At the women's march in January 2017, Janet Mock stood up to speak in front of a crowd of thousands. The words she spoke were for everyone, a sea of pink all around her. We listened, not because of who she was, but because of what she had to say. She talked about speaking up, standing up, and being able to "truly see ourselves and one another." The voices rising up, the ones we need to hear, are trans voices. Trans families. The future is trans-fabulous.

CHANGING VIEWS OF GENDER

You are sitting in an auditorium surrounded by people of all genders. The lights are dimmed as you wait for the speaker to appear. When they step out onto the stage, the audience hushes. No one is thinking about the speaker's gender. They just want to hear what they have to say. In this auditorium, people share a language where pronouns and names match who people are. All of this is possible. This is the future. This is now.

We are already there. The laws and the stories have some catching up to do. People on the street might need some educating, but it is possible. As our stories rise up about our families and our lives, as our parents share their stories, as we do, more people will understand this as part of the spectrum of human experience and not just an anomaly or exception. I used to think I was the only person with a family like mine, but now I know otherwise after talking to trans families from around the country and world.

All around me, people are seeing that being trans is part of our lives.

"There's a kid in my town who's transgender."

"There's someone in my class at school."

"My cousin."

"My best friend."

Kids are growing up in a trans world. They already know more than we do. They are learning early on from friends, from school, from being in the world, that trans is all around us. They already know that the future is trans-fabulous because they are growing up inside it.

There's more to discover, too. We thought we knew everything there was to know about gender, but we didn't. What we know about gender is expanding.

I didn't even know the word "transgender" when my parent transitioned. It wasn't in the dictionary. We had this two-part *Oxford English Dictionary* that my parents used a magnifying glass to read because the print was so small. I liked to hover the magnifying glass over the page, to make the words bigger. The word "transgender" was missing between "transfusive" and "transgress." The word "trans" was in there, though. It means "with the sense across, through, over, to or on the other side of, beyond, outside of, from one place, person, thing, or state to another." Yes—that's what I witnessed—that's what fits.

Trans. Not even transgender, though that's part of it. But simply trans-being. And it's a beautiful thing.

When I was a teenager, I wanted Dana to drop me off 7,000 blocks away from where I was going. Later, I saw that she could see with a wider view and carried a beautiful empathy that I sometimes got to share. All of us are trans at one point or another. We are all crossing over to the other side.

Skyela H. said, "One must learn that there are many types of people in the world, and not just female/male. Be patient and understanding. Be open about your feelings and never feel ashamed."

Jennifer echoed this, and added, "There's not one way to be trans. There's not one universal experience that all of us have had. People transition in so many different ways—so many different degrees of being out." Not everyone chooses to be out. Some want to live their lives in the body that fits without fighting for it every day. "Our stories are so different but equally important." I envision a future where none of us are looking for these gender codes. Where it just doesn't matter. Where having a trans parent is just part of the background of our lives. That is possible, too.

Is it possible to live in a world that's gender blind?

What if we could just forget about gender? Kate V., a trans parent, mentioned how her daughter said that she didn't think of gender at all when talking to her mother, but she thought of it in relation to Kate. Can, we perhaps, forget about gender, and just see each person for who they are?

Morgan was riding in the car with her dad and brother, and something came up about Morgan that her brother thought was boyish.

"You know Morgan," her brother said. "You're a little like a man—you're kind of like a man. Dad, don't you think Morgan's a little like a man?"

"No," her dad said. "I don't think that Morgan's like a man. I think Morgan is a woman, and that's the way that she is a woman."

Her dad was saying that there's no one way to be. "That meant a lot to me to hear that from my dad," Morgan said. "That there isn't one way to be a man or to be a woman. There isn't one way to be non-binary or gender queer—there are infinite ways." When it comes to understanding, "it's really important to listen to the person and how they're identifying themselves, and what being that means to them." Each person is different. None of us fit a mold. "That's the most important thing rather than trying to fit them into a box," Morgan said.

I used to wonder: If gender is a construct, then why change it? Can't we just build it to be what we want? Then I thought of how it would feel to wake up in a boy's body. I would say, "Oh no! What happened?" I would do everything possible to get back. I can be a girl and climb rocks and fix cars (though I don't happen to do those things). It's not about what we do. It's about a feeling of who we are. And it's not one or the other, it's everywhere in between.

How can we break the gender codes in our families? Riley considered this. "What's stopping me from being someone's mom? Just look at mine. He doesn't have breasts anymore or go by 'he', but that's still my mom. It's helped open my eyes about what that relationship actually is. That's just my mom—all the 'typical' pieces that go into it don't matter anymore." His parent being his mom wasn't linked to gender anymore. What is it that makes someone your mom if it's not about gender? I feel the same way—that my mom would have been my mom no matter what gender she lived in. She was just my mom no matter what. The mom-ness wasn't linked to gender somehow.

If we were able to throw out all the gender boxes, where

would you live? I went to a women's college, and the teachers listened to me and took me seriously. After a semester at a co-ed school, I saw the difference. Later, when I was teaching at a college, I sometimes wanted to borrow the white beard of an older male colleague. I thought the students would listen to me then. I shouldn't have to do that, but sometimes, it felt like it might make it easier.

What if the leap wasn't so far? All of us are trans at some point. All of us contain elements of both. It's where our body takes us after that brings us either further away or closer to ourselves. Sometimes, I miss that confident girl I was at age ten—the girl who was ready to take on the world and everyone, who didn't care what people thought. She got the body she wanted, but some things were lost along the way, and maybe I share that with my parent.

PRIDE IN YOUR FAMILY

You might not start out being proud of your family, and you might not always have the perfect relationship with your parent, but you can be proud to be a kid of trans. I know this, because I wanted to hide under a rock for so long when it came to my family, and now I do feel proud. It was a long, squiggly journey to get there and I might not feel it every day, but it's there.

"Although my family structure is different," Cameron V. said, "I have parents that love me very much and I am lucky enough to have all of them in my life."

In high school, while some friends were being bribed by their parents to get better grades or perform better, my parents accepted me just as I was. Even when I brought home a C-minus on my report card—calculus!—they said they knew I was still smart and capable. Both my parents believed in me and my sister whole-heartedly. They had their own struggles, but I never doubted their support.

My parents raised me and my sister to challenge any limits based on gender. To not listen to "Girls can't do that." To not listen to anyone who said, "That's not for girls." At the same time, I did like the so-called girly things: dressing up all fancy with a giant bow on my head, wearing white gloves and patent leather shoes. They didn't tell me not to do that, either. I could wear a giant bow on my head and study advanced math. There was nothing I couldn't do in their minds. No limits.

Jennifer feels like she can talk to her parents about anything. "Within our whole family, it has created such a sense of openness... It has impacted me and my sister to be raised in such an open and caring environment." The openness spread to all aspects of their lives. "She always encouraged us to expose ourselves to all different types of religion and understandings of the world and really think critically and make our own decisions." No matter what, she felt like she could share whatever was going on. "I always felt like I could talk to my parents about anything that came up. I felt like I didn't have to hide stuff." This came out of the open environment created in her family while her parent transitioned. "That is one of the benefits of having this openness and honesty, and kind of open conversation about everything—I think that is a really cool thing. That is a really nice gift that comes out of everything."

Having a trans parent is a gift in our lives. There might be places along the way where it feels otherwise, but we'll come to see parts of our family with pride. "I just love having a trans person in my family," Riley said. "Just that being a unique family is kind of amazing and cool and having a perspective that's different and enriched—it's been a total benefit to me and a total gift."

INTO THE FUTURE

I sometimes wonder if we could have been open and free about who our family was back when my parent transitioned, how that might have been different for all of us. To not have to hide. To not have to try to fit in. It's hard to imagine what it would have been like. A whole other reality.

I like to picture a future society where our families are free to be themselves, where we have that "heavenly understanding" that Jheri Jones talked about in the documentary *The Joneses*, where our understanding of gender has expanded to adapt to all the changes in our families, too. The stories on the news would show our families as an ordinary part of the world, not as a showcase or spotlight of difference. The movies, plays, and books would have our families alongside others. At picnics, we would see families like ours dotted in the field, just like anyone else's. There is no shame or secrets or hiding. The future is trans-fabulous, because our families will not be on the sidelines anymore. We won't be seen as different or separate. We won't be set apart.

A place where no one blinks when you say your parent is trans. A place where we don't split the world in two. It may sound like some future utopia, but it is happening now.

That's the funny thing about the future. Some places get there first. Some people are already living there. Some of us can see it.

The future will still have people who don't get it, who don't understand, but our families will be woven into daily life, part of the landscape, part of reality, part of every day.

Scientists, athletes, inventors, professors, writers, artists, designers, architects, lawyers, pilots. The leaders of the future. It helps to know that your neighbor is trans or your friend's parent is trans, but it also helps to see movers and shakers in the world who are trans, people who are making change.

It's possible that a future exists where people align with their bodies before starting a family. That future is happening now. Where it's possible to be yourself and expand your world. Where it's not such a far-away leap from here to there.

Danielle talked about going to the Trans Wellness Conference in Philadelphia and meeting "multiple pregnant trans men there, and it was like, 'This is so cool—there's so much more.' Granted we have a very long way to go as far as medical accessibility goes, but there's just more. It will be really neat to watch how we see the next generation."

If they made the leap before having a family, they might not bring others on that journey with them, but there would be other shifts and challenges, other difficulties like in any family. There's no perfect family out there, but it's nice to think there could be a world where people get to start families after claiming themselves.

I talked to a parent with a trans child who said that her child has always been the same person, that who her child is has not changed fundamentally from day one. This shone a light on the stories of kids who say their parent changed so much. One expressed a wish for a future where their parent could be themselves before they have kids, "so it's not a transition for the kids."

"I'm hoping that transgender individuals will be able to come out earlier and be themselves and be comfortable by the time they have children," Amy said.

What if our parent could claim the gift of the body that fit at a much younger age? "My hope is that people are able to settle in their identities before they have families," Sarah said, "because I think going through the transition is what's hard on kids, and if your parent has already transitioned or is at least in that ambiguous territory by the time you come around, then I think it would be a lot easier."

Looking at her own family, she wonders about that wish. "Part of me's like, 'Oh, I wish you'd been comfortable to be yourself your whole life,' but my mother and you would definitely have not gotten married and I would definitely not be here, so I guess I'm conflicted about that." Dana has said that to me—that I might not exist had she had the chance to claim her identity sooner. But maybe I would exist. Technology is changing when it comes to starting trans families. Who knows what might have happened?

Acceptance is the future, too. We are mysteries to ourselves, so how can we expect to be able to understand someone else? As Even said, "We have so much trouble understanding ourselves, you know, trying to understand everyone, we would have a really hard time, so acceptance is a much better way to go."

What about us? Where do we fit in this future? What is our place? We don't have to be warriors, as Justin said. We don't have to set right every wrong thing someone says, but we can speak up in small ways that add up. If we don't want anyone in the world to know we have a trans parent, if that's out of the question, if our parents aren't out in our community, we can find anonymous forums to share our stories. Visibility is just starting to be part of our stories, but it doesn't have to be. Visibility isn't the only answer to acceptance. As Julia Serano wrote in a recent article, "Rethinking LGBTQ+ Visibility," "While visibility has played a vital role in enabling contemporary LGBTQ+ people to find one another and share resources, we should reject the premise that it automatically fosters acceptance." I used to wonder why my parent wasn't out in her community, why she didn't share her identity more. In the article, Julia Serano reflected, "Sometimes being more visible simply makes you an easier target for discrimination. And the veneer of visibility may lull those who don't personally face that discrimination into a false sense of progress." We need to move toward a future where we don't expect our parents to be one way or another—in or out, visible to invisible, or somewhere in between. We need to move toward a future where just being is okay in whatever form that takes. Where we aren't asking people to fit in certain lines, even within the LGBTQ+ community.

If you're still making sense of what is going on with your family and your life, you don't have to try to steamroll yourself into the future. Some people talked about accepting every brand of trans in everyone except their parent. When it comes to family, there's more to untangle than just a new vision of gender.

Find some people who get it, who don't ask dumb questions, who let you be yourself. Start there. Find a place to practice being yourself so that, more and more, you can bring that back to your family and into the world.

VOICES OF THE FUTURE

I get excited when I see trans people doing cool things in the world, because it means more people get to have this awareness. In that spirit, I look out for trans celebrities and movers and shakers because they feel like part of my extended family, too, even if they don't know it. Maybe it comes from growing up in a world where I looked at a barren landscape. Who was trans? No one I knew.

As far as I knew in the late '80s, there were maybe six people in the world who were trans: Renée Richards, Christine Jorgensen, the three people the therapist sent over, and my parent. That was all. I've watched that population grow—not just because there are more trans people now, but there are more people willing to say, "I am trans," or just, "I am me." Sometimes, there is a cost that comes from saying that, and not everyone chooses to be out. My parent isn't out in her community. That's not the answer.

I still look across the landscape, though, for people like my parent saying, "This is me." Some of the kids with trans parents used that phrase, too: "*This is me.*" At times, they felt invisible in the transition, not seen or heard. Yet each of us declared this phrase at some point: "*This is who I am.*" We wanted our parents to see us, too.

Here are some trans heroes for my family and me and for other trans families. The following are people who have come up over the course of our lives. There are so many more.

Jan Morris

An essayist who writes about place, history, and her own life, her most recent book, *In My Mind's Eye*, was serialized by BBC radio. Often seen as one of the great travel writers, her works lined the shelf in Dana's home. When Dana came out to Donnie, she did so by saying, "I think I'm a Jan Morris candidate."

He said, "I just thought that meant she wanted to travel."

In a recent *New York Times* profile, "The Many Lives of Jan Morris," Morris said, "I believe in the soul and the spirit more than the body."

When I read that, I felt that the same words could have come from Dana. She has often told me this. It made me see one of the reasons why this writer was a kindred spirit to her over the years. In the article, Morris also talked about what it would be like to live by a code of kindness. That is something Dana often talks about. She told me that my grandmother rarely said goodbye to her—instead she said, "Be kind." She shared this value with Morris.

Kate Bornstein

Kate Bornstein is a gender warrior. She wrote *The Gender Workbook*, a book Dana tried to give to me when I was in college, but I wouldn't touch it with a ten-foot pole. Years later, I ordered the updated edition and saw what a gift it was, opening all the doors to understanding ourselves and others. In her book *A Queer and Pleasant Danger* Bornstein wrote:

> I don't call myself a woman, *and* I know I'm not a man. That's the part that upsets the pope—he's worried that talk like that—*not male, not female*—will shatter the natural order of men and women. I look forward to the day it does.

Dana has always been a big fan of her writing and told me about her for years before I sought her work out for myself.

Nat Titman

Reading Kate Bornstein led me to the work of Nat Titman, who Bornstein quotes in the opening of the new edition of *The Gender Workbook*. Titman, also known online as @quarridors, adapted a *Doctor Who* quote on time to apply to gender: "You see, people assume that gender is a simple progression of masculine to feminine, but actually...from a non-linear, non-normative viewpoint, it's more like a big ball of wibbly wobbly...gender-y blender stuff."

Titman runs the website, *Practical Androgyny*, which is "a resource for those who are comfortably androgynous but struggle with the pressures of the binary gender system, and for those who wish to explore the possibilities of gender ambiguity."

Caroline Cossey, a.k.a. Tula

An English model who appeared in a James Bond film, she went on to be an activist for trans rights and found her way to the European Court of Human Rights to try to claim her true identity. She was Justin's parent's ideal. "See, this is a trans woman who made it," Justin's mom said, showing him photos of Tula.

"Tula was her ideal and thus became mine because I was very young," Justin said.

I hadn't heard of Tula. When I looked her up, I also found a flood of tabloid stories, sensationalized portrayals, and even a clip from an '80s talk show, *Donahue*. Each portrayal, each representation felt personal. I didn't want people asking her dumb questions. *That's my family, too.*

Danica Roem

A journalist and politician who was elected to the Virginia House of Delegates in 2017, Roem is an advocate for change on the local and national level. In responding to readers of a local paper who voted her "Best Local Politician" in 2018, she called for widespread participation in politics—for getting involved:

> If you're well-qualified and you have good ideas, bring your ideas to the table and run for office because of who you are: no matter what you look like, where you come from, how you worship, if you do, or who you love. This is your America, too, and it's time for you to run it.

Andrea Jenkins

Known to most as a politician who was elected to the Minneapolis City Council in 2018, Jenkins is also a poet. She says, "Poetry is my way of distilling and expressing what's around me." She made history as the first openly transgender black woman elected to public office in the United States. Before her election, she shared some of her ideas in an interview with *Auburn Voices*:

> I express gratitude every single morning when I awake. I journal every day, which for me is a spiritual practice. I take long walks in nature, around bodies of water. And bask in that realness; in that mystery of the universe. I try to see the humanity in every person that I encounter and recognize that we are part of a universe.

She brings this view into her work as a politician, writer, poet, and activist.

Cece McDonald

An artist and prison-reform activist, McDonald speaks and works for change in the criminal justice system and larger community. Her writings and voice inspired the #FreeCece movement that led to a film, artwork, and writing across the country. She says, "I want people to not just hear me, but to live through me, to live through this experience to give themselves a platform."

Dean Spade

Writer, teacher, activist, and founder of the Sylvia Rivera Law Center, Spade creates change through organizing, writing, and making films. He has collaborated with other writers and activists to change how we think about the world, trans politics, prisons, and money, among other things. In his essay, "For Lovers and Fighters," he wrote: "Sometimes while I ride the subway I try to look at each person and imagine what they look like to someone who is totally in love with them... I think this fun pastime is a way of cultivating compassion."

Tourmaline, formerly known as Reina Gossett

An artist and filmmaker who has made films that change how

we look at ourselves and the world around us, and who makes us consider the power of everyday resistance. Her short films, *Atlantic Is a Sea of Bones, Salacia, Mary of Ill Fame, The Personal Things*, and others have screened throughout New York City. She collaborated with Sasha Wortzel on *Happy Birthday, Marsha!*, a film that imagines transgender artist and activist "Marsha 'Pay It No Mind' Johnson" in the hours before the 1969 Stonewall Riots in New York City. In an interview in *Mask Magazine*, she said: "I think the everyday ways of being in the world are more important than the times when we're supposedly acting extraordinary. Small things are what are life changing."

Sylvia Rivera

"The revolution is here!" she called out during the Stonewall Riots. She climbed into a closed New York City council meeting through a window when they were debating a gay rights bill. She advocated for the rights of transgender people. She was outspoken in her activism for trans rights, in particular for people of color and low-income members of the community, years before there was any recognition. In a reflection on Stonewall that was aired on National Public Radio in 1989, she said, "I'm not going to change for anybody. If I changed, then I feel that I'm losing what 1969 brought into my life, and that was to be totally free."

For every time there was an internal cheering squad in me for trans politicians, writers, and activists, it was a recognition of the future where this will be part of the background of our lives. Finally, I saw the world coming into line with the inside of my family. That feeling of *it's just us, we're the only ones* faded out when I saw people out there changing the world as themselves.

That was my trans parent, too.

??

Prompts for The Future Is Trans-Fabulous

1. Who are your favorite trans celebrities?
2. Do you see other people starting to understand gender differently?
3. Do you look at gender differently now?
4. What is your hope for the future in your family and the world?

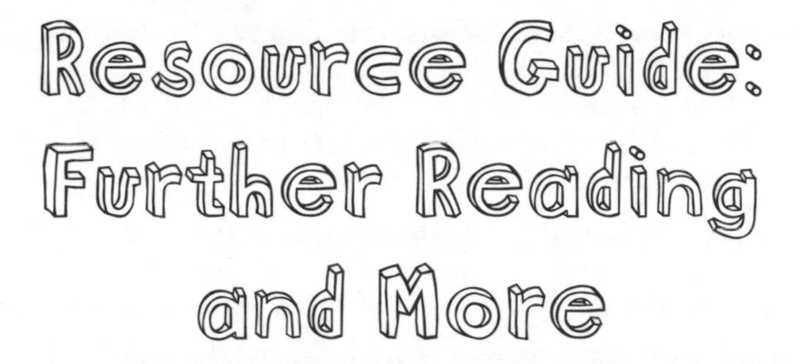

Resource Guide: Further Reading and More

This is a list of recommended books, shows, movies, blogs, and websites from kids of trans parents and trans families around the world.

STORIES BY AND ABOUT KIDS WITH TRANS PARENTS

***Dress Codes* by Noelle Howey, Picador, 2002**

Noelle brings you into her life in suburban Ohio, from the moment she finds out her parent is transgender through her own journey of becoming a young woman. Her story is also featured in this book!

***She's My Dad* by Jonathan Williams, Westminster John Knox Press, 2018**

This book tells the story of Jonathan's experience when his dad, an evangelical pastor, came out as transgender. He takes you through the ups and downs as he comes to a new understanding of his family and religion.

"The Story of a Parent's Transition and a Son's Redemption" by Paula Stone Williams and Jonathan Williams, *TEDWomen*, 2018.

A TED Talk by Jonathan Williams, author of *She's My Dad*, and Paula Stone Williams. Available at www.ted.com/talks/paula_stone_williams_and_jonathan_williams_the_story_of_a_parent_s_transition_and_a_son_s_redemption?language=en

***From This Day Forward* by Sharon Shattuck, Argot Pictures, 2016**

This documentary film tells the story of family ties and growing up with a trans parent. Sharon weaves in her parents' relationship and her own, including the story of her wedding. What is the meaning of commitment and compromise? She explores these and other questions in the film. Her story also appears in this book!

***All About My Father* by Even Benestad, Exposed Film Productions, 2002**
A documentary film about his parent, a prominent Norwegian doctor who identified as a transvestite when Even was young and who starts to shift identity to become more of her female self. Even is also featured in this book!

***When Dad Became Joan* by Cath Lloyd, Librotas, 2017**
This tells the story of Cath's life with a trans parent in England. Cath is a personal coach, and she includes a section on mapping out your own life.

***In the Darkroom* by Susan Faludi, Metropolitan Books, 2016**
An exploration of larger questions of identity inspired in part by her father's trans identity.

"She Killed My Father" by Anonymous, *Beautiful Stories from Anonymous People* podcast, episode 116, 2018
A girl tells the story of her experience when her parent transitions.

"The World in a Box" by Justin Burnell, *The Rumpus*, 2019
A funny, moving story of life with a trans parent from a child's perspective. Available at https://therumpus.net/2019/04/rumpus-original-fiction-a-world-in-a-box

"Coming Out/Betrayal: A Multi-Part Poem" by Justin Burnell, *Hotel*, 2019.
A poem of navigating identity composed in fragments and multiple parts. Available at https://partisanhotel.co.uk/Justin-Burnell

"Crisis of Finite Worlds" by Justin Burnell, *Guernica Magazine*, 2016
Tells the story of growing up with a trans parent in Appalachia. Available at www.guernicamag.com/justin-burnell-crisis-of-finite-worlds

***Kids of Trans Resource Guide* by Monica Canfield-Lenfest, COLAGE, a national organization for children with one or more LGBTQ+ parents, 2008**
Written in 2008, this guide was the original inspiration for this book! Created by and for kids with trans parents to answer any questions and give you tools and resources. Monica's story appears in the guide and also in this book!

***Out of the Ordinary* edited by Noelle Howey and Ellen Samuels, St. Martin's Griffin, 2000**
A collection of essays written and edited by kids with LGBTQ+ parents. Includes essays such as "She'll Always Be My Daddy," "Father's Day," and "Getting Closer." One of the editors, Noelle Howey, is the author of *Dress Codes* and appears in this book, too.

***Raised by Unicorns* edited by Frank Lowe, Cleis Press, 2018**

Essays by kids with LGBTQ+ parents, edited by a "gay-at-home" dad who shares his own story in the introduction. It's primarily about kids with gay parents, but a lot of the emotions and experiences will resonate. It features an interview with a major league baseball player who talks about growing up with lesbian moms in a way that sheds light on many LGBTQ+ family experiences.

***Families Like Mine: Children of Gay Parents Tell It Like It Is* by Abigail Garner, Harper Collins, 2004.**

This book weaves together the story of the author, who grew up with a gay father, with other adult children of LGBTQ+ parents, including those with transgender parents.

***Spawning Generations: Rants and Reflections on Growing Up with LGBTQ+ Parents* edited by Sadie Epstein-Fine and Makeda Zook, Demeter Press, 2018**

This collection includes essays and interviews by queerspawn—another word for kids with LGBTQ+ parents—without glossing over the hard, complicated truths of our family lives. Essays include "Glitter in the Dishwasher," "Roots and Rainbows," and "In between Heart and Break."

***The Adventures of Sebastian Cole* directed by Tod Williams, Paramount Pictures, 1999**

A film about a teen whose step-parent transitions.

***52 Tuesdays* directed by Sophie Hyde, Closer Productions, 2013**

This film tells the story of a teen with a trans parent, and features a clip of Monica Canfield-Lenfest, author of the *Kids of Trans Resource Guide* and one of the kids with trans parents in this book, talking about her experience.

***In My Shoes* directed by Jen Gilomen, New Youth Films, COLAGE Youth Leadership and Action Program, 2005**

A documentary film following the stories of five kids from LGBTQ+ families, including one with a transgender guardian.

COLAGE KidsSafe Blog

A collection of stories by people with one or more LGBTQ+ parents posted to Tumblr and now on Instagram. Available at kidsafe.tumblr.com and at @COLAGENational on Instagram.

COLAGE People with Trans Parents Resources

Selected resources for people with trans parents. Available at www.colage.org/resources/people-with-trans-parents

STORIES BY AND ABOUT TRANS PARENTS

***She's Not There* by Jennifer Finney Boylan, Broadway, 2003**

An essential, desert island read for many kids with trans parents who found that the perspective Jennifer offers helped them understand their parents' lives better.

***Stuck in the Middle with You: A Memoir of Parenting in Three Genders* by Jennifer Finney Boylan, Broadway, 2013**

A story of parenting from across the spectrum of gender by the author of *She's Not There*.

***Born on the Edge of Race and Gender: A Voice for Cultural Competency* by Willy Wilkinson, Hapa Papa Press, 2015**

This book tells the story of Willy's life, while weaving in key perspectives for understanding gender and culture better, including snapshots of a life committed to advocacy and change. The theme of edges fuses Wilkinson's stories together.

***Southern Comfort* directed by Kate Davis, Next Wave Films, 2001**

A moving documentary film that tells the story of a trans parent battling cancer. Features both immediate family members, including his son, and his chosen family in the trans community.

***Transamerica* directed by Duncan Tucker, Belladonna Productions, 2005**

One of the early films I remember seeing that featured a trans parent. In the film, the main character, Bree, played by cisgender actor Felicity Huffman, goes on a road trip to meet her son.

***Transparent* by Jules Rosskam, Frameline, 2005**

No, not the TV show on Amazon. This is a documentary film about 19 trans men living in the United States. "I'll always be their mom," one of the parents says in an interview in the film. It's a film about parenting and the fluidity of gender roles.

***Transgender Parents* by Remy Hubereau, CBC's (Canadian Broadcasting Corporation) Documentary Channel, 2014**

A documentary film about trans families in Canada. Both children and parents are featured in the film, which started as a short film, *Transforming Family*.

***The Nearest Exit May Be Behind You* by S. Bear Bergman, Arsenal Pulp Press, 2010**

A collection of essays about gender, covering a wide range of topics—from women's spaces to becoming a parent.

***Home Fronts: Controversies in Nontraditional Parenting* edited by Jess Wells, Alyson Books, 2000**

A compilation of essays on parenting, including one about trans parents.

***Tales of the City* adapted by Lauren Morelli, Working Title Television, Netflix, 2019**
A great book series by Armistead Maupin adapted into a mini-series with a storyline about a trans parent and other trans characters.

***The Adventures of Priscilla, Queen of the Desert* by Stephan Elliott, PolyGram Filmed Entertainment, 1994**
A road trip film following two drag performers and a transgender woman as they travel and perform across the Australian desert. One of the characters meets her son in the course of the adventures.

***You Don't Know Dick: Courageous Hearts of Transsexual Men* by Bestor Cram, FilmBuff, 1997**
"People would be able to see me more clearly if I had a male body," James says in this documentary that follows six trans men talking about their lives. One of the men has children who appear in the film, too.

STORIES ABOUT TRANS FAMILIES

***The Joneses* by Moby Longinotto, Gravitas Ventures, 2016**
This documentary film follows the story of a family with a trans parent. The identities of all family members are explored and also the question of how to tell your kids when your trans parent becomes a trans grandparent.

***Myth of Father* by Paul Hill, Frameline, 2001**
In this documentary film, Hill deconstructs his family and the identity of his parent before transitioning.

***No Dumb Questions* by Melissa Regan, New Day Films, 2001**
This documentary film tells the story of three sisters whose Uncle Bill is going to be Aunt Barbara. A great resource for younger family members learning about gender.

***Normal* directed by Jane Anderson, HBO Films, 2003**
Set in a small town in the Midwest, this film tells the story of a family and community's response to one character's transition. Adapted from Anderson's own play, *Looking for Normal*.

***Transparent* created by Jill Soloway, Amazon Studios, 2014**
Meet the Pfeffermans. When Mort, played by cisgender actor Jeffrey Tambor, comes out as transgender and starts living as Maura, each family member is going through their own transformations in life, career, and love. The storyline weaves in the family history and a series of trans characters played by trans actors who Maura meets along the way.

***Trans-Kin: A Guide for Family and Friends of Transgender People* edited by Eleanor Hubbard and Cameron T. Whitley, Bolder Press, 2012**
An anthology of stories by significant others, relatives, and friends of transgender people.

***She's a Boy I Knew: An Auto-Ethnography of a Filmmaker's Transition from Male to Female* by Gwen Haworth, Shapeshifter Films, 2007**
A documentary film that explores filmmaker Gwen Haworth's gender transition through a kaleidoscope of perspectives in her family.

***Blood, Marriage, Wine, and Glitter* by S. Bear Bergman, Arsenal Pulp Press, 2013**
A collection of essays on queer family life by S. Bear Bergman, who has written extensively on gender and culture.

***The Argonauts* by Maggie Nelson, Graywolf Press, 2015**
A lyrical story of making a family and navigating a life with her transgender partner.

***Trans Forming Families: Real Stories about Transgender Loved Ones* by Mary Boenke, Oak Knoll Press, 2003**
A collection of stories by families and friends of transgender people, including a letter by a daughter whose parent just came out as transgender.

TRANS MEMOIRS AND NONFICTION

***A Queer and Pleasant Danger: The true story of a nice Jewish boy who joins the Church of Scientology and leaves twelve years later to become the lovely lady she is today* by Kate Bornstein, Beacon Press, 2012**
A hilarious story of growing up, written by the author of *The New Gender Workbook* and *Gender Outlaw*.

***The Gender Games* by Juno Dawson, Two Roads, 2017**
"A great story never starts at the beginning, it starts when something *changes*," Juno tells readers at the start of this funny story of life in a world that has it all wrong.

***Yes, You Are Trans Enough* by Mia Violet, Jessica Kingsley Publishers, 2018**
Mia set out to write her book to balance out the lies and misinformation about trans lives that she saw in the media. A mix of memoir and theory, she chronicles her own life and talks about the issues she faced along the way.

***Becoming a Visible Man* by Jamison Green, Vanderbilt University Press, 2004**
Mixes memoir with social theory to tell the story of the experience of being a male born into a female body, and finding your way back.

***Conundrum* by Jan Morris, Harcourt Brace Jovanovich, 1974**
Jan's 1974 memoir tells the story of her transition and her long-standing partnership and marriage that stayed true as she claimed her own truth in body and mind.

***Gender Outlaw: On Men, Women, and the Rest of Us* by Kate Bornstein, Vintage, 1994**
A mix of memoir and manifesto on gender and sexuality, drawn from her own experience.

***The Last Time I Wore a Dress* by Daphne Scholinski, Riverhead Books, 1997**
A memoir of being institutionalized for not conforming to gender-based expectations. Daphne's therapeutic treatment included being taught to walk and dress in ways that conform to conventional expectations of girls in society.

***Redefining Realness: My Path to Womanhood, Identity, Love, and So Much More* by Janet Mock, Atria Books, 2014**
In her book, Janet talks about the stories we tell and how we can overcome the internal blocks to being ourselves.

***Free Cece!* by Jac Gares, Jac Gares Media, 2016**
A 2016 documentary about the story of CeCe McDonald and the movement she inspired when she was imprisoned after standing up to bullying and harassment.

***Some Assembly Required: The Not-So-Secret Life of a Transgender Teen* by Arin Andrews, Simon & Schuster, 2014**
A memoir by and for teens about growing up in Oklahoma and making the choice to transition in high school.

***Rethinking Normal: A Memoir in Transition* by Katie Rain Hill, Simon & Schuster, 2014**
The first thing Katie tells you in this book is that she hates flies, but as she tells her story, she shares more about her family, life, and friends on her way to becoming.

***Being Jazz: My Life as a (Transgender) Teen* by Jazz Jennings, Random House, 2016**
A memoir by the star of the show *I Am Jazz*, sharing her story and offering perspective for anyone hoping to understand.

***Tango: My Childhood, Backwards and in High Heels* by Justin Vivian Bond, Feminist Press, 2011**
From "Iced Watermelon" Revlon lipstick to performing on stage, Bond tells her story with humor and grace.

***Man Alive: A True Story of Violence, Forgiveness and Becoming a Man* by Thomas Page McBee, City Lights/Sister Spit, 2014**
A beautiful, lyrical story of becoming human with gender as a part of the mix. This was listed among the best books of 2014 by *Publishers Weekly*, *NPR*, and *Kirkus Reviews*.

***To My Trans Sisters* edited by Charlie Craggs, Jessica Kingsley Publishers, 2018**
A collection of letters by trans women to trans women. The advice given here is something we can all take to heart about being yourself and practicing kindness.

***Hiding in Plain Sight* by Zane Thimmesch-Gill, Riverdale Avenue Books, 2015**
A memoir of growing up as a homeless queer teen.

***Balancing on the Mechitza: Transgender in the Jewish Community* edited by Noach Dzmura, Atlantic Books, 2010**
Winner of the 2011 Lambda Literary Award for Trans Nonfiction, this anthology brings together the perspectives of a wide range of people offering trans perspectives in the Jewish community.

***Transposes* by Dylan Edwards, Northwest Press, 2012**
A graphic novel-style book of stories about trans experience.

Tretter Transgender Oral History Project
An oral history project and collection based at University of Minnesota featuring stories on various themes, including "Transgender Family & Children." Available at https://trettertransoralhistory.umn.edu.

America in Transition
A documentary series on relationships, community, and society, featuring trans people of color. Available at americaintransition.org.

STORIES OF GENDER EXPANSIVENESS IN YOUNG ADULT FICTION

***Luna* by Julie Anne Peters, Little, Brown Books for Young Readers, 2008**
"She is me. I am her. I want to be her. I want to be Luna." A novel about a girl with a trans sister named Luna. Tells the story with flashbacks to the early days, and shows a whole family in transition.

***If I Was Your Girl* by Meredith Russo, Flatiron Books, 2016**
What if you were the new girl in school, and all you want is to fit in and make new friends? In this award-winning novel, Russo tells Amanda's story as she gets to know Grant, someone who starts out as a friend, but could be something more.

***I Am J* by Cris Beam, Little, Brown Books for Young Readers, 2011**
"He tried not to think about gender at all, except when the world outside his brain barged in and forced him to," the narrator says about J at the start of this story that takes us into J's life. He's in love with Melissa, who is crushing on someone else. How can J be himself in a world that wants him to be someone else?

***Beautiful Music for Ugly Children* by Kirstin Cronn-Mills, Flux, 2016**
A DJ for a show called *Beautiful Music for Ugly Children*, Gabe describes himself as "like a record. Elizabeth is my A side, the song everybody knows, and Gabe is my B side—not heard as often, but just as good. It's time to let my B side play."

***A Boy Like Me* by Jennie Wood, 215 Ink, 2014**
"I wanted so badly to...run, run away from my own body," Peyton says at the start of this story when he gets his first period in the middle of a school day. That same day, he meets Tara, and quickly falls for her. All Tara wants is for a boy to like her, and all Peyton wants is to be that boy.

GENDER EXPANSIVE FICTION, POETRY, AND FILM

***Seasonal Velocities* by Ryka Aoki, Trans-Genre Press, 2012**
Ryka switches between poetry and prose to tell her story in this beautiful collection.

***Stone Butch Blues* by Leslie Feinberg, Firebrand Books, 1993**
A raw and honest story of a life in transition by an early advocate and leader in the trans community and writing world.

***Tiny Pieces of Skull* by Roz Kaveney, Team Angelica Publishing, 2015**
Winner of the 2016 Lambda Award for Best Trans Fiction, this novel takes us into London and Chicago in the late 1970s with a dash of humor and a dose of reality.

***Little Fish* by Casey Plett, Arsenal Pulp Press, 2018**
An award-winning debut novel about a trans woman who discovers that her late grandfather might also have been trans.

***Wanting in Arabic* by Trish Salah, TSAR Publications, 2013**
Poetry that asks questions about language, self, and identity.

***Trumpet* by Jackie Kay, Pantheon Books, 1998**
A beautiful, poetic book about loss and mourning, and the uncovering of trans identity after death.

***Troubling the Line: Trans and Genderqueer Poetry and Poetics* edited by T.C. Tolbert and Trace Peterson, Nightboat Books, 2013**
A collection featuring 55 poets alongside reflections on poetics, activism, and embodiment.

***Paul Takes the Form of a Mortal Girl* by Andrea Lawlor, Vintage, 2019**
A magical realist adventure in the life of Paul, a shape-shifter who can transform body and gender at will in this cross-country adventure.

***Ma Vie en Rose* by Alain Berliner, Canal +, 1997**
A French film about Ludovic, who is being raised as a boy, but knows deep down she is a girl. She escapes into a world of pink with her Barbie, "Pam," to the place where she can be her true self.

GENDER EXPANSIVE TV SHOWS

***Pose* created by Ryan Murphy, FX Networks, 2018**
A dance musical about the LGBTQ+ ballroom culture scene in New York City in the late '80s and early '90s featuring a large cast of transgender actors.

***I Am Jazz* featuring Jazz Jennings, TLC, 2015**
A docu-series following the life of trans teen Jazz Jennings.

***Supergirl* created by Ali Adler, Greg Berlanti, and Andrew Kreisberg, Berlanti Productions, The CW, 2015**
A show about the legacy of superhuman powers and the search for justice that now features real-life superhero Nicole Maines, who fought for her rights in real life, and plays the role of Nia, "television's first transgender superhero."

PICTURE BOOKS AND CHILDREN'S STORIES ABOUT GENDER AND IDENTITY

***Introducing Teddy: A Gentle Story about Gender and Friendship* by Jessica Walton and Dougal MacPherson, Bloomsbury, 2016**
A picture book about a trans teddy bear, true friendship, and embracing yourself.

***Bunnybear* by Andrea Loney, INDPB, 2017**
Though born a bear, Bunnybear feels more like a bunny. Great story for talking about non-binary identities.

***Backwards Day* by S. Bear Bergman and kd diamond, Flamingo Rampant, 2012**
Each year, Andrea looks forward to "Backwards Day," and being a boy for a day. This year turns out a little differently, though.

***The Adventures of Tulip, Birthday Wish Fairy* by S. Bear Bergman and Suzy Malik, Flamingo Rampant, 2012**
When wish fairy, Tulip, gets a wish from David who wants to be Daniela, Tulip goes to the Wish Fairy Captain and learns something new.

***10,000 Dresses* by Marcus Ewert, Triangle Square, 2008**
Meet Bailey, who dreams of dresses. Tells a story of how friendship and kindness make a difference.

***Red: A Crayon's Story* by Michael Hall, Greenwillow Books, 2015**
Red is wrapped in a red crayon label, but inside is blue. In a world that wants him to be red, how can he accept that he is blue?

***Stacey's Not a Girl* by Colt Keo-Meier, 2017**
A children's book of a gender adventure outside the binary.

TRANS 101: TERMS, DEFINITIONS, AND GENERAL KNOWLEDGE

***Whipping Girl* by Julia Serano, Seal Press, 2007**
Tells it like it is with research woven into personal experience. Links theory with stories from Julia's own life as a trans woman in contemporary society. This is the book I would choose to understand the truth and lies and everything in between.

"Julia's trans, gender, sexuality, and activism glossary!" by Julia Serano, 2019
An extensive online glossary for her third book, *Outspoken*, full of definitions, corrections, and an overall illumination of ideas. Available at www.juliaserano.com/terminology.html

GLAAD Media Reference Guide—Transgender
The resource recommended most for journalists writing about the trans community. Includes terms, definitions, perspectives on media representation, and other helpful information. Available at www.glaad.org/reference/transgender.

***"You're in the Wrong Bathroom": And 20 Other Myths and Misconceptions About Transgender and Gender-Nonconforming People* by Laura Erickson-Schroth and Laura A. Jacobs, Beacon Press, 2017**
A great reference to check out if someone has pulled out a myths like, "All Trans People Want to Be Either Barbie or Ken," "You're Not Really Trans If You Haven't Had 'The Surgery,'" and "It's Rude to Ask How You Should Address Someone." Great research, tips, and information throughout.

***Trans Like Me: Conversations For All of Us* by C.N. Lester, Seal Press, 2018**
A must-read for those who want to challenge their privilege and misconceptions about trans topics throughout culture.

***My New Gender Workbook: A Step by Step Guide to Achieving World Peace through Gender Anarchy and Sex Positivity* by Kate Bornstein, Routledge, 2013**
A funny and comprehensive book about the adventure of gender, sex, and identity.

***The Social Justice Advocate's Handbook: A Guide to Gender* by Sam Killerman, Impetus Books, 2017**
A funny, goofy gender-journey with a social justice training slant.

***The Gender Quest Workbook: A Guide for Teens and Young Adults Exploring Gender Identity* by Rylan Testa and Deborah Coolhart, Instant Help, 2015**
"What is gender, anyway?" the authors of this workbook ask, and answer with many exercises and tips for exploring gender.

***True Selves: Understanding Transsexualism for Family, Friends, Coworkers, and Helping Professionals* by Mildred Brown and Chloe Ann Rounsley, Jossey-Bass, 2003**
An overview of the experience of changing gender by a therapist who has worked with families and individuals in transition for years.

***Transgender Emergence: Therapeutic Guidelines for Working with Gender-Variant People and Their Families* by Arlene Istar Lev, LCSW, CASAC, The Howorth Clinical Practice Press, 2004**
Written by a therapist, this book incorporates her perspective and guidance for trans families.

***Transition and Beyond: Observations on Gender Identity* by R. Vanderburgh, MA, LMFT, 2017**
A look at the process of transitions and more, filling in the gaps from many other guides.

***Trans Bodies, Trans Selves: A Resource for the Transgender Community* edited by Laura Erickson-Schroth. Oxford University Press, 2014.**
Compiles a lot of information about aspects of trans lives from health and wellness to religion and spirituality.

***The Gender Book* by Mel Reiff Hill and Jay Mays, Marshall House Press, 2014**
"A gender 101 for anyone and everyone," this book is a guide to gender in all its diversity, led by Boston, the "gender scout."

***Transgender 101: A Simple Guide to a Complex Issue* by Nicholas Teich, Columbia University Press, 2012**
An introductory guide covering the basics of being transgender.

TRANS HISTORY AND THEORY

***Transgender History: The Roots of Today's Revolution* by Susan Stryker, Seal Press, 2017**
A look at the history of trans culture from post-World War II communities to the present day, with clips from key books and speeches that have influenced change.

***Transgender Warriors: The Making of History from Joan of Arc to Dennis Rodman* by Leslie Feinberg, Beacon Press, 1997**
A historical look at the spectrum of gender and societies that have celebrated gender in all its forms.

***Re-Dressing America's Frontier Past* by Peter Boag, University of California Press, 2012**
A closer look at gender in America's Wild West.

***Sex Changes: Transgender Politics* by Patrick Califia, Cleis Press, 2003**
An in-depth analysis of trans history, politics and literature, challenging easy assumptions about gender.

***Sex/Gender: Biology in a Social World* by Anne Fausto-Sterling, Routledge, 2012**
A look at the development of sex and gender in science and society.

***Transfeminist Perspectives in and beyond Transgender and Gender Studies* by Finn Enke (author called Anne Enke on the book, but prefers Finn), Temple University Press, 2012**
An award-winning compilation of essays challenging ideas and perspectives in gender studies.

***Normal Life* by Dean Spade (Expanded Edition), Duke University Press, 2015**
A theoretical and practical look at how real change can happen in trans communities. Dean explores the systems intended to defend our rights and shows what happens when these systems are broken.

***How Sex Changes: A History of Transsexuality in the United States* by Joanne Meyerowitz, Harvard University Press, 2004**
The story of the physical transformation of sex through the lens of social, cultural, and medical history.

Transgender Archives
The Transgender Archives based at the University of Victoria, Canada preserves key documents and materials in transgender history. Available at www.uvic.ca/transgenderarchives.

TRANS PROFILES AND PORTRAITS

***To Survive on this Shore: Photographs and Interviews with Transgender and Gender Nonconforming Older Adults* by Jess Dugan and Vanessa Fabre, Kehrer Verlag, 2018**
A beautiful compilation of stories and photographs of older transgender people.

***Love Makes a Family: Portraits of Lesbian, Gay, Bisexual, and Transgender Parents and Their Families* by Peggy Gillespie, University of Massachusetts Press, 1999**
Photos and stories of LGBTQ+ families.

***Body Alchemy: Transsexual Portraits* by Loren Cameron, Cleis Press, 1996**
Portraits of trans folks accompanied by notes and short essays.

***Beyond Magenta: Transgender Teens Speak Out* edited by Susan Kulkin, Candlewick, 2015**
Interviews and portraits of trans teens.

***Assume Nothing* by Rebecca Swan, Soft Skull Press, 2010**
A series of photographs across the spectrum of gender that make readers question their assumptions.

***Kate Bornstein is a Queer and Pleasant Danger* by Sam Feder, Moving Train Media, 2014**
A film portrait of Kate Bornstein, author of *Gender Outlaw* and *The New Gender Workbook*.

***MAJOR!* by Annalise Ophelian, What Do We Want Films, 2015**
A film about the life and activism of Miss Major Griffin-Gracy, a transgender activist and hero. Inspiring for anyone who wants to create change.

***Happy Birthday, Marsha!* by Tourmaline and Sasha Wortzel, Frameline, 2018**
A short film imagining the hours before the Stonewall Riots with transgender rights heroes Marsha P. Johnson and Sylvia Rivera.

LEGAL RESOURCES FOR TRANS FAMILIES

***Transgender Family Law: A Guide to Effective Advocacy* by Jennifer Levi & Elizabeth E. Monnin Browder, AuthorHouse, 2012**

Transgender Law and Policy Institute
www.transgenderlaw.org

National Center for Lesbian Rights (NCLR)—Transgender Law
www.nclrights.org

National LGBTQ Task Force
www.thetaskforce.org

Lambda Legal
www.lambdalegal.org

GLAAD
www.glaad.org

Sylvia Rivera Law Project
https://srlp.org

Transgender Law Center
https://transgenderlawcenter.org

Transgender Legal Defense and Education Fund
www.transgenderlegal.org

GET INVOLVED! (ORGANIZATIONS AND GROUPS)

COLAGE
www.colage.org

Family Equality Council
www.familyequality.org

PFLAG
https://pflag.org

National Center for Transgender Equality (NCTE)
https://transequality.org

FORGE—For Ourselves Reworking Gender Expression
https://forge-forward.org

Compiled with the help of people with trans parents and transgender parents from all over the world who shared their stories in interviews and responded to my survey, the *Kids of Trans Resource Guide* from COLAGE, Lambda Literary, *GLAAD Media Reference Guides*, PFLAG, and the book *You're in the Wrong Bathroom*. There are many more stories out there, and many more to come!

References

CHAPTER 1

Learning the basic terms and ideas—what does it mean to be transgender?

"Sex" from GLAAD (Gay and Lesbian Alliance Against Defamation) (2016) Glossary of Terms—Transgender. *GLAAD Media Reference Guide*, 10th Edition, p.10. New York, NY: GLAAD.

"Subconscious Sex" from Julia Serano (2007) Blind Spots: On Subconscious Sex and Gender Entitlement. *Whipping Girl*, p.87. Berkeley, CA: Seal Press.

"Gender Identity" from GLAAD (Gay and Lesbian Alliance Against Defamation) (2016) Glossary of Terms—Transgender. *GLAAD Media Reference Guide*, 10th Edition, p.10. New York, NY: GLAAD.

"Transgender" from GLAAD (Gay and Lesbian Alliance Against Defamation) (2016) Glossary of Terms—Transgender. *GLAAD Media Reference Guide*, 10th Edition, p.10. New York, NY: GLAAD.

"Transsexual" from GLAAD (Gay and Lesbian Alliance Against Defamation) (2016) Glossary of Terms—Transgender. *GLAAD Media Reference Guide, 10th Edition*, p.10. New York, NY: GLAAD.
and Julia Serano (2019) "Julia's trans, gender, sexuality, and activism glossary!" Accessed on 10/17/19 at www.juliaserano.com/terminology.html#T.

"Trans" from GLAAD (Gay and Lesbian Alliance Against Defamation) (2016) Glossary of Terms—Transgender. *GLAAD Media Reference Guide, 10th Edition*, p.10. New York, NY: GLAAD.
and Ruth Pearce (2018) *Understand Trans Health: Discourse, Power, and Possibility*, p.43. Chicago: Policy Press.

"Gender Expansive" from PFLAG National Glossary of Terms (2019). *PFLAG*. Accessed on 10/19/19 at https://pflag.org/glossary.

"Transphobia" from Julia Serano (2019) "Julia's trans, gender, sexuality, and activism glossary!" Accessed on 10/17/19 at www.juliaserano.com/terminology.html#T.

"Microaggression" from Dani Heffernan (2015) "GLAAD Launches Microaggressions Photo Project." *GLAAD*. Accessed on 10/20/19 at www.glaad.org/blog/glaad-launches-trans-microaggressions-photo-project-transwk.

"Gender Confirmation Surgery" from GLAAD (Gay and Lesbian Alliance Against Defamation) (2016) Glossary of Terms—Gender Confirmation Surgery. *GLAAD Media Reference Guide, 10th Edition*, p.11. New York, NY: GLAAD.

"Gender Dysphoria." American Psychiatric Association. (2013) *Diagnostic and Statistical Manual of Mental Disorders, 5th Edition*, p.451. Arlington, VA: American Psychiatric Association.

"Cis" from PFLAG National Glossary of Terms (2019) *PFLAG*. Accessed on 10/19/19 at https://pflag.org/glossary
and Ruth Pearce (2018) *Understand Trans Health: Discourse, Power, and Possibility*, p. 43. Chicago, IL: Policy Press.

"Non-binary" from GLAAD (Gay and Lesbian Alliance Against Defamation) (2016) Glossary of Terms—Transgender. *GLAAD Media Reference Guide, 10th Edition*, p.10. New York, NY: GLAAD
and Julia Serano (2019) "Julia's trans, gender, sexuality, and activism glossary!" Accessed on 10/17/19 at www.juliaserano.com/terminology.html#N.

"Kids of Trans" from Monica Canfield-Lenfest (2008) *Kids of Trans Resource Guide*, p.5. Seattle, WA: COLAGE.

CHAPTER 2

Shifting identities in the LGBTQ+ community

"Real-life test" from Julia Serano (2007) Pathological Science: Debunking Sexological and Sociological Models of Transgenderism. *Whipping Girl*, p.120. Berkeley, CA: Seal Press.

"Young children are better told..." from Richard Green (1969) "Psychiatric Management of Special Problems in Transsexualism," in *Transsexualism and Sex Reassignment*. p.287. Baltimore, Maryland: The Johns Hopkins University Press..

"Coming out" on social media

"Social media is rife with transphobia..." from Ashleigh Kane (2018) Watch This Trans Activist and Her Friends Give Transphobia the Finger. *Dazed Digital*. Accessed on 8/30/19 at www.dazeddigital.com/life-culture/article/40213/1/charlie-craggs-nailtransphobia-trans-activist-the-finger-film.

Social media cheat sheet

Erica L. Ciszek (2017) "Advocacy Communication and Social Identity: An Exploration of Social Media Outreach." *Journal of Homosexuality* 6, 14, 1–18.

Jesse Fox and Rachel Ralston (2016) "Queer Identity Online: Informal Learning and Teaching Experiences of LGBTQ Individuals on Social Media." *Computers in Human Behavior* 65, 635–642.

Andrea D. Kelley (2019) *"We Do Still Call Her Dad, We Just Use Feminine Pronouns": Navigation and Negotiation of Gender, Sexuality, and Family among People with Transgender Parents*. Dissertation, University of Delaware.

Cybersecurity and Infrastructure Security Agency (2019) "Social Media Cybersecurity." Accessed on 2/1/2020 at https://www.cisa.gov/sites/default/files/publications/Social-Media-Cybersecurity-Tip-Sheet-122019-508.pdf.

CHAPTER 3
This is me

"As far as I can tell..." from Noelle Howey (2002) *Dress Codes*, p.307. New York, NY: Picador.

"Be yourself..." from Kali Holloway (2015) Freud Never Said That. *Salon*. Accessed on 9/22/19 at www.salon.com/2015/10/14/freud_never_said_that_19_of_historys_most_famous_misquotes_partner.

CHAPTER 4
Mother's Day/Father's Day

Jane M. Hatch, ed. (1978) *The American Book of Days*, Third Edition. p.574. New York: H.W. Wilson Company.

Eleanor McNulty (1927) "Miss Anna Jarvis Recounts the Founding of Mother's Day," *Children: The Magazine for Parents*. p.30. New York: Parents' Publishing Association, Inc.

CHAPTER 5
The future shape of families

"In any household..." from James Besanville (2018) Trans parents: Don't allow being transgender to scare you from creating a family. *Gay Star News*. Accessed on 8/30/19 at www.gaystarnews.com/article/trans-parents-dont-allow-being-transgender-to-scare-you-from-creating-a-family/#gs.u4dtqy.

CHAPTER 6
A guide to ambiguous loss

Pauline Boss (2009) "The trauma and complicated grief of ambiguous loss." *Pastoral Psychology* 59, 137–145.

Kristen Norwood (2013) "Grieving gender: Trans-identities, transition, and ambiguous loss." *Communication Monographs* 80, 1, 21–45.

Kristen Norwood (2012) "Transitioning meanings? Family members' communicative struggles surrounding transgender identity." *Journal of Family Communication* 12, 75–92.

CHAPTER 9

Transphobia in society

"eating or drinking..." from GLAAD (2017) *Debunking the Bathroom Bill Myth*, p.6. New York, NY: GLAAD.

GLAAD (2018) *More Than a Number: Shifting the Media Narrative on Transgender Homicides*. New York, NY: GLAAD.

Coming to an understanding in religious or spiritual communities

"Heavenly understanding" in Moby Longinotto (2016) *The Joneses*. El Segundo, CA: Gravitas Ventures.

Transphobia in society

"Gender identity disorder" American Psychiatric Association (1994) *Diagnostic and Statistical Manual of Mental Disorders, 4th Edition*. Washington, DC: American Psychiatric Association.

"Gender dysphoria" American Psychiatric Association (2013) *Diagnostic and Statistical Manual of Mental Disorders, 5th Edition*. Arlington, VA: American Psychiatric Association.

Taking action

"I'm from Woodmere, N.Y." Terry Schmitt (1978) photo of Harvey Milk, in Alex Ross (2012) "Love on the March." *The New Yorker*. Accessed on 09/16/19 at www.newyorker.com/magazine/2012/11/12/love-on-the-march.

CHAPTER 10

At the dinner table

"what it meant to be brown and black..." in Janet Mock (2018) "'Pose' Writer Janet Mock on Making History with Trans Storytelling." *Variety*. Accessed on 10/08/19 at https://variety.com/2018/tv/columns/pose-writer-janet-mock-ryan-murphy-column-1202803368.

"I'm Luna" and "I knew zip..." in Cynthia Leitich Smith (2004) Behind the Story: Julie Anne Peters on *Luna*. *Cynsations Blog*. Accessed on 09/03/19 at https://cynthialeitichsmith.com/lit-resources/read/authors/stories-behind/storypeters.

Filling the gap

Ed Webb-Ingall, (2010) *Raising Hell*. London: Ed Webb-Ingall.

CHAPTER 11

Catie L'Heureux (2017) Read Janet Mock's Empowering Speech on Trans Women of Color and Sex Workers. *The Cut*. Accessed on 09/03/19 at www.thecut.com/2017/01/read-janet-mocks-speech-at-the-womens-march-on-washington-trans-women-of-color-sex-workers.html.

Into the future

"Heavenly understanding" in Moby Longinotto (2016) *The Joneses*. El Segundo, CA: Gravitas Ventures.

"While visibility..." in Julia Serano (2019) Rethinking LGBTQ+ Visibility. *Medium*. Accessed on 09/03/19 at https://medium.com/@juliaserano/rethinking-lgbtq-visibility-69e39f36731.

Voices of the future

JAN MORRIS

"I believe in the soul..." in Sarah Lyall (2019) The Many Lives of Jan Morris. *The New York Times*. Accessed on 09/03/19 www.nytimes.com/2019/04/25/books/jan-morris-in-my-minds-eye.html.

KATE BORNSTEIN

"I don't call myself..." in Kate Bornstein (2012) *A Queer and Pleasant Danger: The true story of a nice Jewish boy who joins the Church of Scientology and leaves twelve years later to become the lovely lady she is today*, p.x. Boston, MA: Beacon Press.

NAT TITMAN

"You see, people assume..." from Kate Bornstein (2013) *My New Gender Workbook: A Step by Step Guide to Achieving World Peace through Gender Anarchy and Sex Positivity*, p.xii. New York, NY: Routledge.

"A resource for those who are comfortably androgynous..." from Nat Titman (2017) *Practical Androgyny*. Accessed on 09/03/19 at https://practicalandrogyny.com/about.

CAROLINE COSSEY

James Michael Nichols (2016) This Trans Supermodel Was Outed in the '80s, Lost Everything and Became a Pioneer. *The Huffington Post*. Accessed on 09/03/19 at www.huffpost.com/entry/trans-supermodel-1980s-caroline-cossey_n_575b03dce4b0e39a28ad822e.

DANICA ROEM

Julie Moreau (2017) Transgender Candidate Danica Roem Wins Virginia Primary, Makes History. *NBC News*. Accessed on 09/03/19 at www.nbcnews.com/feature/nbc-out/transgender-candidate-danica-roem-wins-virginia-primary-makes-history-n772486.

John Riley (2018) Danica Roem Voted "Best Local Politician" by Prince William Times Readers. *Metro Weekly*. Accessed on 09/03/19 at www.metroweekly.com/2018/09/danica-roem-voted-best-local-politician-by-prince-william-times-readers.

ANDREA JENKINS

Marwa Eltagouri (2017) Meet Andrea Jenkins, the first openly transgender black woman elected to public office in the U.S. *The Washington Post*. Accessed on 09/03/19 at www.washingtonpost.com/news/the-fix/wp/2017/11/08/meet-andrea-jenkins-the-openly-transgender-black-woman-elected-to-public-office-in-the-u-s/?noredirect=on.

"Poetry..." and "I express gratitude...." from Paul Brandeis Raushenbush (2017) Andrea Jenkins Brings Poetry to the Political—And it is Beautiful. *Auburn Seminary Voices*. Accessed on 09/03/19 at https://auburnseminary.org/voices/andrea-jenkins-brings-poetry-political-beautiful.

CECE MCDONALD

Barnard Center for Research on Women (2018) CeCe McDonald. Accessed on 09/03/19 at http://bcrw.barnard.edu/fellows/cece-mcdonald.

Ankit Jain (2014) Uncommon Interview: CeCe McDonald. *The Chicago Maroon*. Accessed on 09/03/19 at www.chicagomaroon.com/article/2014/10/17/uncommon-interview-cece-mcdonald.

DEAN SPADE

Barnard Center for Research on Women. (2018) Dean Spade. Accessed on 09/03/19 at http://bcrw.barnard.edu/fellows/dean-spade.

"Sometimes while I ride the subway..." from Dean Spade. (2010) For Lovers and Fighters. In Melody Berger (ed.) *We Don't Need Another Wave*, p.38. Berkeley, CA: Seal Press.

Dean Spade (2019) About. Accessed on 09/03/19 at www.deanspade.net/about.

Utne Reader Staff (2009) Tyrone Boucher and Dean Spade: Cocreators, Enough. *Utne Reader*. Accessed on 09/03/19 at www.utne.com/politics/tyrone-boucher-dean-spade-cocreators-enough.

TOURMALINE, FORMERLY KNOWN AS REINA GOSSETT

Tourmaline (2019) Tourmaline: Artist, Filmmaker, Activist. Accessed on 09/03/19 at www.tourmalineproductions.com.

"I think the everyday..." from Jade Marks (2015) Che and Reina Gossett. *Mask Magazine*. Accessed on 09/03/19 at www.maskmagazine.com/the-crossing-paths-issue/life/che-and-reina-gossett.

Tourmaline and Sasha Wortzel (2015) *Happy Birthday, Marsha!* Accessed 09/03/19 at www.happybirthdaymarsha.com.

SYLVIA RIVERA

"The revolution is here!" from Sylvia Rivera (2001) Our Armies Are Rising and We Are Getting Stronger: Talk at The Lesbian and Gay Community Services Center. *History Is a Weapon*. Accessed on 09/03/19 at www.historyisaweapon.com/defcon1/riverarisingandstronger.html

Sylvia Rivera Law Project (SRLP) (2019) Who was Sylvia Rivera? Accessed 09/03/19 at https://srlp.org/about/who-was-sylvia-rivera.

"I'm not going to change..." from Tourmaline (2012) Sylvia Rivera & NYPD Reflect on Stonewall Rebellion. *The Spirit Was...* Accessed 09/03/19 at https://thespiritwas.tumblr.com/post/18108920192/sylvia-rivera-nypd-reflect-on-stonewall

RESOURCE GUIDE—FURTHER READING AND MORE

Stories by and about trans parents

"People would be able to see me more clearly..." from Bestor Cram (1997) *You Don't Know Dick: Courageous Hearts of Transsexual Men*. New York: FilmBuff.

Trans memoirs and nonfiction

"A great story..." from Juno Dawson (2017) *The Gender Games*, p.3. London: Two Roads.

STORIES OF GENDER EXPANSIVENESS IN YOUNG ADULT FICTION

"She is me..." from Julie Anne Peters (2008) *Luna*, p.21. New York., NY: Little, Brown Books for Young Readers.

"He tried not to think..." from Cris Beam (2011) *I Am J*, p.3. New York, NY: Little, Brown Books for Young Readers.

"Like a record. Elizabeth is my..." from Kirstin Cronn-Mills (2016) *Beautiful Music for Ugly Children*, back cover. Mendota Heights, MN: Flux Books.

"I wanted so badly..." from Jennie Wood (2014) *A Boy Like Me*, p.6. Philadelphia, PA: 215 Ink.

GENDER EXPANSIVE TV SHOWS

"Television's first..." GLAAD (Gay and Lesbian Alliance Against Defamation) (2019) *Where We Are on TV: 2018–2019*, p.29. New York: GLAAD.

TRANS 101: TERMS, DEFINITIONS, AND GENERAL KNOWLEDGE

"What is gender..." from Testa, Rylan and Deborah Coolhart (2015) *The Gender Quest Workbook: A Guide for Teens and Young Adults Exploring Gender Identity*, p.1. Oakland, CA: New Harbinger Publications.

"A gender 101..." from *The Gender Book*. Accessed 09/03/19 at www.thegenderbook.com.